2022

M000035883

366 DEVOTIONAL READINGS

LIGHT THROUGH

LITTLE WORD WINDOWS

Two Letter Words from the Bible

For it is the God who commanded light to shine out of darkness, who has shone in our hearts to give the light of the knowledge of the glory of God in the face of Jesus Christ. 2 Corinthians 4:6

Copyright © 2018 Donald L Totten, PhD

All rights reserved. No part of this book may be used or reproduced by any means, graphic, electronic, or mechanical, including photocopying, recording, taping or by any information storage retrieval system without the written permission of the author except in the case of brief quotations embodied in critical articles and reviews.

Scripture taken from the New King James Version*. Copyright © 1982 by Thomas Nelson. Used by permission. All rights reserved.

ISBN: 9781699177853

Library of Congress Control Number: 2018909329

Available through Amazon books

About the author on the last page.

ENDORSEMENTS

As Joan and I were casting about, trying to think of whom we would like to endorse the book, she said, "What better people than our sons and their wives who know us best and are a product of the Holy Spirit's guidance in our privileged role as their parents. They are outstanding examples of disciples who may never be written about in a book of the world's famous but are powerful, professional attractants to life in Christ. This is what they wrote:

"What does a gifted teacher, preacher, counselor, husband and father do in his ninth decade of life? He writes a wonderful devotional book that brings the little words of the Bible alive! This devotional gives an easy and practical way to see scriptures in a new light looking at seemingly overlooked little words in the Bible. Each day brings scripture to life to give us a guide throughout the year. Don't miss his straight-to-the-point style. Dad's wisdom is sharp, practical, timeless, and sprinkled with a bit of humor in this daily devotional. Don't miss September 23 as it's one of my favorites and an example of what you will read throughout the year as the Bible comes alive through his writing." Dr. Douglas Totten, Optometrist.

"After reading this book, I felt a whole new appreciation for God's word. Each chapter leads you down a deeper understanding of the importance that small words have in understanding scripture. The stories included in each chapter are very relevant and help the reader apply a new understanding to their own faith journey." Catherine Totten, Computer Systems Engineer.

"This book of devotions challenges the reader to study the Bible from a number of different angles. The emphasis on little words can provide a big meaning to verses as well as encouraging deeper understanding. Dr. Totten established a good balance between providing sufficient discussion details and holding to an achievable daily devotion." Dr. Jeffrey Totten, Chief Engineer.

"Don has over 30 years of experience in education and is known for teaching in a fun format so that one can learn and remember. After his teaching career, he earned a Ph.D. in counseling and spent the next 20 years as a Christian Psychologist. During those two careers, he included 15+ years in pulpit ministry, serving different churches. I love that he is bringing three passions together in such a unique way. You will love this series of devotions. A must read!" Lori Totten, RDH

DEDICATION

This book of devotions is dedicated to my wife, Joan,

Who is another of God's great gifts to me.

Her knowledge of, and

depth of understanding of the Scriptures,

along with her wisdom of application,

have proved invaluable as she

gave suggestions,

encouragement,

edited,

and

patiently gave me time

to complete this work.

Thanks dear, I love you.

Dr. Donald Totten, PHD, and Joan Totten, MA, have also co-authored The C.H.E.E.S.E Factor – Why You Are The Way You Are. That book explores why Christianity is the best psychology.

Math for Intelligent Students, Parents, Teachers which is filled with games and techniques to prevent math anxiety.

Come and See – Help in growth and witnessing as a Christian.

All available through Amazon Books.

INTRODUCTION

LIGHT THROUGH LITTLE WORD WINDOWS

LITTLE WORDS can be windows through which the light of Christ can shine.

So often we miss the LITTLE WORDS in a verse. This book explores some LITTLE (two letter) WORDS in the Bible that make a BIG difference. Many LITTLE WORDS are explored. Be advised that LITTLE WORDS like "IN," for instance, are used hundreds of times throughout the Bible.

NOTE: The LITTLE WORD for the day is emphasized by presenting it in capital letters. <u>Scripture references are underlined so they pop!</u> *The Scripture verses themselves are in italics so that they will stand out from the rest of the text.* Paraphrased references are in parentheses. LITTLE WORDS that refer to a member of the Godhead, such as Me, My, or He, are not referenced. Some references are simply part of the narrative. Because of the intent of the book, the usual rules regarding capitalization of two letter words are discarded.

All scriptural passages are taken from the New Kings James Version published by Thomas Nelson. This twelve month collection of verses, which represent nuggets in the gold mine of the Word of God, is intended to be an <u>instructive</u> devotional study for individuals, couples, families, and/or groups, to strengthen personal faith, and to enable the readers to share the Gospel with others.

> *… it seemed good to me also, having had perfect understanding of all things from the very first, to write to you an orderly account, most excellent Theophilus, that you may know the certainty of those things IN which you were instructed* <u>Luke 1:3-4</u>.

> IN as IN-structed. We are to be Jesus' house and a temple of the Holy Spirit. We are a temple in-habited by God in the form of His Spirit. In order to be this structure, we need to be in-structed (con-structed that is with-structure) using material from His word.

Notice in the above verse there are several LITTLE WORDS – IT, TO, ME, OF, and AN. By no means will all LITTLE WORDS be explored in a particular verse. Each LITTLE WORD will get its turn in the month dedicated to it. You may have a favorite word or verse that is not explored in any month. By all means, add them to your list.

When several LITTLE WORDS are used in the same passage, a major word is chosen to fit the theme for that month. There will be repeated thoughts from time to time to refresh our knowledge.

Also, there will be times when a verse is used more than once to use a different LITTLE WORD or to solidify a point. Peter set the precedent for this explaining that even though the truths were known and firmly fixed, he was not going to shirk his duty to continue to bring them to the reader's attention (2 Peter 1:12).

Many important verses are used several times in the hope that by the end of a year, they will be fixed in your minds. The Holy Spirit has greatly increased my depth of knowledge and application of the Scriptures during the preparation of this devotional book.

I have found that paying attention to LITTLE WORDS gives more powerful meaning to Bible passages. I have had great joy as I worked in bringing this book to you. Hopefully, after reading some of the LITTLE WORD items in this book, the LITTLE WORDS will jump out at you and be more helpful in your understanding, getting more meaning out of your Bible study. So, enjoy the impact of LITTLE WORDS.

The format of each day's reading will be:

A key word to carry through the day, followed by a verse or verses to explore.

Background or definitions on occasion.

A "Q" introduces a question that brings out the importance of the verse. The <u>WOW</u>!

There follows an answer to the question and how that important concept impacts our lives. The <u>HOW</u>.

An exploration of the day's verse.

A prayer of application to everyday life.

Please note: Space is provided in the margins for your notes, birthdays, etc.

The primary goal of this book of devotions is to show light on our way as we walk with God. This will be helped by a secondary goal of making your meditation more fruitful. Several definitions and suggestions are given to this end, starting with ten tips to improve meditation, understanding, and utilization of our faith. Each month will begin with information about the month's LITTLE WORD: what it is and how it is used in verses. Meditation is to the soul what medication is to the body and mind.

Here is a list of the little words used, in the order of months.

1. January ------- IN
2. February ------ IF
3. March --------- AT GO ME MY NO ON UP
4. April ------------ IS
5. May------------SO
6. June ---------- WE/US
7. July ------------ TO
8. August -------- AM AS IT
9. September --- DO
10. October ------- OF
11. November ---- BY
12. December --- BE

Ten Tips for Terrific Meditation

1. Pray for the Holy Spirit's interpretation at this time and place.

2. Use an adverbial approach: Ask - who, what, why, how, when, and where?

3. Leave out a word or phrase and see how the meaning changes.

4. Meditate and memorize.

5. Check Scripture before and after the passage. Scripture sharpens Scripture.

6. Don't get caught up in disputable matters like food and days.

7. Watch for words like "therefore," "so that," "because of," etc. These indicate the preceding material sets up that which follows.

8. Emphasize one word at a time.

THE Lord is my shepherd, The LORD is my shepherd, The Lord IS my shepherd, etc.

9. Don't "proof-text" to use a passage outside its meaning.

10. As you mature in Christ, verses will take on a clearer and deeper meaning.

Many of these tips are utilized in the presentation of verses.

Remember to keep your Bible handy because there are many references for extended growth.

Also, remember: You have Christian rights which may or may not exist in our court system:

1.) Anything we confess will be forgiven; we will be cleansed of all unrighteousness. (See 1 John 1:9).
2.) We have the privilege of an Advocate (attorney). (See 1 John 2:1b).
3.) We can make a phone call. (See Jeremiah 33:3).

Because – He (Jesus) was wounded for our transgressions (Isaiah 53:5).

A criminal often returns to the scene of the crime. The crime often returns to the victim through flashbacks and other PTSD symptoms.

In Christ we have the ability to turn the matter over to God, forgive the perpetrator and live a life of joy and peace. See Philippians 4:6-7.

When we remember unforgiven abuse or neglect with emotional pain, it is as if the incident is happening all over again, AND AGAIN, while the perpetrator often has no regret about what he or she has done.

We know when we have forgiven when we can remember the incident without undue negative emotions.

This often is excruciating as was Christ's act of forgiveness on the cross, but it is the solution to a life filled with agonizing memories. See Colossians 1:24.

JANUARY

IN

Study and Meditation Guide

The word IN is a Preposition. A preposition (pre-position) usually is a word used "pre," that is, before a noun or pronoun to form a phrase that modifies (qualifies, describes, or limits) some aspect of the sentence. The object of the preposition could be a noun, a verb, or an adjective. Check the objects of the preposition IN to understand its impact.

Uses of IN - included – within - among - an intimate part of.

Example:

IN the beginning was the word … John 1:1a.

IN the beginning is a prepositional phrase where the object of the preposition is the *beginning*. The phrase modifies *word*. It describes when the word existed.

Preposition	-	IN
Object	-	beginning
Modifies	-	word
Describes	-	when existed

As we spend part of each day reading the day's Scripture

and employing the study and meditation guides,

we become more IN Him and He becomes more IN us.

Therefore, if anyone is IN Christ, he is a new creation; old things have passed away; behold, all things have become new 2 Corinthians 5:17.

Each new year and new day brings new beginnings.

HAPPY NEW YEAR!

January 1   Begin

Genesis 1:1 *IN the beginning God created the heavens and the earth.*

John 1:1b-2 *IN the beginning was the Word, and the Word was God. He was IN the beginning with God.*

Philippians 1:6 *He who has begun a good work IN you will complete it until the day of Jesus Christ …*

Q Who has begun this good work *IN* us?

God, Who created the earth, came to us in human form, and works in us. Note the similarities in darkness becoming light.

There was darkness, then He brought light (Genesis 1:2-4).

The life of Christ brings light into darkness (John 1:4-5).

We are moved from darkness into light (Ephesians 5:8).

Let it be clearly understood that God has no beginning. There is no "beginning of time". For you mathematicians, God is like the real number set going from zero infinitely positive and infinitely negative. You may think of Jesus' birth as being a zero point, hence BC and AD.

The beginnings discussed in Genesis, John, and Philippians are first, earth; second, Christ on earth; and then Christ in us. In like fashion, we were reborn; we learned about the truths of Christianity; and we come alive in Him (Ephesians 2:1).

Our experience in Christ is very similar to the creation of the world. In our beginning is the Word and He begins a good work in us. In our new year, we need to focus on every day, and our constant, new beginnings in Christ.

Prayer – Dear Father, thank You for giving us Your Word, Jesus, and Your word, the Bible.

January 2   Creations

<u>2 Corinthians 5:17</u>   *If anyone is IN Christ, that person is a new creation, the old is gone, the new has come.*

Q How do we become new creations?

> We become new creations by being IN Christ.

> We now have the question of how we gain the spiritual condition of being *IN Christ*. Here is the answer – If we receive Him into our lives we are God's children (John 1:12). It is important to realize that before we receive Christ, we are NOT God's children. The doctrine of Universal Salvation is a terrible lie.

> Think of a clear glass pitcher filled with, and immersed in, clear water. The vague outline of the pitcher is visible (we don't lose our identity and power of choice) but it is surrounded by, and filled with, clear water. When we are IN Christ, we are in union with Him in thought and actions. We are a new creation – we are born again. We are no longer ruled by an outer set of do's and don'ts, but by the Spirit's inner direction. We now have "inside information". The Holy Spirit will live in us and will be our constant companion and helper (John 14:15-16).

> Father, Son, and Spirit are involved. Christ is in us through the Person of the Holy Spirit. As Christ and the Holy Spirit are in us, and we in Them, we see that Christianity is more than a religion; Christianity is a relationship. Relationship is the genius of Christianity. Christianity is the only form of faith that has constant and instant new beginnings because it is based on God's grace, not our efforts. We are constantly new creations IN Christ. Rejoice in grace, live in grace.

> *The old is gone.* Don't hang on to guilt and regrets. These are Satan's tools. The past presents lessons learned but we cannot and should not live in the past. Open yourself to newness led by the Holy Spirit in love, joy, and peace. Windshields are bigger than rear view mirrors because we are to focus on where we are now and what lies ahead. There is only an occasional glance at the past to make sure nothing is sneaking up on us.

Prayer - Dear Father, Help me, each day, to recognize my constant newness IN Christ.

January 3   Mangers

Luke 2:7 *And she brought forth her firstborn Son, and wrapped Him IN swaddling cloths, and laid Him IN a manger, because there was no room for them IN the inn.*

Q How are our hearts like the manger?

If we look at this passage as a living parable, we can think of a messy, smelly stable and a busy uncaring Inn being like a person's life. The world is so busy and filled with such turmoil, Jesus is often relegated to a lesser part of people's lives, unknown or ignored. As with so many lives, there is NO room. However, God will find a safe place in our minds and hearts and place Jesus IN us if we are aware and willing. We can be an In(n).

When we look at this passage as a fulfillment of the many Old Testament prophecies of a Messiah, God's saving presence in Person, we see the beginning of Christ's time with us in human form (John 1:14).

Jesus took the shape and substance of human form, so that He could communicate person to person and give credibility to His message. We now have the word in written form and the Word in our form.

It was necessary for Jesus to come to earth in human form with human frailties so that people would know that He, being subjected to the same temptations as we, would be able to grant mercy to those of us who experience temptation (Hebrews 2:17-18). In Hebrews 4:15 we are told that because Jesus experienced the same temptations we do, that He can have sympathy for us. We should not let our imaginations run wild at this point, but we need to know that God's understanding of our frailties took on a personal nature.

God did not need to find out what it was like to be a fallible human. What is important to us is that we find out what it is to have an infallible God.

Prayer - Dear Father, allow my entire "manger," and life, to be open to welcome and celebrate the life of Christ in me.

January 4   Blessed

Psalm 1:1-2 *Blessed is the man who walks not IN the counsel of the ungodly, nor stands IN the paths of sinners, nor sits IN the seat of the scornful, but his delight is IN the law of the Lord, and IN His law he meditates day and night.*

Q How can I be blessed by God?

If the nots and the nors of ungodly counsel, crooked paths, and scorn are exchanged for delight and meditation IN God's law, I will be blessed.

Avoid ungodly people, sinful people, and scornful people. Instead, find light in, and meditate on, God's laws in all circumstances. A firefly backed into a fan and was de-lighted. Don't fly with scoffers.

One of my client's stories serves as an example of what happens to those who are victimized by peer pressure: My client didn't own the drugs. He didn't even know they were in the car but had been pulled over because of a broken tail light. He was presumed guilty with no chance of being believed innocent. Unfortunately, his passenger friend had a record of drug possession and sale so my client lost his car, his license, and a large sum of money. Don't place yourself in the power of ungodly people. Stay out or have an out.

Don't seek out an ungodly man for council. You will both end up in error. Don't traffic with those who walk in harmful and destructive behaviors. You will both come to a dead end. Don't join with those with contagious negative attitudes. You will both have a miserable life.

When you are in their company, though, greet them with Christ's love, never with condemnation. Spend each day delightfully, with no regrets, living in God's light. Constantly think on His Word and let Him direct your steps so that His light will shine through you.

Prayer – Dear Father, I delight in your law. Help me identify negative influences so I can avoid evil, walk in Your paths, heed Your counsel, and delight in Your word.

January 5   Peace

Philippians 4:6-7 *Be anxious for nothing, but IN everything, by prayer and supplication, with thanksgiving, let your requests be made known to God. And the peace of God, which surpasses all understanding, will guard your hearts and minds through Christ Jesus.*

Q How do I avoid anxiety?   Trust that God is present IN everything,

Be thankful IN all circumstances, and make all your requests to Him. Only then will His peace, which is beyond our ability to comprehend, keep us safe and sound in Christ. God will help us discern His will by responding Go, Slow, Grow, or No. But He always answers! Go, do it; this is what I want. Or Slow, don't get ahead of Me. Or Grow, this is a learning experience. Or No, this is not what I have in mind for you. Teach these precepts to your children. Nothing enters your life that He doesn't allow. Never waste a seemingly negative experience. Sometimes, for a different perspective, we need to ask, "Why is this the best possible thing that could happen?"

Note: It says *IN everything*, not FOR *everything*. Many readers miss IN, this very important pre-position. If we are thankful regardless of circumstances, He will show us a positive cause and/or give us growth (Matthew 6:34c). We need to thank God for His grow lessons. If we are anxious or resentful about what is happening in our lives, we miss the possible blessing that God will give us. We certainly won't have His peace. This directive does not mean we have to put up with situations that can be corrected.

When we love God and have dedicated our lives to look for His plan and purposes, we know that, when the whole picture puzzle comes together, God can bring good from anything (Romans 8:28). What!? Well, God is a God of love, joy, and peace. If we allow a circumstance to take away love, joy, and peace, we make IT to be our god and suffer the consequences. We need a guard because we are under attack by Satan. Satan wants us to lose our peace, but, we will not lose God's peace if we are thankful. We don't have to understand God's peace; we just have it when we offer up prayers of supplication with thanksgiving. We need to know that we aren't experiencing anything unusual. God always provides ways to handle a situation or the way to remove ourselves from a difficult circumstance (1 Corinthians 10:13). Don't worry, accept His peace.

Prayer – Dear Father, guard my thoughts and help me look for Your peace in everything.

January 6   Do

Philippians 4:9 *The things which you learned and received and heard and saw IN me, these do, and the God of peace will be with you.*   WOW!!

This is a verse that I have accepted as a motto that I may not lead others astray by my actions. What I teach, what people hear about me, and what they see in me should be an accurate picture of God.

Q How do we have the *God of peace* in our lives?

In our verse today we are told to do certain things so that we will have the *God of peace* with us. What are these things? Verse 9 follows vs6-8 both of which encourage: a lack of anxiety, being thankful, making requests to God, dealing with issues through Christ Jesus, and thinking positive thoughts. Verse 9 gives Paul's recipe for a model life.   *Learned* – Read Paul's writings as instruction. What we learn from his writings can save us learning from experience.
        Received – Don't just read or listen but accept what Paul is offering as God's instruction. He was inspired and directed by the Holy Spirit. Some people's message is not received because their actions speak louder than their words. We can't trust a source like that.   *Heard* – What he said may be read and studied.
        Saw – People need to see believers who walk the walk. When we are least aware of our impact, we have the most impact. We walk in Christ, away from home or in a place where there is no one to watch.   Evil people watch to find error to accuse us so they can satisfy their negative mindsets and use information to undercut our witness to others. Seekers, on the other hand, are watching - longing to know that there is truth, value, and hope for their own lives. We are the only Bible the world reads. What they think about Christians is what they think about Christianity. Is what is seen or heard in us an OUCH? Or a WOW!

Don't be anxious; meditate on, and make the teachings in Philippians 4:6-9 part of your life and you will have the *peace of God* and the *God of peace* in your life.

Prayer – Dear Father, may others see the truth about You in me and want what I have.

January 7   Things

2 Corinthians 6:5   *But IN all things we commend ourselves as ministers of God: IN much patience, IN tribulations, IN needs, IN distresses, IN stripes, IN imprisonments, IN tumults, IN labors, IN sleeplessness, IN fastings ...*

Q How does Paul commend himself as a minister of God?

IN one positive, and nine negative items, Paul saw *things* as opportunities to show the grace and presence of God. See 2 Corinthians 11:22-29 for a list of some of the *things* Paul experienced in his ministry. The average person would consider most of what is listed as negative experiences. But Paul trusted God so he worked in all these things through Christ to grow in grace.

In one circumstance we find prisoners listening to Paul and Silas as they sang hymns to God while being shackled in a prison cell (Acts 16:25). Paul and Silas were in prison because Paul had cast a demon out of a slave girl. They had been beaten with many stripes and had their feet fastened with stocks. Did they gripe or despair? No, they sang hymns and were heard by other prisoners. (Forty lashes less one because the prisoner got to strike back any excess stripes.)   Other people notice our reaction to adversity. They either hear words of complaint or find how God gives more grace. Our witness is stronger when we handle tribulation with the same grace that we have in less trying times.

Paul begged God to relieve him from something that was really bugging him. God told Paul that His grace was more than enough for anyone to make it through any difficulty and that would prove that no human weakness is more than His perfect grace can handle (2 Corinthians 12:7-10). Paul then accepted the fact that he could show God's power and comfort in any situation (vs9-10). Paul stated that the experiences he had, taught him to be content regardless of what was going on in his life (Philippians 4:11b).

2 Corinthians was written around AD 55-56; Philippians around AD 60-63. Thus Philippians was written after 2 Corinthians. It is likely that, in this four to eight year period, Paul had experienced growth in his grasp of Christ's intention for our lives when it comes to tribulation. The secret is to be thankful IN everything (Philippians 4:6-7).

Prayer- Dear Father, Help me to seek Your will in tribulations for Your glory.

January 8   One

John 17:20-23 *I do not pray for these alone, but also for those who will believe IN Me through their word; that they all may be one, as You, Father, are IN Me, and I IN You ... that they also may be one IN Us ... that they may be one just as We are one: I IN them, and You IN Me, that they may be made perfect IN one ...*

Q What does You IN Me - I IN You - I IN them - mean?

> This magnificent concept, unique to Christianity, means that God is IN Christ; Christ is IN us, therefore God is IN us. A = B, B = C, therefore A = C. We are His house, we are His temple. God is *IN* Christ but separate from Him. He is *IN* us but separate from us. We are *IN* Him but we are not Him.

> God, Christ, and believers are one in agreement with their actions and approach to life. Do you get the idea that the concept of "IN" is an important element in Jesus' belief and teaching? We do not have ideas about Christ, we have Christ IN us.

> Remember the clear glass pitcher, filled and immersed. While we choose to be in union with God, we still have control of our thoughts and decisions, but, being one means there is no division of purpose.

> There is oneness of thought and action. God and Christ are in complete agreement, Christ subjecting His will to God's will. God, Jesus, and the Holy Spirit function in one accord, uniting people with them through Their different roles. We invite Christ and the Holy Spirit into our lives and live according to Their will and desires in like manner.

> One of the great parts of Jesus' prayer is that it is *for those who will believe* bringing us, those who believe, into oneness with God so that we become His voice, hands, and feet in ministry.

> Think of a four horse team with God, Christ, the Holy Spirit pulling together and one horse hitched backwards. That is me, and all people, if we are not in agreement with the Godhead. We need to be newly created, facing the right way, all pulling together.

Prayer – Dear Father, remove any wicked way from me; fill me with Your Spirit; and let every aspect of my life be one IN You.

January 9   Life

<u>Galatians 2:20</u> *I have been crucified with Christ; it is no longer I who live but Christ lives IN me.*

Q How can I have Christ living in me?

> I gain LIFE by dying to the world and coming to life IN Him and He IN me. I no longer listen to the counsel of the ungodly or stand in the way of sinners or sit in the seat of the scornful (Psalm 1).

> Christ living in me. ACTUALLY!! Christ, the Son of God, living in me. WOW!

> We become His house when we have *hope* and firmly grasp an enduring faith filled with assurance and a joyful heart (Hebrews 3:6b). It is silly to think that those in Christ will take advantage of grace to sin. That is a lie promoted by outsiders who have not experienced oneness with Christ.

> Think of your life as a house. I, Jesus, am knocking at your door. If you are listening for Me, and open the door, I'll come in and live every part of your life with you (Revelation 3:20). He will dwell with us. He follows our invitation by entering our lives and becoming one with us. We become part of God's presence in the world.

> By means of Christ's crucifixion, our sins are removed and, we have the opportunity to become purified vessels for His indwelling presence. We join with Him by crucifying our desires for anything that is contrary to God's will.

> To have the fullness of God in our lives, we need to give every aspect of our lives to Him. We can check each area of our lives using the concept of armor outlined in (Ephesians 6:13ff): a belt so we won't be caught with our pants down, our emotions kept in line by the breastplate of righteousness, our feet directed by the Gospel of peace, our mind and mouth protected by the helmet of salvation, a shield of impenetrable faith, and the Bible as our offensive weapon – all supported by Spirit filled prayer.

Prayer – Dear Father, crucify any aspect of my life that would prevent Christ from living fully in me.

January 10   Healed

1 Peter 2:24 *He, Himself, bore our sins IN His own body on the tree, that we, having died to sins, might live for righteousness; by Whose stripes you were healed.*

Q How can we live for righteousness?

First we need to believe in Him and accept His sacrifice for our sins, taking them from us and making us pure in God's eyes. There is nothing we need to do except to accept.

Then, we need to die to sin. One good thing about dying to sin is we don't have to sin anymore. Sin no longer controls us; we don't have to give in to temptation (Romans 6:1-14). We now have the response-ability to live the right way - not to sin. INSTANT REPLAY – We now have the response-ability to live the right way - not to sin. WOW!

He was without sin but took our sin to the cross so we could receive righteousness in God. A powerful thought to know is that He not only bore our sins, He became our sin (2 Corinthians 5:21).

Once we accept that we are dead to sin, we must be sure not to take it back again like the person in Matthew12:45, who ended up worse off with seven more demons along with the one that was cast out.

Perhaps we can be like the fish, which when released, simply lies still in the water until it realizes it is free. Then, like the fish, we can dart off in newness of life.

When I was a Middle School teacher there was often a problem of messy floors. I began standing at the door with a waste basket. At end of class, each student had to put in a scrap from the floor as a ticket to get out. They would bring grains of sand! I had the cleanest room in school. Jesus takes all our sins away and leaves us clean.

Realizing that we are pure helps motivate us to keep on being pure. We now have the power and teaching of the Holy Spirit to help us avoid sin and walk in righteousness.

Prayer – Dear Father, thank You for making me righteous in your eyes. May I continually invite the Holy Spirit to guide my feet in paths of righteousness.

January 11   Overcome

<u>John 16:33b</u> *IN this world you will have tribulations; but be of good cheer, I have overcome the world.*

Q Are tribulations inevitable?

According to Jesus, the answer is, "Yes." As long as we live IN this world we will have tribulation.

Will have, not may have. Too many people reject Christianity because they think God is awful because bad things happen. But God often does not prevent troubles; He helps us in times of trouble. One of Satan's lies is that our troubles are over once we become Christians, however, God is a God of comfort as well as a God who prevents troubles that would overwhelm us. Whenever we would grow in grace, Satan will increase his meddling in our lives but Jesus is the Overcomer.

IN <u>this</u> *world* is important because the Bible teaches that in heaven there will be no more pain (Revelation 21:4b). Stuff happens. If we are honest, a lot of bad things are a result of bad choices. However, there are those who have a problem with natural disasters, innocent bystanders, and those who haven't heard the Good News. My thought is that God is love, what He does is the best thing (Revelation 19:2), and I don't need to worry about it. Sometimes we need to ask, "Why is this the best thing that could have happened?" This helps us look for good and opens pathways to healing. The writers Paul, Peter, and James did not fret about tribulations. Instead, they spoke about how to deal with them and what benefit could come from them. Hear what they have to say:

> Paul rejoiced in tribulations because he knew that overcoming problems produced *perseverance* (Romans 5:3).

> Peter felt that success in overcoming trials proved our faith to be real and that problems produced *praise* (1 Peter 1:6b).

> James believed we were to rejoice when we faced trouble because problems produced *patience* and *perfection* (James 1:2-4).

So let us live with *perseverance, praise* and *patience* as we go on to *perfection*.

Prayer – Dear Father, Help me not to be swayed by tribulations but to accept Your care and consolation in them that I might grow in grace.

January 12   Love

<u>1 John 3:18</u> ... *let us not love IN word or IN tongue, but IN deed and IN truth.*

Paul echoed this thought in Colossians 3:17 adding that all of this is done when we adopt the nature of Christ.

Word and deed must have been a common theme because both John and Paul used it.

Q How should we love?

We should love *IN deed* - what we do, and *IN truth* – with honesty.

The implication of the first part of this verse is that our life in Christ should not just be a thing of conversation. It stands to reason that we should have words, but our deeds should give life to our words.

The verse clearly means we should live by putting hands and feet on our words. If our faith doesn't result in Godly work, it has no life (James 2:17). We plan our work; we work our plan. The *word/tongue* can be hollow while *deed/truth* are productive.

We can't just talk the talk. We should <u>not</u> be like the brother in Jesus' parable who said he would do his father's bidding but didn't (Matthew 21:30).

We need to <u>WALK</u> the walk - proceed on the path - emphasis on our physical movements. We need to walk the <u>WALK</u> - produce on the path - emphasis on the tasks to be accomplished. Our walk is much easier if we *live* and *walk* with the guidance of the Holy Spirit (Galatians 5:25). Life is so much easier if we never do anything we feel we will need to lie about.

Prayer – Dear Father, May the words of my mouth and the actions of my body be delightful in Your sight.

Tomorrow Paul goes into detail with instructions to Timothy.

January 13   Example

1 Timothy 4:12 ... *Be an example ... IN word, IN conduct, IN love, IN spirit, IN faith, IN purity.*

Be an example. What is an example? An example illustrates or represents an object, action, or person. The example, in this case, gives behavior for fellow Christians to copy.

Q How can we be an example of Christ?

The fourth and fifth chapters of the book of Ephesians have a wealth of instruction about Christian conduct. See what Paul told the Ephesians about what he told Timothy.

IN word –   4:29 – edify - build up - impart grace.

IN conduct –   4:24 – put on the new man (Colossians 3:10-17).

IN love –   5:2 – walk in love – forgive – eliminate barriers.

IN spirit –   5:18 – squeeze out any negative emotion.

IN faith –   4:23 – let faith control your thinking – God is good.

IN purity –   4:22 – put off corruption and lust – clean up mind
and mouth.

This is what we should do to attract people to Christ. We are to be winsome witnesses. And, this is what we should do to show baby Christians how to act. They need to see possessing Christians in action. Satan would like the opposite of all these things.

I was working in a construction crew when I met a person who had something that I knew I needed to have. His life was an example as presented above. I then asked him how to get what he had and he led me to John 1:12 which essentially says that whoever receives Jesus and believes in His nature are legally adopted into God's family. I believed and received. We have something that others need. Let's live it and give it.

Prayer – Dear Father, may the words of my mouth, the emotions of my heart, the actions of my body, and the thoughts of my mind be delightful in Your sight. (Used throughout the book and based on Psalm 19:14.)

January 14   Proof

John 20:6-7 Peter *saw the linen cloths lying there and the handkerchief that had been around His head ... folded together IN a place by itself.*

Q Why is the condition and location of the handkerchief important?

It is one of the proofs of the resurrection of Jesus Christ.

The folded head cloth is one of the compelling proofs of the resurrection. If the body had been taken in haste, the handkerchief would not have been removed and folded.

Other facts contribute to the truth of the resurrection. The soldiers were ordered to make the grave secure with a possible penalty of death if the body were stolen (Matthew 27:62-66).

The women came with spices to anoint Jesus' body. They didn't know He was already embalmed (Luke 24:1, John 19:39-40).

The disciples didn't believe the women who had come first to the tomb. They had run away and were in mourning and hiding for fear for their own lives (Luke 24:11).

The followers were scattered; some were even returning to their homes and jobs (Luke 24:13).

It took an incredible event to bring them together and radically change their thoughts and actions (John 20:19). They were transformed from being frightened to being faithful.

A great proof is that we were dead and rose into newness of life (Ephesians 2:1).

There is now a life of productivity and joy. The Spirit leaps within us when we hear a certain hymn or verse. We feel kinship with Christ when we see love in a Christian circle. There is a feeling of being alive, living as purified people, being acceptable to God when our log is in the fire.

We have inside information.

Prayer – Dear Father, let the resurrection of Jesus have a daily impact on my life.

January 15   Completion

<u>Philippians 1:6</u> *He (God) Who has begun a good work IN you will complete it until the day of Jesus Christ's coming.*

Q What is the *good work*?

> The *good work* is spelled out as Paul goes on ... (1) that you have love that abounds in knowledge and understanding ... (2) that you promote the finer things ... (3) that you be dedicated and faultless to the end ... (4) and that you may bear the fruit that comes from living in the right way... (vs. 9-11). (Numbers inserted).

> Remember *Who* is doing the *good work*. Let us not get in the way. At any point from beginning to completion, God is working. Your house (life) is being reconstructed: the foundation is Christ - the roof and walls are God's protection – the rooms are different areas of life.

> In a construction project, there may be snags. Some toxic substance may be found. But we are too precious to God to be condemned and abandoned. The enemy may try to interrupt and delay. We need continually to live joyously in our purity in Christ and newness of life each day. Don't try to live joyously in the sewer of a sinful mistake. Repent, turn again, and let the construction continue.

> The foundation has been laid. We need to go beyond the basic teachings of Christ. Let us go about the process of sanctification (Hebrews 6:1b). We can do that by utilizing the four elements stated above.

> The *good work* is our relationship with God and in becoming like Christ in love, excellence, and sincerity. We now can produce fruits of righteousness that last for eternity.

Prayer – Dear Father, help me recognize and get rid of any habit or act that may delay Your good work in me.

January 16   Strength

Ephesians 3:16 ... *to be strengthened with might through His spirit IN the inner man, that Christ may dwell IN your hearts ... being rooted and grounded IN love.*

Q How does Christ come to dwell in our hearts with strength?

One of the benefits of being filled with the Spirit is power for living (Acts 1:8).

Our verse of the day refers to hearts (emotions). The focus here is on emotions that are described as being the source of our actions.

Ask Him to come in. He wills to do this. Open your heart and mind and trust Him to work His will. If we confess and believe, we will be saved (Romans 10:9-10).

The *inner man* is the well spring, the true being, the essence of a person. Think of an artesian well that gives pure water of its own accord, not needing pipes and pumps.

Jesus wants to provide that water so that which flows from us will be living water from that well Who is the living Christ (John 4:14b).

When we believe in Jesus our hearts become a gushing artesian well (John 7:38).

We will be rooted and grounded in love. Our hearts become the ground from which Jesus produces a harvest (Matthew 13:8).

We will have strength and might in our inner person so that when the erosive forces of life wear us down to that inner core, there will not be weakness and wavering but strength and power.

Prayer – Dear Father, I open my heart to You so that what flows out will be pure.

January 17   Magnified

Philippians 1:20 ... IN *nothing shall I be ashamed ... so now also Christ will be magnified in my body ...*

IN – not part of - to avoid shame, to magnify Christ.

Q How do we avoid shame?

Don't do anything you think you are going to have to lie about.

In working with clients the above thought came to me. Don't do ANYTHING you think you are going to have to lie about - to God, to yourself, or to others. The main thing is to think! Think through your idea and imagine the worst possible thing that could happen which is possibly what will happen. Then, live in truth, the Truth.

When I was a child, for whatever reason, I frequently lied. I knew I was lying, others knew I was lying, but I kept on lying and had to make up new lies to try to cover the old ones. Unfortunately, this habit carried on into adult relationships with predictable results. I finally decided I would stop lying but a lie would come out before I thought. I even started saying, "No, that's a lie" which shocked people but wasn't entirely effective. Then, Don't do anything you think you are going to have to lie about came to me. Much better results! If I had lived by THAT motto as a child, I would have saved myself a world of hurt. If you live by it as a motto, you will save yourself a world of hurt!

We should not do anything we will be ashamed of - anything - nothing. Paul wrote in Romans 6:21, Looking back, what benefit do you have from those things that experience has taught you were shameful? Poison trees bear poisoned fruit. So often what turns out to be a disaster, seemed to be the reasonable thing to do at the time. If you have a problem in this area, practice thinking ahead when not under stress so you will be able to think ahead when tempted to say or do something shameful.

In games and in war we have drills to prepare us for actual combat. We get good at what we practice - so practice good.

Prayer – Dear Father, may the actions of my body magnify Christ and be delightful to You.

January 18   I AM

Mark 1:11 *Then a voice came from heaven, "This is My beloved Son IN Whom I am well pleased."*

Q Who is Jesus?

Jesus is God's beloved Son – God was very pleased with Jesus. Jesus accepted His Father's esteem and worked out His Father's will.

The genealogy of Jesus is God by means of the Holy Spirit (Luke 1:35b). The people listed in Matthew and Luke are Joseph's ancestors. The human side of Jesus could be traced back through his mother, Mary.

In the verse in Exodus 3:14, God defined Himself as, "*I AM WHO I AM*" to show He always is and always was. God defined Jesus as His Son. Jesus accepted this anointing and referred to Himself as noted in several passages in the Gospel of John. I AM the:

(6:35)   bread – as the manna in the wilderness.

(8:12)   light – a light to our path, *Let there be light.*

(8:58)   preexisting – a member of the eternal Trinity.

(10:7)   door – protecting His sheep.

(10:11) shepherd – Who fulfills Psalm 23.

(11:25) resurrection – in Him is life.

(14:6)   Way, Truth, Life – He is everything we need.

(15:1)   vine – we are grafted into Him and thus bear fruit.

When we are in Christ we are God's children, esteemed by Him – valued. People who know they are esteemed are far less likely to make harmful decisions or to mistreat their bodies. If we esteem our children, they will see themselves as lovable and loved. They will love themselves appropriately.

Prayer – Dear Father, help me to let Your love define me so that I might live in joy as Your child.

January 19   Life

<u>Acts 17:28</u> ... *for IN Him we live and move and have our being ...*

Q How can our being be IN Christ?

> We are grafted into Christ.

> *In Him we live and move.* How can we be a branch when we are not naturally part of the Vine? As an example, we have an apple tree that bears five different kinds of apples. Five different branches are grafted in a common root stock. In like manner we are grafted into Christ and thus *live and move* in Him.

> Grafting, at that time, was being offered to Roman Gentiles. Today it extends to all people, all different national and ethnic groups, and, to you and me. In Him we *have our being* – we are human <u>beings</u>, through grace, not human <u>doings</u>, by works. INSTANT REPLAY - We are not human doings to gain God's favor, we are human beings IN God's favor.

> Jesus compared our lives together like a branch and a vine. Unless it is intimately connected, so that the branch receives sustenance from the vine, it will be barren (John 15:4). All things come through the root (Jesus) to us.

> At all times, good and bad, we need to know, and practice, that our source of life and actions are based in Christ. Rule # 1, we live and move in Him. Rule # 2, if at any time we are tempted by Satan to rely on our own works, or any other thing, see rule # 1. All of our life, moves and beings are *in Him.*

Prayer – Dear Father, thank you for making Christ's action total and sufficient. Help me always to give my life into His care and leading.

January 20   Welcome

1 Thessalonians 2:13 ... *when you received the word of God ... you welcomed it not as the word of men, but as it is IN truth, the word of God, which also effectively works IN you who believe.*

Q How should we receive the work of the word?

> We welcome it! COME ON IN!

> The word is the truth and it works effectively like yeast that causes us to rise up and grow into greater likeness of Christ. It is jokingly said that when a baby is born, a book of instructions should come out with the child. In truth, many baby books have been written by well-intentioned authors. What we need to know, and use, is the ultimate Book of instructions – the Bible. In the Bible we find all the dos and don'ts for life on earth and life for eternity.

> The word of God is powerful; it comes with a guarantee -- *So shall My word be that goes forth from My mouth; it shall not return to Me void, but it shall accomplish what I please, and it shall prosper IN the thing for which I sent It* Isaiah 55:11.

> The writer of Hebrews enlarges the words of Isaiah: *For the word of God is living and powerful, and sharper than any two edged sword ... and is a discerner of the thoughts and intents of the heart* Hebrews 4:12.

> *A discerner of the thoughts and intents of the heart* – the innermost generator of actions. The heart is one of the engines that pulls the train. To discern is to see clearly. We need to know the word so we can hold our thoughts and intents up to the "Light of the world." Then, we are able to separate earthly matters from that which has eternal value.

Prayer – Dear Father, help me to study and know Your word so that it can work effectively in me.

January 21   Light

Ephesians 5:8 *For you were once darkness, but now you are light IN the Lord.   WOW!*

Q How do we get from darkness to light?

To get out of darkness we need to recognize that we are *darkness*, want to get out of *darkness*, see Christ as the Way out, confess our sins, accept His grace, and live according to the leading of the Holy Spirit. PLEASE READ AGAIN.

We were not just in darkness, we were darkness.

There are dire consequences to being in the dark. Some people, those who are evil, prefer the dark. They choose to be darkness so they choose to die in darkness. However, there are those who are tired of stumbling in darkness.

For them there is good news.

Jesus gave us this insightful message, God is pure light and there is not so much as a shadow in Him (1John 1:5).

The good news goes on.

Christ is light and His light gives life to us (John 1:4).

When we know that we are forgiven and purified in Christ, we can move into the light of Christ. We can now live in the light and are proud of what we do in Christ, inspired by the Holy Spirit.

And on --

Jesus describes Himself as being the light (John 14:6) and we not only reflect His light, we have His light shining through us.

When we are in Him, and He in us, we can show His light to the world.

Prayer – Dear Father, thank you for Your Light, for helping me see the Light, and giving me Your Holy Spirit to lead me in the Light.

January 22   Abound

Romans 6:1 *What shall we say then? Shall we continue IN sin that grace may abound?*

Sin is thoughts or actions that go against the will of God.

Q Should grace be increased by intentional sin?

Paul answers his own question: Are you kidding?! How on earth can we be dead to sin and still live in it? Don't be ridiculous! (Romans 6:2).

When we can be purified of sin, walk in the light, and be empowered by the Holy Spirit, why on earth would we return to darkness?

We are not like the pigs who return to their wallow; or like the dogs who return to their vomit (2 Peter 2:22). When we are in Christ we abhor sin.

Moses was used as an example of one who chose suffering over temporary pleasure (Hebrews 11:24). Sin may seem to be pleasurable at the time, but, sin leads to an unfulfilling life and ultimately *death* (Romans 6:23). Think of all the famous people who have committed suicide.

Some people, who haven't given themselves totally to Christ, try to justify their sinful choices by rationalizing, "God wants us to be happy" or as one of my clients said, "God allowed me to do it, so it must be okay."

When we are seeking to justify a decision, we can be pretty sure what we are thinking about is sin. We have to be aware that we should not violate clear definitions of wrong doing. When we ask the Holy Spirit, He will guide us in right living.

A person was being followed by a bear. He thought, "The bear likes to follow my tracks, I'll make more tracks for it to follow." Some people apply this error of thinking to God, "God wants to forgive my sin so I'll give Him sins to forgive." What a terrible thought!

Prayer – Dear Father Help me not to presume upon Your grace. May I hate sin as You do.

January 23   Abide

1 John 3:24 *Now he who keeps His commandments abides IN Him, and He IN him. And by this we know that He abides IN us by the Spirit Whom He has given us.*

Today we consider several verses emphasizing the importance of the Holy Spirit.

Q How do we know that we are IN Christ?

When we are IN Him, we are motivated by His Spirit within us to keep his commandments. We make following and obeying His commandments our constant interaction. Jesus wants us to have the Holy Spirit in us so that He can be our constant helper and companion (John 14:16). Therefore, we should ask Him to come in, then listen to Him. God truly wants to give His Spirit to anyone who will ask for Him to be in their lives - (Luke 11:13b). These two verses are a double witness to God's desire that we have the Holy Spirit in us.

The Holy Spirit, along with our spirits, are also a double witness that we are God's children (Romans 8:16). The Holy Spirit is God's active agent in the lives of Christians today. Therefore, it stands to reason that Satan will do everything he can to reduce the Spirit's influence. Satan will say the Holy Spirit isn't necessary, that the trinity is not a reasonable explanation of the Godhead, that those who have the Spirit do weird things, and any other defamatory thing he can think of.

We don't need to, and actually won't accept what the world calls true. We don't get information from the wiles of the world, we depend on God for the more than generous, no strings attached, gift of His Spirit (1 Corinthians 2:12).

We need to ask the Holy Spirit to guide us every time we read the Bible. He will then bring to our remembrance those things that are helpful. The Holy Spirit is sent to us with the authority of Christ and will not only be our tutor, He will help us remember the instructions of Christ (John 14:26). We need to become His residence, not a hotel stop. Churches should be hospitals for sinners, not hotels for saints.

Prayer – Dear Father, help me read Your word, directed by Your Spirit, that I might have His full power and assistance in my life.

January 24   Therefore

<u>Romans 1:24-26</u> *Therefore God also gave them up to uncleanness, IN the lusts of their hearts ... For this reason God gave them up to vile passions.*

Q What would cause God to give people up to their evil desires?

> Before we explore that awful consequence, we need to be aware that this is not what God intends as the result of a person's life. God will stick to His promises and will give people every chance to turn to Him. He doesn't want anybody to live in eternity without Him. He wants everyone to come to Him with repentance and have eternal life (2 Peter 3:9). However, we need to realize the reality of the consequences of choosing a life of sin. With all the good news we need to know that there is a dark side which we need to avoid.

Paul describes *them* as people who are ungrateful and spiritually blind (Romans 1:21). They called the truth about God a lie and chose to worship created things instead of Him who created them (Romans 1:25). We become what we worship.

And to top it all off - they knew they were wrong and that they deserved to die. Yet they continued to sin and even applauded others who lived lives of evil (Romans 1:32). That seems to be preposterous but we see evil, and those who cheer evil on, all around us.

We need to know what choices and activities are displeasing to God. One list of wickedness is given in Romans 1:28-32. See also Ephesians 5:3-7, Galatians 5:19-21.

God is a Gentleman. He does not force Himself on people. He does not condemn anyone to Hell. He gives us a choice. If we choose the life described in the above passages, we choose the consequence.

<u>Ephesians 5:8</u> should be our choice – *For you were once darkness, but now you are light to the Lord. Walk as children of light for the fruit of the Spirit is IN all goodness, righteousness, and truth, finding out what is acceptable to the Lord. And have no fellowship with the unfruitful works of darkness ...*

Prayer – Dear Father, may I never select anything or activity that would force You to give up on me.

January 25　　Joy

<u>John 15:11</u> *These things have I spoken to you that My joy may remain IN you and that your joy may be full.*

Q How do we get the full joy of Jesus?

The joy of Jesus is part of the fruit of the Spirit (Galatians 5:22). When you want joy - pray to be filled with the Spirit.

We find out about Jesus' joy by believing it is possible and paying heed to the things He has spoken. We read the Bible, we listen to, and observe possessing Christians. We obtain Jesus' joy by confessing sins, receiving forgiveness, and knowing we are forgiven.

Jesus loved us more than His life. He loved us <u>with</u> His life.

When we realize the extent of His love, we will have joy beyond measure.　　　　Love begets joy. Joy begets love.

When we have Jesus, we have His joy. In Matthew 7:7-8 we are told to diligently search out the truth about Christ. We are promised that, upon our request, we will receive the truth and that it will be made clear to us.

Ask, seek, believe, and receive joy.

Jeremiah extolled God's word as joy in both its noun and verb form. Joy as a fact and joy as an operating force in his inner being (Jeremiah 15:16b).

Read, believe, and receive joy.

What is the joy of Jesus like? How can it be defined? The joy of Jesus cannot be expressed in words (1 Peter 1:8b). That's it – the joy of Jesus is *inexpressible* – it cannot be defined, it can only be felt – deep in our hearts. We have hearts and minds. Things of the mind can be understood and explained in words. Things solely of the heart can only be felt. Joy is a thing of the heart.

Prayer – Dear Father, fill me with your Spirit that I might have the fullness of Jesus' joy!!

January 26   Hope

Romans 5:3 *And not only that, but we also glory IN tribulations, knowing that tribulation produces perseverance; and perseverance, character; and character, hope. Now hope does not disappoint ...*

Q How should we react to tribulations?

> We *glory IN tribulations* – we give triumphant praise beyond measure because He is with us in everything.

> We demonstrate visible witness to the power of the indwelling Holy Spirit.

> We need to know that tribulation produces a chain of activities and emotions that lead to *hope that does not disappoint.*

> First - *Perseverance* - which is steadfast in spite of difficulty - stick-to-it- ive-ness.

>> And *perseverance produces*:

>>> *Character* – good reputation,

>>> And *character produces*:

>>>> *Hope* – desired expectation – confidence.

> Later in Romans, Paul caps off the verses between Romans 5:3 and 12:12 with - exuberant exaltation, repurposing tribulation as the root of perseverance, character, and hope, and having a strong prayer life - ACTS (Romans 12:12).

>> Adoration

>> Confession

>> Thanksgiving

>> Supplication.

Prayer – Dear Father, instead of provoking resentment, help me let tribulation do its good work.

January 27   Conquerors

Romans 8:37 *Yet, IN all these things we are more than conquerors through Him who loves us.*

Q How do we become *more than conquerors*?

We go beyond victory when we are totally in Christ. (Look back at the promises in Philippians 4:7 and 1 Corinthians 10:13). Notice, we go *through* Christ; He is our means of escape and victory. See the list of *things* in Romans 8:35b.

Consider four conditions of mankind:

Victims - Victims have given up. They are overcome by adversity. They feel out of control of things going on in their lives, their lives are overcome by *all these things* mentioned above. They are without hope and without God (Ephesians 2:12).

Survivors – Survivors plod through a joyless life. They are overcome by sorrow. Consider a plow horse which has lost its spirit, lunging ahead and barely keeping up with its feet. It persists, but only because a ration of oats waits at the end of the day. And then, another day – more of the same.

Conquerors – Conquerors overcome adversaries by force. Conquerors feel they have it made. They are self-made. They often are overcome by possessions. Sometimes they have abused people and resources in their quest for that which perishes. But their lives are filled with constant striving to maintain what they have and to gain more worldly possessions.

How do we become more than conquerors?

And then there are *More than conquerors* – More than conquerors are overcome by love. They have all the benefits of abiding in Christ, empowered by the Holy Spirit. We are *more than conquerors* in spiritual warfare, through faith in Him.

Prayer – Dear Father, thank You for making me more than a conqueror through Christ.

January 28   Appointments

1 Corinthians 12:28 *And God has appointed these IN the church: first apostles, second prophets, third teachers, after that miracles, then gifts of healings, helps, administrations, varieties of tongues ...*

Q What are the differences between appointments, miracles, and gifts?

Before we discuss the differences, let us be thankful that God has provided all these helps in our personal and corporate life, given according to His desires.

First apostles, second prophets, third teachers ... The appointments are based on talents that have been achieved by developing genetic factors with which we are born. *After that miracles* – things that happen that can't be explained by natural causes.

Then gifts provided by God (see verses 7-11. See also 1 Peter 4:10-11, Ephesians 4:11-12, and Romans 12:6-8 regarding gifts.)

Gifts are abilities that we do not develop. They are given to us by God to fulfill a need. They may be a one-time thing or a lifetime experience. There are those who encourage us to "Discover our gift" as if it were something within us. Again, the gifts are given. They are given, not achieved.

We have to be careful in thinking we can't be used in healing because we don't have the *gift of healing*. Don't confuse a gift with a talent. You may not have a medical degree but God may use you in an act of healing. You may be sitting on a plane with someone who doesn't speak your language and God may gift you with a *tongue*.

In one of the churches I pastored, I visited a man with a traumatic blood flow that required surgery. I prayed for his healing. I went back the next day and he had been sent home, completely healed, with no surgery. The doctors couldn't figure it out. A specific gift for a specific time.

Be open to God for whatever gift He may give for a specific need at a specific time.

Prayer – Dear Father, I open my life for You to use with any gift for any time.

January 29   Shame

Romans 6:21 *What fruit did you have then IN the things of which you are now ashamed?*

Q What good thing did you think would happen?

Sometimes, after we realize that we have messed up, we ask, "What was I thinking?" The fact is, if we were thinking at all, we were operating under the knowledge and emotion we had at that time. The Bible often links the mind and the heart as both affect our actions. Our mind may have overruled our emotion or our emotion may have overruled our mind, but we act according to our accumulated knowledge and feelings.

> We say, "It seemed to be the reasonable thing to do at the time." Whatever stupid, outlandish thing we did, it seemed to be the best choice of action – at that time. But, sometimes it brings shame. Many of my clients denied that what they did was "reasonable at the time." But they did it. Then, we discussed their reasons.

> We learn by observing others; we learn by listening to others. Quite often, we learn from experience. Experience is the best teacher – if we survive. From observation, listening, or experience we gain knowledge. Knowledge is what we know; wisdom is what we do with what we know. And emotion sometimes overpowers both. Anyway, we learn as we go and, hopefully, act with improved reason.

> As Christians, we have the added advantage that we are led by the Spirit and we have the advantage of being able to think as Jesus thinks (1 Corinthians 2:16b). I know this sounds almost impossible, but this ability is given to us as children of God. We need to be alert to the guidance of the Holy Spirit. If we feel a warning tinge, and He will tinge us if we haven't hardened our hearts, we need to count the cost - think of possible consequences. We need to heed the same instruction about the use of commas, given by my high school composition teacher – when in doubt, leave it out. If we are wise, we will follow teaching we find in the Bible. If God says, "No", there is a good reason not to. We may not see the reason at the time but His word is reason enough.

> The fruit we are supposed to seek is the fruit of the Spirit.

Prayer – Dear Father, help me be tuned in to the Holy Spirit so I do what is right in Your eyes instead of what may seem reasonable to me.

January 30   Yes

2 Corinthians 1:19b-20 *For the Son of God ... was not Yes and No, but IN Him was Yes. For all the promises of God IN Him are Yes, and IN Him, Amen, to the glory of God through us.*

Q What is the YES in Christ?

The first, and biggest Yes is salvation and relationship with God (John 3:16). Another big Yes is all the benefits of the Holy Spirit (John 14:16). There are many more "yeses" in Scripture!

We have eternal life through belief in Christ (John 3:16). I never tire of seeing, hearing, or thinking about this verse. It might be, and should be, the most popular verse in the world.

The second fantastic Yes is the gift of the Holy Spirit Who lives with us, and even more, is IN us, to help us every day of our lives. We know we have the gift of the Spirit because Jesus asked His Father, our God, to gift us with Him (John 14:16).

Jesus not only prayed for his followers at that time, He prayed for anyone in the future that may believe in Him (John 17:20-23). That includes us. It is God's deep desire that we ask for, and receive, the Holy Spirit (Luke 11:13b).

Not only do we have salvation leading to everlasting life, but power, gifts, and the fruit of the Spirit to help us in our life on earth -

power, gifts, and fruit!   Oh, my!

Q How do we get the YES? We get the *Yes* by confessing and believing.

... if you confess with your mouth the Lord Jesus and believe in your heart that God has raised Him from the dead, you will be saved. For with the heart one believes unto righteousness, and with the mouth confession is made unto salvation Romans 10:9-10. We need to remind ourselves of the requirements and the results of this verse quite often. INSTANT REPLAY - We need to remind ourselves of the requirements and the results of this verse quite often. All the promises of God are ours. Claim them and live in them.

Prayer – Dear Father, words cannot express my gratitude, hopefully my life will.

January 31   Confess

Matthew 10:32 *Therefore whoever confesses Me before men, him I will also confess before My Father Who is IN heaven.*

> To confess is to witness, admit to, to claim, to acknowledge one's belief in what one sees or knows by personal presence or perception.

Q Who will Jesus confess before His Father?

> He will confess those who confess Him before men.

Peter was identified as a companion of Christ by his association with Jesus and by his Galilean accent, but he denied with cursing and swearing (Mark 14:71). If you were accused of being a Christian would there be enough evidence to get a conviction? We may not curse or swear but sometimes we deny by our silence or by avoiding a situation.

We need to realize that the Holy Spirit convicts people of sin, righteousness, and judgment and brings them before Christians who have been prepared to witness about Jesus to them. It is our part to study and be prepared to deliver our witness (1Peter 3:15-16).You may stammer or stutter at first but practice makes good enough. If a job is worth doing, it is worth doing poorly, Yes, poorly, until we get good at it.

> Give them simple answers. They need Spiritual milk. When their eyes glaze over, wait until they are ready for more.

> As the joke goes, a little boy asked his father where he came from. His father took a deep breath, got out all the charts and pictures of birds and bees, etc. When he was finished, the boy said, "That is interesting but Willie said he was from Toledo".

> This is not a do-it-yourself project. Be sure to pray and enlist the aid of the Holy Spirit. It is through the indwelling and prompting of the Holy Spirit that we confess Jesus as our Lord (1 Corinthians 12:3b). We are not alone.

> If we confess Him, He will confess us! What a wonderful promise!

> Let us joyfully and strongly confess Him as our Lord and Savior.

Prayer- Dear Father, help me never to deny by words or actions but to affirm Christ as I confess with my words and actions that Christ is my life.

FEBRUARY

IF

Meditation Aids

This month's LITTLE WORD is IF. IF is a powerful word and, though only two letters long, is often the most important word in a verse.

Remember, the verse is chosen because of its importance and the narrative explains its importance and how it is applied to everyday life. Other little words in the verse often support the dominant word.

IF is a subordinating conjunction (con-junction means with junction, like the junction of two roads coming together). "Con" means "with," i.e. chili con carne – beans with meat. So a con-junction is a "with" junction. The word IF is a junction between two thoughts. IF is subordinate in that it is beneath or subject to another thought.

IF requires a THEN which is the commanding or dominant thought.

Uses of IF: provided that, a condition to be met that has a consequence.

IF the "IF" isn't satisfied, then the "then" cannot come into being.

The power of the meaning of IF is in the following phrase:

IF _____ then _____.

The impact of the power is brought home by taking the negative of IF.

IF not _____ then not _____.

Example:

… IF you love Me, keep My commandments … John 14:15-16.

Then is understood.

IF you love me, THEN you will keep my commandments.

IF you don't keep the commandments, THEN you don't love Me.

February 1   Confess

<u>1 John 1:9</u> *IF we confess our sins, He is faithful and just, and will forgive us our sins and purify us of all unrighteousness.*

Q What is the result of our confession?

IF there is confession, then forgiveness and purification are the results.

This is one of the significant relationship passages in the New Testament. Use it for yourself and memorize it to share with others. It applies not only to our pre-Christian experience but to our everyday walk with Christ. It is true for both abuse and neglect.

If we/us (all believers/confessors) confess, we admit to having deeds or thoughts that separate us from God. Then he grants to us a purity that is equal to the purity of Christ. He will remove <u>all</u> of the unrighteousness that we have accumulated in our lives – everything we have done that we should not have done - everything we didn't do that we should have done – everything that was done to us (abuse) that should not have been done - everything that should have been done for us (neglect) that wasn't done.

Example: A client thought she must have been a terrible person or the abuse wouldn't have happened. She felt "filthy". The problem was, there was no reasonable explanation for the offense. People tend to take blame on themselves to try to make sense of the world. This is trying to make sense out of nonsense. INSTANT REPLAY - This is trying to make sense out of nonsense. Applying today's verse to her pain, and knowing that she was cleansed of the abuse - pure, gave her peace with the memory.

All it takes to be as pure as Christ is to hope in Him (1John 3:3). If I define myself as impure, it is easier to have impure thoughts and do impure acts. If I accept God's word as true, then I am as pure as Christ and do not want to choose sin. I will work to keep my life clean.

Now we know is that God will forgive and purify us when we confess. How pure do you think you are? Do you immediately think, "No, I'm not pure?" <u>Seriously</u>? If you start listing sins, you place yourself under law instead of grace. Do you hope in Christ? Then you are as pure as Christ!   WOW!

Prayer - Dear Father, give me the good sense to admit my need for forgiveness, the humility to confess, and the faith to accept the purity You give. Forgive me for retaining my sins against myself.

February 2   Believe

Romans 10:9 ... that IF you *confess with your mouth the Lord Jesus and believe in your heart that God has raised Him from the dead, you will be saved.*

Q Why is confession and belief necessary? IF we confess and believe then we are saved.

This is another salvation verse to be used and shared.

Salvation means we are brought into union with God. He now dwells in and directs our inner person. The act of salvation is necessary because, outside of Christ, we are impure. Salvation is the salve that heals the sickness of sin.

It is as if our sins never happened. We have purity and freedom that only Christ can give (1John 3:3). Do not let the world define you. Accept God's definition of who you are in Him.

It must be clearly understood that Christianity is a relationship with God, NOT a religion to be practiced. I can be religious about brushing my teeth but that doesn't make me a dentist. People can be religious about going to "church," but that doesn't necessarily mean they are Christians.

Quite often people want to accept Jesus as Savior but not as Lord, or ruler, of their lives. The two go together. You don't have one without the other.

We need to believe in our hearts. While the brain is the center of thought, the heart is considered to be the controller of emotions because it reacts so quickly to adrenalin. Jesus needs to be given our hearts, the seat of our emotions.

Jesus must be actively involved with our salvation relationship. His action is complete and sufficient. People who reject Christ are not in relationship with God. We come to God by way of Jesus. Do not fret because Jesus is the only way; instead rejoice that God has given us a way that accounts for our sin and still gives relationship with Him. God acts with grace and gives us His Spirit to guide our steps.

Prayer - Dear Father, grant me the humility to confess my sins and sinfulness, and the good sense to believe and accept salvation through Christ.

February 3   Risen

1 Corinthians 15:12-19   *IF v12 Christ is preached as risen ... (BUT) v13 ...
IF there is no resurrection of the dead, then Christ is not risen. v14 And IF
Christ is not risen, then our preaching is empty and your faith is also empty.
v17 And IF Christ is not risen, your faith is futile; you are still in your sins! v19
IF in this life only we have hope in Christ, we are of all men the most pitiable
v20 But now, Christ is risen from the dead!* (Verses numbered for emphasis.)

Q What is the importance of the resurrection of Jesus Christ?

If He is not risen then Christianity lumps in with the religions of the world and
we are to be pitied. Note: Again, Christianity is not a religion, it is a
relationship. A religion is a set of exterior rules to be followed. Our
relationship with God is an interior relationship - Christ IN us.

There are a lot of IFs in these verses with dire consequences. The truth and
meaning of Christianity depends on the reality of the resurrection of Jesus
Christ from the dead. If Jesus didn't rise, as He said He would, then He was
just a visionary with a lot of good ideas. People can go on their eat, drink, and
be merry ways with no thought of relationship with God, either that He
doesn't exist, or that He is a benevolent being who smiles and tolerates their
deviant behavior.

Although Paul was writing of his time, these IFs still need to be examined
today. The resurrection is presented as an historical event. Paul's argument
is that IF there is no resurrection of Jesus, then we are still mired in the
hopeless quagmire of separation from God. Then we, who have expressed
faith in Him, are considered to be the most pitiful of people.

BUT!! v20, He IS risen from the dead! Therefore, our preaching is
meaningful, our faith is full of truth, our sins are dismissed, and we have
certainty of eternal life. We are amongst all people most to be envied with all
kinds of positive consequences. Hallelujah and AMEN!   WOW!

Paul went all in with Jesus. Paul suffered beatings, stoning, shipwreck, jail,
starvation, vilification etc., but did not consider himself to be pitiful. Instead,
he said he had learned the secret of contentment – he could do anything
through the strength that Christ gave him (Philippians 4:11-13).

Prayer - Dear Father, keep me aware that I serve a risen Savior and that He
has chosen to be risen in me. Help me live out the impact that Jesus'
resurrection makes on my life and choices.

February 4   Witness

Romans 8:17 *The Spirit Himself bears witness with our spirit that we are children of God, and IF children then heirs, joint heirs with Christ.*

Q How do we know if we are joint heirs with Christ?

The Bible tells us IF we are *children of God* then we are *joint heirs* with Christ.

The Holy Spirit bears witness (testifies) with our inner being. The Holy Spirit is the best and most faithful witness to our adoption, both seeing and testifying to the fact of our adoption.

We become siblings of Christ and joint heirs with Him of God's blessings. Heirs of the kingdom, WOW! That is beyond my wildest imagination but it is true through faith in Jesus Christ.

A person is not naturally one of God's children but when we are born again, we are one of God's children, not with human parents, or somehow by our own devices, or by anyone else's wishes, but, we are born *of God* (John 1:13). We need to be reborn. We find in Hebrews 9:17 that it is our fate to die once. If we are only born once, we die twice, physically and spiritually. But, if we are born twice, physically and spiritually, we only die once, physically. As God's children, we have eternal life beginning at our second birth date. We receive adoption, our second birth, as a gift. We can celebrate both birth dates!

Our spirit and the Holy Spirit need to be on speaking terms. He is always available, and not just for 911 calls. This is not a long distance call, the Holy Spirit lives in us. In each moment and circumstance of the day, we can talk with Him.

God is constantly communicating His love and power to us. We need to keep the lines of communication open through the Bible, with our possessing brothers and sisters in Christ, and through our inner spiritual voice, and know that we are constantly new creations in Christ (2 Corinthians 5:17).

Prayer – Dear Father, thank you God; help me identify with, and live in, my status as Your child.

February 5   Know

1 John 3:19-20 *By this we know that we are of* the truth, *and shall assure our hearts before Him. For IF our heart condemns us; God is greater than our heart and He knows everything. Beloved, IF our heart does not condemn us, we have confidence toward God.* (Emphasis added.)

Q How do we overcome the doubt brought about by a condemning heart?

God overrules our heart. Trust God, not your heart.

IF in our heart, our emotional being, we feel condemned, then God's greatness overcomes that feeling of condemnation. We should not have faith in ourselves, instead we believe what God says.

The word this, in *by this* in today's Scripture, is the fact, as the verse says, that God is greater than our hearts and He knows everything. We know because He knows. It is not a fabrication or wishful thinking. We didn't make up the promises of God. He knows we are pure in His Son when we have faith in Him.

Jesus said, *"I am the way,* the truth, *and the life. No man comes unto the Father except through Me"* John 14:6. Because of God's greatness we have the truth in Christ. The Holy Spirit witnesses with our spirits to the truth of Christ giving us an inner sense of joy and peace.

We, as believers, have knowledge of the truth that places us in God's plan. Part of His plan is that He overrules any doubt or fear that Satan may generate in our hearts. Satan attempts to destroy us by deception, distractions, and discouragement but our focus, our faith, and our fidelity are towards Jesus Who has overcome the world.

There are so many lies and false claims in the world, it is good to know that Christ Jesus is the truth and we are in Christ. We are of the truth. Being of the truth gives our hearts assurance so that we have confidence before God and others.

The main thing is to make the main thing the main thing. The main thing here is that Jesus is the truth.

Prayer – Dear Father, help me keep the eyes of my heart focused on the truth.

February 6   Choice

Proverbs 1:10 *My son, IF sinners entice you, do not consent.*

Q How do we refuse to consent to enticement?

IF you are enticed, it is your response-ability to simply refuse to consent. We have the choice of giving in, or not giving in, to temptation. There is no "loss of control" unless we fall in a heap and babble meaningless phrases. We need to be aware that the enemy is always at work. The enticement is not always obvious and up-front. Don't be blind-sided but realize that we are in a continual war against evil. Sometimes a seemingly simple step on the slippery slope of sin can lead to sorrow.

In the first place, don't put yourself in tempting situations. Ask the Spirit to guide your thoughts and actions. If your spiritual footing is uncertain, don't go on a path of temptation. Walk where healing is possible so as to prevent further damage (Hebrews 12:12b, see Psalm 18:36). Through God's cleansing and grace, we will not desire our old sinful ways and by His grace our "*feet*" are healed.

Some say if we, as Christians, are saved by grace not by works, then it doesn't matter if we sin. However – Does it make sense to attempt to increase grace by continuing in sin? Heavens no!! We are dead to sin. Where is the logic to living in sin? (Romans 6:1-2). While we are saved by grace, grace is not permission to sin.

Quite often, the body juices released by anxiety over careless sin can be linked to a physical or mental illness. As my wife says, "The sickness of the soul will manifest itself in an illness of the body". It is also true that what we hate in ourselves, we project on to others. If you often find fault with another person, ask God to examine your heart. People who are pure project purity.

We need to surround ourselves with redeemed and cleansed companions. We should not become actively involved in/with those who entice us to sin (1 Corinthians 15:33). It is not a good idea to spend time with those who defame God by their actions except with the intent of leading them to Christ.

As Christians, we don't go around looking for how we can sin and get away with it. INSTANT REPLAY - As Christians, we don't go around looking for how we can sin and get away with it. When we are in Christ, we don't try to play on both sides of the fence.

Prayer – Dear Father, help me not to let Satan, others, or myself lead me into temptation.

February 7   Advocate

1 John 2:1b *IF anyone sins, we have an Advocate with the Father, Jesus Christ the righteous.*

An advocate is like a lawyer or intercessor – one who says, "Let me do the talking".

Q What should we do if we relapse and sin?

IF we confess, He purifies (1 John 1:9). Don't presume upon His grace. We should also use the love and support of advocates in the body of Christ. Siblings in Christ should not have a pocket full of stones (John 8:7).

It is important to know that one slip does not need to lead to another and put us on a downward path. If you are wading in water in the dark of night, and the water is gradually getting deeper, back out. The next step may be devastating.

There is great power in Romans 8:1 that promises we are not condemned if we are in Christ and walk, led by the Spirit. There is NO condemnation, not from God, or from others, and there should not even be our own condemnation of ourselves. Paul essentially said, "God is my judge. You, the court system, or even myself, don't have the qualifications to pass eternal judgment on anybody" (1 Corinthians 4:3-4). And God has deemed us pure if we hope in Christ (1 John 3:3).

Self-condemnation is a lack of trust in the grace that God offers us through Christ's sacrifice. Self-condemnation keeps us from having love, joy, and peace and from being winsome witnesses. Who wants what a self-condemner does? If we have God in our lives, who can be successful in being against us? (Romans 8:31b). No one, including ourselves. Above all, do not accept judgment from a non-Christian or a non-Christian source. INSTANT REPLAY – do not accept judgment from a non-Christian or a non-Christian source.

We, as Christians in general, often need an Advocate Who personally stands beside us. This is so much better than wallowing in remorse, beating ourselves up, and forfeiting the joy given to us through Christ's sacrifice.

Prayer – Dear Father, when I falter, may I quickly claim Christ as my Advocate. May I not presume upon Your grace and continue in sin. May I continue to strive to live righteously.

February 8   Forgive

Luke 17:4 *Jesus said to the disciples, "And IF he sins against you seven times in a day, and seven times in a day returns to you, saying 'I repent', you shall forgive him."*

Q When and how many times should I forgive? IF a person sins against you seven times with repentance, then forgive each time.

Then Peter came to Jesus and asked if there were a limit to how many times we should forgive someone. Jesus basically said we should forgive an unlimited number of times, 490 times, which was considered to be a perfect number (Matthew 18:21-22).

This is a bit difficult to believe; not so much the forgiveness but that someone has to be forgiven for something that often – but - hold on, wait a second – how many times, over a lifetime, do we have to be forgiven for a sin against others, or God? In Luke, the admonition is for a day; In Matthew there is no time limit.

Seventy times seven is expressed as a perfect number. If Jesus taught His disciples to forgive up to seventy times seven then we can rest assured that God will extend the same grace to us. We also need to take heed of the admonition that we are to repent - turn 180 degrees. Just don't do it again. However, in addition, this repentance should be with Godly sorrow.

(2 Corinthians 7:9-11) gives a helpful discussion about repentance, comparing sincere sorrow with worldly sorrow that is insincere. What is the worldly sorrow? It is often the sorrow of getting caught. Sometimes it is the sorrow of losing an intended personal gain of fame or property. Paul goes on to give the earmarks of sorrow that is real (See 2 Corinthians 7:11). Godly sorrow comes when we realize our sins are ultimately against God.

We do need to realize that forgiveness is not always an easy thing to do. Sometimes it is soul wrenching. Remember, it took the sacrifice of Christ to bring about our forgiveness. There are times when we feel in ourselves the *afflictions of Christ* for the good of His body (Colossians 1:24). The cross was the affliction of Christ – when we are in Him, we take other's sins upon ourselves. This may be painful but it is a good thing and necessary for relationship. In a sense, we "take one for the team".

Prayer – Dear Father, help me, with Godly sorrow, to forgive as I have been forgiven.

February 9   Blameless

Colossians 1:22 ...*To present you holy and blameless IF indeed you continue in the faith...*

Q What is the benefit of continuing in the faith?

IF we continue in the faith then we are presented holy and blameless. How does that sound to you? Holy and blameless, WOW! Is this possible?

IS THIS POSSIBLE?

YES! Consider a three step process.

Step 1. Accept God's grace gift of faith (Ephesians 2:8-9).

God gives us saving faith. We can't boast of having more and/or different faith and our works are of no account. If there is any scrap of boasting, we forfeit grace and exclude ourselves from God's family. Ask for, receive, and act in relationship faith.

Step 2. Accept the Holy Spirit into your life and allow the process of sanctification to proceed (Philippians 1:6).

God works in our dedicated lives to perform His purposes. Allow the Holy Spirit to be effective with power (Acts 1:8), gifts (1 Corinthians 12), and fruit (Galatians 5:22-23). IF we allow Him to do His work, the work will be completed. We will be so far above normal, we will seem to the world to be abnormal.

Step 3. Use every resource to understand and apply the truths of Christianity throughout your life. (Matthew 10:22).

At one time we were separated from God but Christ's sacrifice brought us together. We will be able to say, "Whether you compare life in Christ to be a war, or an athletic completion, or a test of faith, I did it right. I found that my faith in God allowed me to apply His truths and they have served me all my life" (2 Timothy 4:7). Our choice is to continue to become holy and blameless as we continue in *the faith* according to the teachings of the Word (Jesus) and the word (the Bible).

Prayer – Dear Father, help me make every day holy and blameless.

February 10   Forgive

John 20:23 *IF you forgive the sins of any, they are forgiven. IF you retain the sins of any, they are retained.*

Q What are the meanings of *forgive* and *retain* another's sin?

To forgive, in its purest form, is to live as if the offense never happened. To retain is to wear the sin and to forever be resentful.

Whether the sins are against us or are sins in general, to forgive does not mean we have the power to forgive as God forgives. We forgive to avoid carrying an ever increasing load of resentment. Our forgiveness of others sets us free from their abuse and we do not have the Post-traumatic Stress Disorder (PTSD) symptom of flashback occurrences of negative events.

A different way to look at retain is to hold, or keep possession, for ones' self. IF we, as victims, retain anyone's sins then the sins are retained on us, not on them. The abuser continues to offend the victim every time an abuse is re-membered (put arms and legs on them). The offense does not go back on the offender. It becomes the property of the abused person. Quite often, the offender couldn't care less and he/she may not even want or accept your forgiveness. The genius of Christianity is newness, the old is gone. To retain offenses is to make them "not gone" and prevents fellowship, joy, and peace.

Some people retain their own sins against themselves. They confess their sins but are not released from the memories. They believe but don't receive. They wallow in sorrow instead of rejoicing in renewal. Somehow, it seems as though they must be smarter than God Who has forgiven them. God has forgiven another's (and our) sins. We don't act as obedient followers of Christ if we don't follow His ways and teachings about forgiveness for others and for ourselves.

To retain the sins of any is to keep them in your mind and not forgive. Essentially, it is a nasty way of wreaking vengeance on ourselves. What we don't like in others may be what we don't like about ourselves. We need to remember that when we point a finger at others we have three fingers pointing back at ourselves (Matthew 7:5).

Prayer – Dear Father, help me avoid the foolishness of allowing another's, or my own, transgressions to decrease my love, joy, peace and witness.

February 11   Forgive

Matthew 6:15 *IF you do not forgive men their trespasses; neither will God forgive your trespasses.*

Q What if we don't forgive? IF we are not forgiving then we are not forgiven. OUCH!

Although simply stated, this is a powerful statement and needs intense investigation and application. Forgiveness is more for the giver than for the forgiven. They may not accept your forgiveness but that is on them. Forgiveness unloads the burden of the need for vengeance and releases one for joy and peace. There is neither joy nor peace in hate.

What happens if we retain another's aggression/abuse against us or even if we retain our own sins against others or ourselves? We have a double whammy – we replay the abuse each time we remember it and, suffer lack of forgiveness. Remember, the first thought is Satan's responsibility, the second thought is ours. We have to be persistent with our prayers of, and for, forgiveness. Lack of forgiveness is contagious. Lack of forgiveness generalizes to other real or imagined insults. It is contagious to our thoughts as we develop a negative approach to the world. It is contagious to people around us. When we don't forgive others, they quite often return in kind to us and to others.

What do we do so we don't retain bad memories? We can ignore the triggers. We can switch our thoughts to things that are … *true … noble … just … pure … lovely … of good report … of virtue … praiseworthy - meditate on these things.* Philippians 4:8-9. (The Nice Juicy Plum, Lovely, Good, Very Purple. Make up your own acronym.)

God knows all the facts, and His wisdom is pure so you can trust His judgments (Revelation 19:2). (See Romans 12:19 quoted from Deuteronomy 32:35). My judgments may be neither true nor righteous. Only God knows what is behind people's thoughts and actions. Let God deal justice. He will. Relieve yourself of the dreadful burden of condemning others. When there is no emotional reaction to a memory we know the resentment is gone. We are in control instead of being controlled by a bad memory. PTSD symptoms decrease.

Prayer – Dear Father, forgive my sinfulness and cleanse me of resentment. Let me leave judgment to You.

February 12   Gifts

<u>Luke 11:11-13</u> *IF you, being evil, know how to give good gifts to your children, how much more will your heavenly Father give the Holy Spirit to those who ask Him.*

Q How do we receive the gift of the Holy Spirit?

IF we ask, then we will be given the Holy Spirit.

The Holy Spirit is a good gift! We need to remember that the Holy Spirit is a gift to give us abilities we cannot achieve by our own efforts.

Why is there so much confusion about the Holy Spirit? Why are there so many religious split offs from Christianity that don't embrace the Spirit or include Him in the Trinity? Because, Satan tries to destroy anything that is good (John 10:10a), that's why. The better a gift is, the more Satan will attempt to corrupt it. Marriage, salvation, the presence and work of the Holy Spirit are all under attack. Do not accept the world's, or even some denominations' view of the Holy Spirit. Seek the truth in God's word.

Does God want you to receive the Holy Spirit? <u>YES</u>, the Holy Spirit is a good gift. Many people shy away from the blessings of the Holy Spirit because of misunderstandings about His ways and works. We need to have a thoughtful, Biblical approach to understanding and receiving the good gift of the Holy Spirit.

Jesus wants us to have the Holy Spirit. He told His followers that He would ask His Father to give help and guidance in their walk with Him, letting them know that God would give them a constant helper, His Spirit, Who could be depended on to guide them in the truth (John 14:16). This is also true for us today. He will always be with us! <u>The Holy Spirit is a helper</u>. Also, how great it is, in this world of lies and half-truths, to have the Holy Spirit Who will show us what is really true.

You don't have the Holy Spirit? Ask your heavenly Father for Him. Don't be afraid. ASK FOR HIM! Ask and you will receive. Know that God keeps His promises. Then trust that you have the Spirit within you and live accordingly.

Prayer – Dear Father, help me understand Who and What the Holy Spirit is and help me allow Him to grant all His power, gifts, and fruit to me.

February 13   Walk

<u>Galatians 5:25</u> *IF we live in the Spirit, let us also walk in the Spirit.*

Q How do we live in the Spirit?

When we walk in the Spirit, we live in the Spirit.

If we walk according to this instruction, we will be less likely to give in to negative temptations (Galatians 5:16). What a great promise for living in this world that is flooded with immorality.

What is the difference between living and walking? Perhaps living is having the Spirit in us, while walking is an outward manifestation of His presence. We walk the walk, not just talk the talk.

Think of the causes that people support. Some fans are rabid about their team. Clothes, bumper stickers, flags, and other lawn and household decorations proclaim their devotion. They are obvious at sporting events. And then there are grandparents ---. Should we not be enthusiastic about, and dedicated to, the Holy Spirit with all that God has given to us through Him?

In order to walk in the Spirit we need to have the Spirit dwell within us. Remember, Christianity is an intimate relationship, not a religion. It is not a list of do's and don'ts but a response to grace.

Whatever path you take, look for God's guidance and He will show you the correct way to go (Proverbs 3:6). This is not a complicated instruction. If we do this, He will give us direction for every aspect of our lives. We should not pick and choose how to acknowledge God.

We should make a habit of constant discussion with the Holy Spirit, our good and faithful Companion, about every decision of consequence. In so doing, we will never know how much trouble we avoid.

Prayer – Dear Father, fill me with Your Spirit and may I walk in Him, in all my ways, every second of every day.

February 14   Love

Philippians 2:1 *Therefore, IF there is any consolation in Christ, IF any comfort of love, IF any fellowship of the Spirit, IF any affection and mercy, fulfill my joy by being like-minded, having the same love, being of one accord, of one mind.*

These are rhetorical IFs. That is, the concepts obviously exist and are true.

Q Are there conditions to being of *one accord*?

IF there is any *consolation/comfort/fellowship/affection/mercy* then there is one accord.

This is one of the rhetorical statements found in the Bible. Another is – "Do all perform miracles?" (1 Corinthians 12:29). The obvious answer is, "No, not everyone performs miracles". Some rhetorical statements have obvious No answers while others are obviously Yes, like in today's verse. *Is there consolation comfort*, etc.? Yes, all of these help us be *like minded* - in Christ.

Here we find a powerful recipe for love for Christians to use so they can avoid controversies that cause the world to question the worth of Christianity. Love includes support, encouragement, fellowship, agreement, kindness, and undeserved favor. If these attributes of love are shown in the body of believers, it would go a long way towards making Christianity more attractive to the world. People would see the power of God in believers. Churches with the above named characteristics will be winsome witnesses. We need this super goal to be met. Be of one accord!

We need to get out of the judgment business, present the truth of the Gospel, and cooperate with the work of the Holy Spirit. We so often bind people in their sins. We need a church where people will feel free to go and get help with their deepest troubles. No longer will the local bartender be called upon to fill that role.

Prayer – Dear Father, help me be seen as one with whom a person feels safe with anything they may say.

Happy Valentine's Day.

February 15   Life

Matthew 19:17 ... *IF you would enter into life, keep the commandments.*

Q How do we *enter into life*?

IF we want real *life* then we need to keep the commandments.

It is important to realize that this is a response to grace, not a substitution for Jesus' sacrifice. Outside of Christ we are dead and practice deadly activities. We become what we worship. INSTANT REPLAY- We become what we worship. When we disobey the commandments we practice death. Life and truth, on the other hand, are found only in Christ Jesus (John 14:6). He is our guide to truth.

Most people have heard of the 10 Commandments (Exodus 20) but many of them feel they are the 10 "suggestions." One comedian quipped he agreed with God on seven out of ten. In the world's eyes, people are accepted if they profane the commandments; unfortunately they are often idolized when they break them.

You shall love the Lord your God with all your heart, with all your soul, with all your strength, and with all your mind, and your neighbor as yourself Luke 10:27. (Combined from Deuteronomy 6:5 and Leviticus 19:18).

These verses are like a digested version of the 10 commandments. They fit the acronym SPICE – Spiritual - soul, Physical - strength, Intellectual - mind, Community - neighbor, and Emotional - heart, all the aspects of our being. We are to love God with our total being such that each SPICE element, Spiritual, Physical, Intellectual, Community, and Emotional, gives honor and glory to Him.

Jesus added something new to the list of commandments when He told the disciples to love people the way He did (John 13:34). We are to love others as He loves us. The old commandment said, "*You shall love your neighbor as yourself.*" The new commandment goes beyond that and instructs us to love others as Jesus loves us.

Jesus fulfilled His own commandment by giving His *life* on the cross for us.

Prayer – Dear Father, Thank you for *life*. I commit my total self to You in response to Your grace.

February 16   Thirst

John 7:37 *Jesus said, "IF anyone thirsts, let him come unto Me and drink."*

Q What should we do if we have spiritual thirst?

> Drink the spiritual water of life offered by Jesus.

> *Whoever drinks of the water that I shall give him will never thirst, But the water that I shall give him will become in him a fountain of water springing up into everlasting life* John 4:14.

> If you have spiritual thirst, then go to Jesus to satisfy that thirst (Matthew 5:6). Jesus is the source of spiritual food and drink. Water is a necessity for life. We can go without food far longer than we can go without water. Spiritual water is necessary for eternal life. When we drink from Jesus' well, we have everlasting life. Jesus spoke of the water of life, that begetting our relationship with God through grace rather than by keeping the law.

> The water of life gives us the beginning to eternal life. But, we need to go on from this. Peter adds another beverage: *IF indeed you have tasted that the Lord is good, desire the sincere milk of the word that you might grow thereby* 1 Peter 2:3.

> Got milk? The Bible offers a rich variety of spiritual foods to satisfy the discriminating appetite. Partaking of the word (Bible) helps us grow in our baby steps as Christians - and beyond milk is solid food. Babies have limited ability and are limited in the food they can consume. Let us go on to maturity so God can give us a full menu of His grace (Hebrews 5:14).

> The water of life and the milk of the word are two powerful metaphors. Let us thoughtfully study, understand, and faithfully use each as they apply to life.

Prayer – Dear Father, thank you for filling my spiritual thirst with the water of life and for the milk and solid food of the word.

February 17   There

Psalm 139:8 *IF I ascend into heaven, You are there; IF I make my bed in hell, behold, You are there.*

Q Is there a place where God isn't? No. Wherever we ascend or descend, God is there.

This is a great promise because we often find ourselves in difficult circumstances. We are like sheep that nibble their way into trouble without a thought of the consequences (Isaiah 53:6). A sheep may see a tempting bit of grass on a ledge, jump down to it, and then find itself unable to get back up. Without even knowing it, sheep become lost. And, unfortunately, there are those of us who deliberately choose to be lost.

If we have nibbled our way into danger, unlike sheep, we are capable of responding to God. He beats off our enemies with His rod and rescues us with His staff (Psalm 23).

There is an old adage, you have made your own bed, lie in it. Thankfully, God gives the permission and power to rise up and walk through His power and presence (John 5:8).

When we respond to the conviction of the Spirit we have the opportunity to enter relationship with God. He may work through people, circumstance, or natural events, but He always speaks. He convicts of righteousness (John 16:8) so that we know what manner of life we should have. The caterpillar can know what is in store for the butterfly.

One of the primary activities of Christ on earth was to search out lost sheep (Luke 19:10b). What does it mean to be lost? It means we have made our *bed in hell*. The KISS definition (Keep it Simple Slave - We are slaves of Christ.) is that we are separated from God – out of relationship with Him. So why do we spend so much effort to remain lost? Why should we avoid being found? It is such a wonderful feeling to look up and see God's available saving grace. Unlike sheep, we have a deep sense of relief when we look up and see the compassionate shepherd rescuing us. God is always with us even if we aren't with Him.

Prayer – Dear Father, keep me in tune with the Holy Spirit so I can know when I am wandering in dangerous territory; then lead me to safety in righteousness.

February 18   Follow

Matthew 16:24   *IF anyone desires to come after Me, let him deny himself, and take up his cross, and follow Me.*

We need to know, that if Jesus told us to deny ourselves and take up our crosses, that these are good things. Jesus doesn't ask us to do bad things.

Q What action is necessary if you desire to follow Christ?

IF you desire to follow Christ, then self-denial and dedication to life in Christ is needed. The self is the combination of the spiritual, physical, intellectual, community, and emotional aspects of a person. If any aspect of the self is contrary to God or others, it is to be denied. "IF" puts it back on us, our decision.

To deny ourselves is to do our best to make each aspect of our living fit God's agenda. We now love others as Jesus loves. Under His direction we sometimes say, "No" to self and "Yes" to God. Deny any evil tendency – crucify, take up your cross and put to death, evil thoughts and actions – walk in Jesus' footsteps. To take up our cross is to become dead to the evil aspects of the world and to become alive in Him.

In another situation a young man, seeking justification, asked Jesus what he needed to do to inherit eternal life. He was told to prove his intent by selling off everything he had, give the results to those in need, and join with Jesus' followers. The man couldn't part with his worldly goods because they were more important to him than his heavenly reward, so he walked away grieving (Matthew 19:16-22).

This seems to be a parallel verse to Matthew16:24 but it has an entirely different objective. To deny our self is an instruction for sincere followers. The directive to sell everything you have exposed an insincere person who was attempting to justify himself by his works. In brief, the young man said he had kept the "love your neighbor" commandments, but Jesus asked for him to love the Lord instead of his possessions.

Jesus recognized that, in this person's life, great possessions got in the way of total commitment. The young man's possessions were material goods but whatever is treasure to us - material things, bitterness, lack of forgiveness of self or others, retaining our sins - whatever we are hanging on to that keeps us from following. We need to be rid of those things.

Prayer – Dear Father, Help me not to sell out to possessions but to give myself fully to You.

February 19   What

Matthew 26:15 *And Judas said, "What are you willing to give me IF I give Him to you?"*

Q What deal are we willing to make with Satan that betrays Christ?

Judas wanted money. What is our if - then?

This is how Judas responded when the chief priests, the scribes, and the elders plotted to kill Jesus. Judas was the treasurer of the disciples and wanted money for himself (John 12:6). But, what could we possibly gain in exchange for the loss of our soul (Mark 8:36-37)? The whole world – money, cities, countries, companies, - the whole nine yards - all of this is in this life and ends with physical death. The things of this earth end for us when we die. We can't take it with us.

Before the betrayal, greed took over Judas' thinking. Judas opened the door for Satan, then, later, Judas saw his error. Too late, he realized the horrible consequence of his decision. Tragically, although Judas had remorse, his remorse led him to suicide instead of salvation (Matthew 27:3-5). So many people today take the same path when they consider what they have done or what was done to them. They need to hear of, and believe in, the purification that comes from Jesus (1 John 1:9 and 3:3).

As we consider this event, WE NEED TO KNOW, if (when) we betray Jesus, we can receive forgiveness for the denial. Jesus, Himself, will advocate for us. Grace upon grace!! Judas hanged himself. He didn't do as Peter had done and repented. Judas didn't know he was forgiven; therefore he retained his sin against himself.

Unfortunately, we have help in making bad decisions. Whenever something good can happen, Satan is right there to mess things up if we allow him into our lives. When we are tempted to betray Jesus and enter into sin we need to consider the following question. What means more to us than life in Christ? We can betray Jesus in any of the SPICE areas: Spiritual, Physical, Intellectual, Community, or Emotional. Each day we need to pray for the Spirit within us to guide our decisions so that we have commitment, not betrayal.

Prayer – Dear Father, warn me of potential betrayal and help me to resist Satan.

February 20　　　　　　Behind

Luke 4: 6 Satan speaking: *All this authority I will give You IF you will worship before me, all will be Yours. Jesus said, "Get behind Me Satan."*

Q What is Satan's promise?

IF You will worship before me then I will give you everything.

Satan could offer Jesus authority because Satan is the ruler of this world (John 12:31b). We need to be careful not to underestimate Satan's power.

Satan is so bold he even tried to tempt the Son of God. Jesus had been led into the wilderness to be tested. He went without food for 40 days and probably had intense hunger. Satan will come to us in troubling times and we will be tested. He will tempt us in our weaknesses and/or in our strengths.

Jesus was tempted by Satan in three different ways, He was offered food after a 40 day fast; He could have had authority over all the kingdoms of the world; and He could have felt the human temptation to test God with an inappropriate action (Luke 4:1-13). Jesus rejected them all with scriptural quotes. We are to worship God and serve Him only (Luke 4:8b).

Satan had run out of ideas so he took a time out to come up with another time and plan to discredit Jesus (Luke 4:13). A significant time and place came in the Garden of Gethsemane where Jesus' sweat was like drops of blood. Again, Jesus obeyed God.

Quite often, the trials we face early in life prepare us for what comes later. If there are no early trials, later shock can be devastating. We face temptations every day but we are assured that God will always provide the way to deal with them (1 Corinthians 10:13).

Prayer – Dear Father, thank You for showing me how to resist Satan. Give me scripture to fend him off. Thank You for trials that strengthen me in my faith.

February 21   Fruitful

2 Peter 1:5-8 ... *faith, virtue, knowledge, self-control, perseverance, godliness, brotherly kindness, love – For IF these things are yours and abound, you will be neither barren nor unfruitful in the knowledge of our Lord Jesus Christ.*

Q How can we be fruitful in Christ?

IF we abound in the listed virtues, then we will be fruitful in the knowledge of Jesus.

Peter knew that having these characteristics would enhance our ability to know, and to take on, the nature of Christ. We will not be barren, instead we will be fruitful in our own lives and productive in leading others to life in Christ.

Peter's list of spiritual characteristics is similar to Paul's statement about spiritual fruit. His list includes love, joy, peace, long-suffering, kindness, goodness, faithfulness, gentleness, and self-control (Galatians 5:22-23). Peter's offering adds a few characteristics to Paul's list. Take a few moments to make sticky notes and tape them on the bathroom mirror and the refrigerator. Then, tape them on your heart.

Virtue, for example, is becoming more rare in the world as shown by the way people dress and the ridicule expressed by many groups towards those who are modest in dress and behavior. Brotherly kindness is especially helpful in the fellowship of believers.

Self-control is the opposite of so-called loss of control. "I lost control" is an attempt to excuse bad behavior. For example: "I lost control and hit him in the nose." Hmmm, "Where did you hit him?" Seems like pretty good control to me. When it comes to lust, people don't lose control, they choose to give control away. When in a position of choice of giving in to lust or following Christ, we need to ask to be filled with the spirit, and we will have all the self-control we need.

Prayer – Dear Father, help me practice these virtues in my life so that I will bear fruit for You.

February 22   Hear

Revelation 3:20 *IF anyone hears My voice and opens the door, I will come in to him and dine with him, and he with Me.*

Q How do we have Jesus' intimate presence in our lives?

IF we hear His voice and open up to Him, then He will enter every aspect of our lives.

How do we hear Jesus today? We have the Word (Jesus), the word (the Bible), and the Holy Spirit Who was given as an indwelling presence when Jesus left the earth. When Christ becomes the Lord of our lives, we are told we have His mind (1 Corinthians 2:16). And, then we know from God's word that we have a helper to guide us (John 16:7 and John 16:13*)*.

The Holy Spirit, as our Helper, has God's seal of approval. Part of the help the Holy Spirit gives is to teach us new things we need to know as well as remind us of everything Jesus taught us (John 14:26). This is one reason to be well versed in the Bible so we have something to be prompted to remember.

Is anyone listening? The main complaint that parents have about children is that they don't listen to them. The main complaint that children have about parents is that they don't listen to them. No baby book tells about the time Baby first listened. Might God feel that way about His children? How do we hear His voice? Listen. Listen! We can talk with Him in regular conversation. Ask for specific instructions and then listen. If you don't get a clear response, ask a yes or no question. Should I -----? Then listen.

The door opens both ways. If we open the door, He comes in to eat with us, and, we can go in to Him and find sustenance *(*John 10:9*)*. Jesus specifically called Himself the good Shepherd and the doorway to the Father. The shepherd sleeps in the entrance to the sheepfold to ensure that nothing bad enters and nothing good wanders away. When we open up to Christ, He comes into us. Those who trust in Jesus recognize His loving call, come to, and follow, Him. Jesus is always open for us to enter into Him.

Prayer – Dear Father, teach me that You will guide and direct me. Enter into me and help me to enter into You and listen for Your voice, however it may come.

February 23   With

Colossians 2:20 *IF with Christ you died to the elemental things of the universe, why do you live as IF you still belong to the world?*

Q How might we still belong to the world?

Simply put, IF we haven't yet died with Christ, then we are still making worldly things our god. We become what we worship. If we are banking on the things of the world we will worship the things of the world and be ashamed of God.

Do not love the world or the things in the world. If anyone loves the world, the love of the Father is not in him. For all that is in the world – the lust of the flesh, the lust of the eyes, and the pride of life – is not of the Father but is of the world 1 John 2:15-17.

John mentions several elemental things that we do that may tie us to the world. Those things may be material, physical, or emotional. If we love the world, or the things of the world such as adultery, fornication, pornography, and taking pride in things the world prizes, then we don't love God. But, why would we choose some elemental thing instead of God? We have made some lesser "god" the object of our time and affections.

There is an inclination towards evil in all of us. It is described as the doctrine of original sin. We don't have to teach children to be bad. Many people today try to excuse their choices by saying they were born that way, or some environmental force was responsible, or the flip saying, "The devil made me do it." Some may say that even murder is not our fault if we had a bad childhood, etc. But, evil action is still a choice. It's just that people want an excuse for their evil choices. Evil may involve alcohol, sex, drugs, etc. but whatever goes against the teachings in God's word is evil and we choose the consequences if we deviate from God's direction for our lives.

We have to die to elemental things and live in Christ.

Prayer – Dear Father, may I stop living by the world's example and let Your love and teachings direct me.

February 24   Both

Matthew 15:14   *IF the blind lead the blind, both will fall into a ditch.*

Q What is the problem of following someone who cannot see?

The implication is that the blind leader doesn't know where he/she is going. This is so true of people outside of the truth. IF you are following someone who can't see; then both of you will stumble. If we know someone is spiritually blind, why follow him? "There are none so blind as those who refuse to see," is a popular saying. While not from the Bible, it has a clear application to spiritual truth. Speaking of the Pharisees, *Jesus said, "Let them alone, they are blind leaders of the blind"* Matthew 15:14. Unfortunately, we have to say that of some churches and preachers today.

Another old saying is, "My mind is made up, don't confuse me with facts". This suggests a mindset. When we have a mindset we will accept any scrap of information that supports it and ignore a mountain of information that goes against it. INSTANT REPLAY - When we have a mindset we will accept any scrap of information that supports it and ignore a mountain of information that goes against it. The more imbedded the mindset, the more these statements are true. This is true for evil and for good.

There are those who insist on doing evil. Their mind is set in ungodliness. Those who exchange whatever truth about God for a lie are given the choice to live in the mess they make for themselves (Romans 1:25). It seems the greater the life-lies, the more lies it takes to cling to it. If we choose to live without God, we choose to die without God. What an ugly mindset-choice! Jesus gives us a life line, not a life lie.

To be given up by God is a terrible consequence. However, if people insist on living in a sinful condition, God will let them go. They are playing a strange game where there is really no good prize to be found. Do not follow someone who has given himself up to uncleanness. He should say, "Don't follow me, I'm lost."

We know Jesus is of the truth because He rose from the dead. We are amongst all men most to be envied!!

Prayer – Dear Father, help me to know Jesus as the truth and to follow Him faithfully in every step and decision.

February 25   Hear

1 Samuel 3:9 ... *IF He calls you, then you must say, "Speak, Lord, for your servant hears."*

Q What should we do when God calls us?

IF God calls then we are to listen.

Samuel was given to Eli as a servant to fulfill a vow his mother had made in order to become pregnant (1 Samuel 1:11). In this instance, God had called Samuel twice and Samuel had responded to Eli. Eli then knew it was God calling and gave instructions to Samuel to respond to God's instruction.

Isaiah was another person who heard the call of God. He said, *"Here am I, send me"* Isaiah 6:8. Isaiah heard the voice of God and responded with obedience.

Ananias, who lived at Damascus (a God-incident, not a coincidence) also answered the call. He responded to a vision of God by placing himself at God's disposal (Acts 9:10).

In both the Old and New Testaments, God calls people to action. God still calls His people to action in many ways. We can hear through the Bible, through nature, through visions, dreams, through circumstances, and through others. We have to be listening. We just have to be sure that when we open the door for the cat that the skunk doesn't come in instead. Satan will take every opportunity and use any means to lie and cheat us out of obedience to God.

How do we know it is God calling? His call must agree with complete Scripture, not just a proof-text. It must agree with the considerations of possessing Christians. It must build up ourselves and the fellowship of believers. Ask the Spirit if the message is from God. If it agrees with the power, gifts, and fruit, of the Spirit, it is of God.

Prayer – Dear Father, help me always to call on You and to be listening for Your directions. Help me be aware of when You are calling me.

February 26   Serve

Joshua 24:15 *IF it seems evil for you to serve the Lord, choose for yourselves this day whom you will serve ... As for me and my house we will serve the Lord.*

Q Are there those who think it evil to serve God?

Unfortunately, yes.

IF it seems evil to serve God! Come on now; this is unthinkable! The opposite is true. Not to serve God is evil. Joshua placed himself and his family in God's service.

We can follow a step by step process in our desire to serve God. Because He cares so much for us, we can *cast* all of our cares on Him (1 Peter 5:7). CAST is an acronym that will help us remember how to utilize His care. – Choose, Avoid evil, Seek God's wisdom, Trust in Him.

1. First make a firm, conscious choice. Choose whom you serve thoughtfully; this is serious business. Consider the possible consequences of the choices that are being considered.

2. Avoid evil - Satan wants to destroy us, if not with laziness, then with busy-ness. ... *the cares of this world, the deceitfulness of riches, and the desires for other things entering in, choke the word, and it becomes unfruitful* Mark 4:19.

3. Seek God's advice. If you don't know what to do in a given situation, ask God. He won't make you beg or feel embarrassed. He will give you the best answer to your problem (James 1:5-6).

4. Trust in God, We are admonished to place heartfelt trust in God and not to depend on our own thoughts (Proverbs 3:5). You may have to step away from the crowd and what they say is right. Beware of crowd, or mob, thinking.

    If there are any problems, start over at step 1. Not to choose is to choose.

Prayer – Dear Father, as for me and my house we will serve you, O God.

February 27   Will

Matthew 26:39 Jesus prayed, *"O My Father, IF it is possible, let this cup pass from Me, nevertheless, not as I will, but as You will."*

Q Why wasn't it possible to avoid crucifixion?

Because God's will was/is that the placement of our sin on Christ would allow us to have relationship with Him.

Jesus was in the Garden of Gethsemane which became a Garden of Decision. He was facing crucifixion, the Golgotha of death, which is not a pleasant way to die. However, in the economy of God, and the world for that matter, wrong doing demands consequences of punishment. Again, God wanted relationship with us so much that He chose the incredible sacrifice of punishment to His Son for our sins.

God will not allow sin to interfere with His relationship with us. There are many people who are unclear about what sin is. (See Romans 1:28-33, Matthew 15:19, Galatians 5:19-21, and Colossians 3:8-9 for lists of depraved activities).

Jesus had not sinned in any way but He knew that God couldn't have relationship with sinful people so He literally became our sin so that we could have the righteousness necessary to have fellowship with God (2 Corinthians 5:21). Jesus became all the ugly, disgusting things listed including all your and my transgressions.

Jesus *became* sin. He didn't just take our sins on His body, He *became sin*. He was temporarily forsaken by God because of this (Matthew 27:46). Then, on the cross, Jesus accomplished His mission and He and God were reunited.

We need to confess our sins and accept His sacrificial gift of grace with the utmost gratitude and humility.

Prayer – Dear Father, help me consider the cost of my salvation and live in appreciation of relationship with You.

February 28   Cleanse

1John 1:7 *But IF we walk in the light as He is in the light, we have fellowship with one another, and the blood of Jesus Christ His Son cleanses us from all sin.*

Q What happens when we walk as He walked?

IF we walk in His light then we have fellowship and cleansing.

I am the light of the world. He who follows Me shall not walk in darkness, but have the light of life John 8:12.

When we follow Jesus we share in His blessings and have all that He has to give.

We have fellowship in the Church, big C - God's children, not the church, little c – the building. Why would we want to have fellowship with a building? We need to fellowship with the Body of Christ and be in agreement with a common cause - like minded in our intent to have relationship with God and each other. This super goal eradicates all petty, personal priorities. It is important to remember that we are the Body of Christ. A church may be a group of people, but, unfortunately, that doesn't necessarily mean they are part of the Body.

We are cleansed of ALL sin: Cleansed and purified. This cannot be emphasized enough. Do not retain your sins against yourself. You are purified in Christ.

If Jesus is in us, Jesus will shine forth from us. Jesus is Light; Jesus gives us light; we become light to everyone around us (Matthew 5:14).

We are light! If you don't feel like light, get with the program. Ask God what is keeping you in the dark. Let the light of Christ extinguish the darkness and move you into the light of life in Christ.

In the olden days a window was called a "light." Jesus is light, When Jesus enters into us, we become light. Light shines through us so that people will see Jesus through what we do and say.

Prayer – Dear Father, I choose to walk in the Light, kept from darkness, so that Your light may be shown to others through me.

February 29   House

Hebrews 3:6 ... *Whose house we are IF we hold fast the confidence and the rejoicing of the hope firm to the end.*

Q How does Jesus become our house?

IF we hold fast and firm then He lives in us and we are His house.

A house is a building in which someone lives. Christ lives in us so it is an apt metaphor that we are His house. "In Christ" and "Christ in us" are common themes in the New Testament. Think of the different rooms in a house: living, sleeping, eating, office, etc. Christ is to live in every "room" of our lives.

Our bodies are also called temples of the Holy Spirit (1 Corinthians 6:19). A house is for living while a temple is for worship. All our rooms need to be open – no secret or hidden rooms. And we don't need to wait until they are all neat and pretty (Romans 5:8). He will help us clean house.

We should decorate our house with *confidence and rejoicing.* Confidence comes from "con" – with, and "fidelity" – loyalty. Rejoicing is part of the fruit of the Spirit. We need to serve Him with fidelity and joyousness. Take a few moments and see what the Master Decorator wants in your house. What delightful pictures and furnishings does He provide? What does He suggest you throw out?

Jesus referred to the temple as a place where prayers are to lifted up to God (Isaiah 56:7b Quoted in Matthew 21:13). Jesus applied this verse to the synagogue but it also can be used to describe our bodies as His house. Our bodies can be a continual fragrant prayer offered up to Him.

Prayer – Dear Father, my body is an open house for you. Please occupy every room.

MARCH

Miscellaneous LITTLE WORDS

Meditation Aids

Uses and examples:

AT - preposition – a place occupied – (Matthew 26:58).

GO - imperative verb – to move or depart, to continue, to change from A to B – (John 14:2-4).

ME – personal pronoun – the objective case of "I" – (1 Chronicles 4:10).

MY – personal pronoun – the possessive case of "I" – (Lamentations 3:22-23).

NO – adverb – dissent, denial, refusal, to qualify a previous statement – (John 6:37).

ON – preposition – about, above and in contact –
        (Philippians 4:8).

UP – adverb, preposition, or adjective - to, toward, or in a more elevated position – (Mark 8:34).

March 1   Go

<u>John 6:68</u> *But Simon Peter answered Him, "Lord to whom shall we GO? You have the words of eternal life."*

> Jesus had compared following Him to eating His flesh, and many found this too hard to swallow. So they left Him. Jesus then explained that He was speaking of His teachings and asked the disciples if they too were going to go away (vs65-67).

> GO – Jesus is the best one to follow. No one else is worth following.

Q Is there any other way to have a right relationship with God?   No.

> Eternal life is a promise that came into greater prominence with the advent of Jesus. The prospect of eternal life, with or without the presence of God, needs to be considered. Eternal life in relationship with God begins when we enter the "In Christ" relationship.

> *To whom shall we go?* The person or "ism" you go to depends on what they, or it, offers. Peter had heard Jesus' promise as stated in John 3:16, and wanted what Jesus had to offer. Several bits of evidence of Jesus' offerings are given in John, chapters 3 thru 6. Some believed, some left – which are you? If you haven't closely studied the first six chapters of John, it would be a good idea to do so. John was the only Gospel written for Gentiles so it is more clearly directed to non-Jewish people. Read the short version of the Christmas story in John 1:1 and Hebrews 1:1-2 comparing the coming of Christ into the world with His help in creating the world.

> People often make idols of rock stars, actors, actresses, athletes – the rich and famous. They buy sweatshirts, albums, pictures – all sorts of stuff – and even try to act like their idol. Be it known: Jesus is the ONE to be adored and Who is the best model for our behavior.

> The disciples believed that Jesus was the Messiah and that He had the promise of eternal life. We, also, can GO to Jesus for the certainty of eternal life.

> *To whom shall we go?* This question is still critical for this life and the next. As we give it the attention it deserves, we agree with Peter and go with Jesus.

Prayer – Dear Father, thank You for the truth of *the words of eternal life.*

March 2   Saved

John 10:9 *I am the door, if anyone enters by Me, he will be saved, and will GO in and out and find pasture.*

GO means to move freely.

Q What is the importance of this door?

If we enter through Jesus, then we will be saved. This is the critical first step in an if/then experience.

Jesus is the door to salvation. The shepherd literally was the door to the sheep fold. He would lie down to sleep in the entrance to keep the sheep in and harm out. If we make Him our door, our lives will be safe and "pastureful."

The "in door" of Jesus is always open. It is important to note that we must first go in. We have studied much about the "in Christ" relationship. Once we are in Christ, all the benefits that God gives us through the Holy Spirit are ours for the asking and receiving.

The "out door" of Jesus opens to abundant life. If we have gone in, then we can go out, loving God with all our heart, soul, mind, and strength. That is the most loving, joyful, and peaceful way to live. Once in – that is, saved, we can safely go out, leading a Godly life. And continue to go in and out.

When we go in, we find salvation and safety, so that when we go out we will find helpful pasture as indicated in Psalm 23:3. (Pasture is an inclusive term for life's needs.) If we accept Him as our Shepherd, we will live as God intended when He first created us.

Prayer – Dear Father, thank You for salvation, for safety, and for green pastures.

March 3   Blessings

1 Chronicles 4:10 *Oh that You would bless ME indeed, and enlarge my territory, that Your hand would be with ME, and that You would keep ME from evil, that I may not cause pain!*

You can read about Jabez, his mother, and his brothers in 1 Chronicles 4:9.

Q What did Jabez ask for?

> The "Prayer of Jabez" has become popular in some circles because people want God's blessing. He asked for a blessing that would: give him large territory, provide him with God's help, protect him from evil, and that he wouldn't hurt others. Property, Power, Protection, and Painless.

> We also find blessings in the New Testament that God grants to us, listed in the beatitudes, *... the kingdom of heaven ... comfort ... an inheritance ... being filled with righteousness ... mercy ... to see God ... to be called sons of God ... and to have a great reward in heaven* Matthew 5:3-11 (Short version).

> Jabez prayed for enlarged territory, God gives us the kingdom of heaven. Jabez prayed for God's help. God gives us His Spirit to guide and assist us in every area of life. Jabez prayed to be protected from evil. God gives us spiritual armor. Jabez prayed not to cause pain. God wants us to give comfort in any trouble or tribulation in the same way He comforts us (2 Corinthians 1:4).

> It is important to realize that the prayer of Jabez was an Old Testament prayer, before Christ and the Holy Spirit. We now have the "much more" of the fulfillment of the Old Testament prophecies. We can pray for, and be thankful for, the blessings of the beatitudes (Be-attitudes). What is your prayer?

Prayer - Dear Father, thank You for the blessing of salvation through Christ, the infilling of the Holy Spirit, and all the blessings that result from our life in Them.

March 4   Mercy

Lamentations 3:22-23 *Through the Lord's mercies we are not consumed, because His compassions fail not. They are new every morning: Great is Your faithfulness. "The Lord is MY portion," says MY soul, "Therefore I hope in Him!"*

MY – shows ownership.

Q What does morning bring for you?

God's mercies and compassions - breakfast food for the soul. Good, Lord, it is morning.

Regardless of what may have happened the day before, whatever way we may have erred or failed, His mercies and compassion are new. It is of no benefit to us to wallow in our inadequacies - learn and live on. He wants us to enjoy the love, joy, and peace of relationship with Him. Windshields are bigger than rear view mirrors for a reason.

Mercies are not getting what we deserve. *We are not consumed*, swallowed up by regrets and self-loathing.

Compassions are empathy for and consideration of all the factors that affect our lives. The word em-path-y has the meaning of being "in a path." Jesus had to take on the form of humanity so that we would know about God, so that we would know that He understood what it was like to be tempted, so that He could help those who are tempted, that He would know suffering, and to know that He is merciful (Hebrews 2:17-18). Sympathy means someone feels sorrow for us. Empathy means they feel our sorrow. Jesus suffered like us so He has empathy. Because of His compassion, we can live with positive passion fueled by love, joy, and peace.

GREAT is His faithfulness, so His mercies and compassions are infallible. Our benefit is not dependent on anything we do except hope in Him. There is nothing we need to do except to accept. Then live in His grace.

The Lord is my portion! He is proportionately above all else. *Therefore, I hope in Him* because of His mercies, compassions, newness, and faithfulness.

Prayer – Dear Father, thank You for being my portion.

March 5   Prepare

<u>John 14:2-4</u> *In My Father's house are many mansions, if it were not so, I would have told you. I GO to prepare a place for you. And if I GO and prepare a place for you, I will come again and receive you to Myself; that where I am there you may be also.*

Mansions are palatial rooms.

GO – move to.

Q What will be our heavenly address?

God's house.

Jesus is telling us that He is preparing a magnificent place for us in the eternal Kingdom of God. *If it were not so*, and *if I go*, are not questions about whether or not these things will happen, but definite statements about the "places." The emphasis is on the places, not the ifs. We have the historical perspective of seeing beyond His present tense statements. After His resurrection, He went to prepare a place for us and, having prepared the place, He promised to come again and receive us to be with Him.

In order for all of this to occur, we must enter into relationship with Jesus. Being a child of God is a right given to us by Jesus. There should not be a sense of entitlement on our part. We get the right by believing and receiving Him (John 1:12). If we *receive* Him, He will *receive* us.

To *receive* Him is to take Him into our minds, hearts, and lives. Once we have received Him, whether He comes before or after our physical death, He will receive us to Himself.

Instead of just come and *GO*, Jesus' promise is to come, and *GO*, and *come again* to take us to the place He has prepared for us.

Have you entered into relationship with Jesus? Are you ready to move into your mansion when He comes to get you? If not, *receive* and *believe* - make John 1:12 your beginning in Christ.

Prayer – Dear Father, thank You for the place you have for me in this life and the next.

March 6   Repent

Luke 5:32 *Jesus answered, "Those who are well have NO need of a physician, but those who are sick. I have not come to call the righteous, but sinners to repentance."*

NO refers to misguided thinking.

Q What is our spiritual health?

We need to recognize that outside of Christ we suffer from two maladies, we are all sinners, and we all fall short of God's glory (Romans 3:23*).*

The scribes and Pharisees had complained that the disciples were eating with undesirable characters (Luke5:30). There seemed to be two committees. One to criticize if Jesus, or the followers, did one thing and another committee to criticize if they did the opposite.

The humor in the Bible is often subtle and is somewhat different from the gut busting stories that we deem to be funny. Here, Jesus was speaking tongue in cheek. *Those who are well* refers to those who think they are well. The fifty cent word for the humorous thought that they think they are well is "facetious". This is irony in its highest form. It is a lesson for us not to concentrate our efforts on *those who are well.* Jesus dismissed the unrepentant as people who look good on the outside but have cadaver bones and untold filthiness on the inside (Matthew 23:27b).

Those of us who are *sick* and realize it, are invited to respond to Jesus' call to repent which is to turn 180 degrees. Instead of going away from God, we need to go towards Him. Then, after we have been made *well*, we can share the good news with others.

Without Christ, no one is *well.* No one, without God, is spiritually healthy, but not everyone admits they are sinners. Because of their spiritual blindness, they miss out on salvation and eternal life with God.

Prayer – Dear Father, thank You for helping me realize my spiritual illness and for healing me through Christ.

March 7   Distance

<u>Matthew 26:58</u> *But Peter followed Him AT a distance …*

Peter wanted a safe distance so as not to be recognized as a disciple. Sound familiar?

Q How close are we following?

So often, we follow at a distance where we will not be noticed by the world.

Peter was in fear for his physical life. He knew the hatred the Pharisees had for Jesus and he also knew the capabilities of a mob when adrenalin overcomes reason. It is to his credit that he did follow, even if it were at a distance. Later on he came close.

Peter may have been remembering walking on water, the healings, the miracles, and the teachings of Jesus. He may even have remembered when Jesus accused him of being Satan because Peter was thinking on his terms instead of understanding God's plan (Matthew 16:23). Eventually Peter would deny <u>any</u> relationship with Jesus.

Then, came transformation. Peter had met Jesus' eyes as Jesus was taken to His earthly judgment and could see forgiveness in them. He had visited the empty tomb, and had met and talked with Jesus in the post-resurrection experiences. So, in haste, he dove into the water to join Jesus on the shore of the Sea of Tiberias (John 21:1). He then knew that the magnitude of his spiritual life transcended any threat to his physical life and obeyed Jesus' command to follow Him (John 21:19).

My experience, and perhaps yours, is so like Peter's. So many times I have followed at a distance. So often I have been mindful of the things of men. But I have looked into His eyes and found mercy and compassion. I so want to obey His commands and follow Him. If you haven't seen compassion in His eyes, look now! Then follow closely by meditating on His word, prayer, and by staying constantly aware of the ways that God is blessing and protecting.

Prayer – Dear Father, thank You for not giving up on me.

March 8   Yielded

Matthew 27:50 *And Jesus cried out again with a loud voice, and yielded UP His spirit.*

Yielded UP indicates a purposeful act.

Q Was Jesus' life taken from Him?   No!

His life was not taken from Him; He yielded it UP for us. Each time He cried out, it was with a loud forceful voice indicating strength.

Earlier, *Jesus cried out with a loud voice, saying … "My God, My God, why have You forsaken Me?"* Matthew 27:46b. *… He said, "It is finished!" And bowing His head, He gave up His spirit* John 19:30. *And when Jesus had cried out with a loud voice, He said, "Father, into Your hands I commit My spirit," Having said this, He breathed His last* Luke 23:46.

It seems logical that the three sayings follow the order given here. First Matthew - Jesus felt *forsaken* because our sins separated Him from God. Then John - He indicated His life giving purpose had been accomplished – our sins were removed by His grace. Finally, Luke - He committed His spirit to His Father and was reunited with Him.

The reason Jesus was forsaken was because He became my sin, your sin, and the sins of the world for all time. God is too pure to be present in evil, therefore Christ, Who came to *be sin*, was abandoned temporarily. After having finished His work, Jesus was reunited with God in the continuing mystery of the Trinity.

So much of God's work is God's work, not ours, and while beyond our total comprehension and understanding, it is well within our ability to accept and enjoy. It is ours to know that through the cross we achieve relationship with our Creator that can be enjoyed now and continues for eternity.

Our sin separates us from God. Jesus took our sins away on the cross. As we accept His death for us, we begin life in Him.

Prayer – Dear Father, it is beyond my understanding why You would love me so. But You do. I thank You for doing the incredible - to bring me unto Yourself. WOW!

March 9   Light

1 John 1:5b *God is light and in Him is NO darkness at all.*

NO means none.

Q Is there any darkness in God?   NO!

We don't really appreciate light if we haven't experienced darkness. That is one of the reasons bad things exist. We wouldn't know good things if there weren't bad things. We don't know the fullness of the grace of God if we haven't recognized the awful darkness of Satan. Thanks be to God that the Holy Spirit convicts us of sin, righteousness, and judgment (John 16:8) and gives us understanding of grace, mercy, and eternal life. Look around you and let the Holy Spirit convince you of sin. People are condemned because they ignore the light of Christ, love darkness, and perform evil acts (John 3:19-20).

Being in total darkness is like being blind. It is impossible for a blind person to describe light. Those who choose spiritual darkness have no way of seeing the light of Christ until the Holy Spirit convicts them. He may use a "sighted" person to describe it to them. When we choose to believe in Christ we can literally "see the light". I wouldn't have seen it if I hadn't believed it.

Some people are so evil that they even harm loved ones to prevent evidence from being given against them. Most criminals aren't sorry for what they have done, they are sorry they got caught. They just don't want their misdeeds to be known.

Think through the consequences of the evil that enters your mind and the negative emotions that come from your heart. So often, what seems to be reasonable to do at the time has nasty results. One of the characteristic of Attention Deficit Hyperactive Disorder is impulsivity. Let's not be ADHD in our life in Christ. It is best never to do anything that you think you are going to have to lie about. This could help us to think before doing anything when it would be wrong or harmful.

People who are in Christ have come out of darkness, have become light, and are walking in the light that Jesus gives them (Ephesians 5:8).

Prayer – Dear Father, I love light, Jesus is the light of the world, I love Jesus.

March 10   Epistle

2 Corinthians 3:3 *… clearly you are an epistle of Christ, … written not with ink but by the Spirit of the living God, not ON tablets of stone but ON tablets … of the heart.*

ON means installed.

Q What is one of the ways God communicates with people?

By His living epistles – Christ in us.

We may be the only Bible that others around us read. We are an epistle, a living letter, (a loving letter) showing and telling people about the Gospel. But, how can the Spirit write on our hearts if we don't have Him in our lives? If you don't have Him, ask, and God will give Him to you immediately (Luke 11:13).

Clearly you are an epistle – really? Hopefully! Not only should this thought be clear to us, it follows that our message should be clear to others. What is the condition of our writing surface? Is it full of smudges and hard to read? Are we confusing to others?

Have you ever tried to write on a soggy, soiled sheet of paper? Not much fun - soggy paper may not even take ink. *The heart is deceitful above all things, and desperately wicked; Who can know it?* Jeremiah 17:9. Who can write on a heart like that? Nobody can know the message if the writing material is compromised. Christ makes our writing material perfect.

What words about Christ are in our letter, written on our hearts by the Spirit of the living God? There were tablets of stone with 10 commandments, which are wonderful "shalt nots" to keep us safe. Now, the truth about Jesus is written on the *tablets of our hearts* so others can "read" the "shalls" of love, joy, and peace.

Prayer – Dear Father, dwell in and cleanse my heart so that the letter written on it may clearly proclaim the good news of Christ.

March 11   Believe

Romans 10:14-15 *How then shall they call ON Him in Whom they have not believed? And how shall they believe in Him of Whom they have not heard?*

ON – in reference to Christ.

Q Do you believe there is a Savior?

Question 1 - How shall they call if they haven't believed?

Who? Those who need to believe in Jesus.

What? Call on Him – Jesus.

Why? So they can believe.

How? Someone has to tell them.

When? Any opportune time.

Where? Wherever they are in time and place.

Question 2 - How shall they believe if they haven't heard?

Who? Those who need to hear. How did you hear?

What? Hear of Him and believe in Him.

Why? They can't believe if they haven't heard.

How? We need to tell them so they can hear.

When? After they hear.

Where? In their hearts and minds.

The disciples told of Jesus, and His story has been passed on through a chain of witnesses up to you and me. It is so wonderful to be another link in the chain and that the chain can be extended through us. Who do you want to be the next link?

Prayer – Dear Father, help me, at all times, to show and tell the Good News of salvation and life in Christ to those whom You send my way.

March 12   Steadfast

Luke 9:51b ... *when the time had come for Him to be received up, that He steadfastly set His face to GO to Jerusalem.*

> GO means move towards.

Q What does it mean to set one's face?

> To be steadfast in resolve and intention: stead = position; fast = solidly in place. We can apply this verse to Jesus and to ourselves.

> Who? Jesus.

> What? To be crucified and resurrected.

> Why? For our salvation.

> How? *He steadfastly set His face.*

> When? In the fullness of time.

> Where? To go to His death in Jerusalem.

> It wasn't going to be fun but it was going to be joy. This was why Jesus came into the world in human form. He was determined to bring us into relationship with God.

> For what purpose? So we would not perish! Why could He? Because He is God. How could He? In love, by taking punishment for our sin and making us righteous.

> Has your time come to be delivered from sin? To set your face to follow Jesus? The time to accept Jesus as Savior and Lord is when the Spirit has gotten your attention. Like, NOW! If you put it off, Satan will try to prevent another entrance time (2 Corinthians 6:2b). There are times we need to set our faces; the task will be joyful even if it seems scary or difficult.

Prayer – Dear Father, let there be no thing between my life and my intention to follow You.

March 13   Comes

John 6:37 *All that the Father gives Me will come to Me, and the one who comes to Me I will by NO means cast out* ...

NO refers to unwavering acceptance.

Q Will Jesus reject you?

NO!! Not if you come to Him. This is GOOD NEWS!

The words *all* and *one* are interesting. All refers to the whole of humanity. *All* people have the possibility of life in Christ. *One* refers to each individual, you or me. The ones who come make up the all who are welcome. It is important that all sin, for all time, is forgiven by the one act of Christ. However, the transaction is only complete when sins are confessed and the sacrifice is accepted. It is when He is believed and received that we become children of God (John 1:12).

There are those who think they have to clean up their act before they are acceptable to God. This is not possible or necessary (Romans 5:8). The basic fact is that they can't possibly be clean enough on their own terms to be acceptable. The good news is that Christ has made us clean. There is nothing we need to do except to accept.

The invitation, in truth, is come-as-you-are. Once we are in Christ, and He in us, salvation has occurred; the process of sanctification can begin.

If you haven't come to Jesus – if you need to accept Christ, and didn't do it yesterday, here is another chance, now, today, NOW (2 Corinthians 6:2b). What a wonderful day this can be! Tell others the good news! Send out announcements. They did when you were born. Why not when you are born again!

Prayer – Dear Father, thank You for accepting me just as I was.

March 14   In

<u>Romans 8:1</u> *There is therefore now NO condemnation for those who are in Christ Jesus.*

NO – means none whatsoever.

Q Is there condemnation?

Not if we are *in Christ Jesus.*

Not only are all called as individuals, each one has no condemnation – spot free! Several products, from those that clean cars to those that clean dishes, are trumpeted as leaving no spots. This is a good and desirable thing. Jesus is the ultimate spot remover. As noted in Ephesians 5:26-27. He presents the church to Himself without *spot or wrinkle.*

Should we condemn ourselves? No, there is <u>NO</u> condemnation. Not others, nor should we condemn our self. Paul declared the only One Who was qualified to judge him was God (1 Corinthians 4:3b-4). And the Lord declared Paul, and us, pure! WOW!

The *therefore,* in our verse for the day, refers to our deliverance through Christ. If you have any struggle or doubt within yourself, realize this is a tool of Satan to destroy your joy and peace. God's grace is sufficient. That means it is enough. No amount of remorse on our part will do what His grace has already done. INSTANT REPLAY - NO AMOUNT OF REMOSE ON OUR PART WILL DO WHAT HIS GRACE HAS ALREADY DONE. Don't abuse His grace; don't presume upon it; just accept it; be thankful for it; and live in His marvelous grace.

Are you one of *those who are in Christ Jesus*? If not, why not? Give yourself to Him now and accept Him into your mind, heart, and life.

If we ... *are in Christ* ... we are in Him for now and for eternity.

Prayer – Dear Father, thank You for bringing us into Christ.

March 15   On

<u>Colossians 3:12</u> ... *put ON tender mercies, kindness, humility, meekness, longsuffering, bearing with one another and forgiving one another ...*

> Put ON means to make these virtues a part of our life.
>
> Paul uses a metaphor of clothing in Colossians 3:8-14. There are things to put off and things to put on. The instruction is that we have the power and responsibility to do this. We need to make a conscious choice to put virtues on the inside that show themselves as actions on the outside.

Q What virtues should we *put on?*

> *Tender mercies* – gentle and loving care.
>
> *Kindness* – sympathy with consideration.
>
> *Humility* – without arrogance.
>
> *Meekness* – mild and unassuming.
>
> *Longsuffering* – patient and tolerant.
>
> *Bearing with* – Putting up with differences.
>
> *Forgiving* – as if it never happened.
>
> *To top it all off, to bind everything together, make your spiritual garment the power of love* <u>Colossians 3:14</u>.
>
> Compare with 1 Corinthians 13:4-10, Galatians 5:22-23, and Matthew 5:3 -10.
>
> When His love is observed in us, it is very winsome to others. Meditate on these things. Meditation is medication for the soul.

Prayer – Dear Father, thank you for "clothing" that makes me look like a million loves (intended).

March 16   Good

<u>Ephesians 4:29</u> *Let NO corrupt word proceed out of your mouth, but what is good for necessary edification.*

Corrupt - that which is fraudulent or causes rot.

NO means not any – none.

Q Should we use corrupt words? No. This verse is edification medication.

What is the source of corrupt words? The heart produces evil thoughts, including blasphemy - any negative thoughts about God, Christ, or the Holy Spirit (Matthew 15:19).

A corrupt heart produces corrupt and corrupting words. Corrupt words corrupt the environment around us. If sewage is spewed into an area, that area becomes repulsive. We have the power to corrupt friends, family, and our life space. Should we?

If you are hearing corrupt words, you know the person with that behavior is outside of Christ at that time. We are to witness to, but not fellowship with, such people if they continue to use corrupt words.

The word *let* means we have control, which is ours if we have the fruit of the Spirit (Galatians 5:22-23). If people are having trouble with what is coming out of their mouths, they need to subject their tongues to the healing power of the Holy Spirit.

But no man can tame the tongue. It is an unruly evil, full of deadly poison. With it we bless our God and Father, and with it we curse men, who have been made in the similitude of God. Out of the same mouth proceed blessing and cursing. My brethren, these things ought not to be so <u>James 3:8-10</u>. We can't control our tongue but God can. Give your tongue to Him every moment. And don't take it back.

The word *but* gives us the good news that there is an alternative to corruption. The alternative is edification – *necessary edification.* Edification (growth from instruction) is not optional. Sometimes we need to set ourselves down and have a little self-talk. Play nice. When we give our tongue to God, He changes corruption to edification.

Prayer – Dear Father, let the words of my mouth be delightful in Your sight.

March 17   Trust

<u>Proverbs 3:5</u> *Trust in the Lord with all your heart. And lean not ON your own understanding; in all your ways acknowledge Him, and He shall direct your paths.*

    ON means our understanding may be suspect.

Q How can we avoid going astray?

    Acknowledge Him in <u>everything</u>.

    It is interesting how often the word *all* shows up in Scripture. We are not to be half-hearted in our acknowledgement of God. He certainly isn't half-hearted with us.

    All includes all <u>S</u>piritual, <u>P</u>hysical, <u>I</u>ntellectual, <u>C</u>ommunity, and <u>E</u>motional activities, the whole SPICE rack. I don't really want to take a chance of getting messed up because of faulty thinking and then having to have Him bail me out. I'll start with Him and avoid negative consequences. We don't want to lean on our own understanding. What is <u>under</u> our <u>standing</u> is the foundation of our success in life and we certainly want a foundation in which we can trust. We have all leaned on something, at one time or another that gave way. In Christ we have the best and lasting solid foundation that possibly could be provided   (1 Corinthians 3:11).

    Have you ever leaned on someone and have him impishly move? That can be unsettling if not dangerous. Have you ever leaned on something and have it give way? Not fun. Our *understanding* is questionable at best. We need to lean on, rely on, *trust in the Lord.*

    We are to trust Him because our way of thinking is faulty. Man's best thinking is a one way street to death (Proverbs 14:12). Rest on His foundation – *He shall direct your paths.*

    (1) *Trust in the Lord*, (2) *with all your heart*, (3) He will show you <u>His</u> way

1 – 2 – 3 Go!

Prayer – Dear Father, I want Your guidance in ALL my ways, depending on <u>Your</u> understanding.

March 18   New

Mark 2:21 *No one sews a piece of unshrunk cloth ON an old garment or else the new piece pulls away from the old, and the tear is made worse.*

ON means the new is attached to the old.

Q What is the meaning of this parable?

One lesson is that Jesus is the new cloth. We are the old garment, torn and in need of fixing. If we try to patch Jesus on us, instead of in us, we may be pulled in different directions. Jesus was referring to those who were attempting to integrate Christianity with Judaism. Even today, some are trying to combine Christianity with some religion. Much is said about that in Paul's writings, see Galatians for instance.

For those of you who don't know anything about shrinking, it means the garment fits until you wash it and then it may only fit your younger sibling, if you are lucky. My mother attempted to weave a rug using all kinds of rags she had from new and old stuff she had saved in a basket. She even added in some nylons that had runs in them. It looked wonderful. Then she washed it. Oh, my! – what a wrinkled up mess. It was painful to see and more painful to walk on. If we try to mix Christ in with our old selves, our experience in the "washer of life" will be filled with lumps.

We need to be new creations. There are ordinances in many cities that prohibit the use of old materials in new construction. To paraphrase a phrase - Don't try to put new boards on an old building. I doubt those laws were based on 2 Corinthians 5:17 but they could have been. In Him all of the old goes to the dump and entirely new things, *all things,* are fresh, clean, and *new.* Too often there is an attempt to combine Christianity with old beliefs or habits. This will likely lead to life like a wheel that is out of balance; (New parable) things get really bumpy.

I don't want to try to somehow incorporate Christ into the existing framework of my life or to dilute life in Him with weeds. The new life in Christ is too wonderfully fantastic. I want to incorporate my life into Christ so that everything is new! Every once in a while we should take a trip through our life and see if anything is there that should have been left behind.

Prayer – Dear Father, help me to start each day all new in Christ.

March 19   Think

Philippians 4:8 ... think ON these things: True, Noble, Just, Pure, Lovely, Good report, Virtue, Praiseworthy...

ON – namely about good stuff – The following acronym, or make up your own, helps us to remember the attributes named in today's verse. The Nice Juicy Plum Looks Good, Very Purple.

Q What is ON your mind?

The implication is that we can choose to think the opposites of each - false, base, unfair, etc. It is our choice with which we fill our minds. Both positive and negative thoughts are available. We need to control our thoughts, Put on your sheriff's hat and badge and arrest any deviant thought and train it to be obedient to Christ (2 Corinthians 10:5).

If our minds are filled with these things, there is no room for mental garbage. The best way to have a weedless lawn is to have healthy grass.

True – anything to do with Jesus is the truth.

Noble – that which is dignified and decent.

Just – honorable and righteous.

Pure – wholesome and uncorrupted.

Lovely – delightful and pleasant.

Good report – wonderful to be told.

Virtue – moral and good.

Praiseworthy – admirable and to be commended.

Think on these things. Meditate.

Prayer – Dear Father, purify my mind with noble, praiseworthy things of good report.

March 20   Dwell

Revelation 21:3b-4 *Behold, the tabernacle of God is with men, and He will dwell with them, and they shall be His people. God Himself will be with them and be their God. And God will wipe away every tear from their eyes; there shall be NO more death, nor sorrow, nor crying. There shall be NO more pain, for the former things have passed away.*

NO means none of the negative things.

Q Will there be hardship in heaven?

No.

God will be with us and *dwell* (tabernacle) with us: no tears, no death, no sadness, no pain. The final words of Revelation are words of wonderful encouragement. Meanwhile, while we are on earth, tears are God's method of washing our brains.

No more death – Spiritual death stings because it has strength given by the law. Victorious life comes through the Lord Jesus and for that, we give thanks to God (1 Corinthians 15:56). Our main enemy is sin and, in Christ, we have victory over sin.

The bottom line is that heaven is God's place where His will is perfectly accomplished (Matthew 6:10). Therefore, heaven is good. In Christ, we don't have to be concerned about where we are or have been and we don't have to worry about where or when we are going. All the questions about the how, when, where, etc. of His coming can be put to rest and we can relax in knowing that it is all in His hands and that God is good.

Behold! Take solace, the tabernacle of God is with us. The former things, that is, the tribulations we experienced in life will be gone. He will live with us as His *people.* He is our God. He is with us. Whatever your present problem, God is with you now and will sustain you until earthly problems have finished their work. It is important to remember that whatever trials we have as Christians, are far less than the problems that people outside of Christ bring upon themselves.

Prayer – Dear Father, thank You for all the good that You have done for us and all the wonderful promises you have for our future in this life and the next.

March 21   Loose

<u>John 11:44</u> *Lazarus came forth bound hand and foot with grave clothes, and his face was wrapped with a cloth. Jesus said to them, "Loose him and let him GO."*

> GO means it is our job as Christian siblings to loosen the bonds of those who enter the family.

Q Why did Jesus ask others to set Lazarus free from his bonds?

He wanted them to come close, recognize Lazarus as alive, and take responsibility for his release. This is another one of the living parables Jesus gave to us. It is the parable of us and our work in the Body of Christ. Lazarus, symbolically bound by grave clothes - old dead acts - was brought forth, his face wrapped with a separate cloth similar to the burial treatment of Jesus. Jesus could have removed the burial cloths but told the onlookers, "*Loose him and let him go.*" In the narrative of Ananias and Paul, we find an amazing example. Ananias actually called Saul (soon to be Paul) his brother (Acts 9:17). Brother? After all Paul had done? This brother had been a big bother. <u>Brother</u>? But God had told Ananias all that Paul would do as a family member in the Body of Christ. Do you know any "brothers"?

So often, after Christ has set a person free from their sins, we keep that person bound in past sins because we fail to forgive and we remember their sins against them. Whether we don't appreciate our own deliverance, or perhaps, we have never forgiven ourselves, we may be in the same condition as Lazarus. Is it time for you to be loosed? Are you still bound, or binding others in sin? Is it time to release someone you have bound?

We were serving a church during our seminary experience. After visiting a family, and inviting them to come to church, they came and were met at the door by a regular who said to them, "I never thought you would darken the door of a church." Really! The family turned, left and never came back.

Remember, we are required to forgive, but not necessarily reconcile if the other person doesn't join in the transaction (across-action). Forgiveness is a one way street and gives both parties release. Reconciliation is a two way street and restores relationship. We are reconciled with God (2 Corinthians 5:19). Loosen others, loosen yourself. GO to newness of life in Christ. Love.

Prayer – Dear Father, may Your grace <u>to me</u> extend <u>through me</u> to those in need.

March 22   Turned

Luke 22:61 *And the Lord turned and looked AT Peter.*

AT indicates their eyes met. Note: Jesus took the initiative.

Q What might be our reaction if we were looking at Jesus after denying Him?

With Peter and Judas we have two reactions to the crucifixion events. Peter hung around Jesus all this eventful night. Jesus had told him that before the rooster announced the dawn, he would voice three denials, a verbal betrayal (Matthew 26:34). Meanwhile, Judas, scheming how he could make a little money on the side, went to the rulers and made a deal to exchange Jesus for 30 silver coins, a financial betrayal (Matthew 26:15-16). What a horrific bargain; he didn't give Jesus much value.

Peter followed, but far off, and made his three denials as Jesus had predicted. Judas went to the garden to betray Jesus for 30 pieces of silver. Later on, Jesus turned His face toward Peter and, evidently, Peter saw love, compassion, and forgiveness because he turned towards Jesus. Judas went back to the Pharisees. They turned a cold shoulder to him and he threw the coins on the floor (Matthew 27:5).

Peter went out and wept bitterly, repented, and became a pillar of the early church. Judas, a thief in disciple's clothing, never got the point about the Kingdom of God, saw no future in it, and went out and hanged himself.

Jesus saw the potential of Peter and persevered in relationship with him. The Pharisees used Judas' greed to get what they wanted and then didn't want anything more to do with him. Jesus delivered Peter from his weakness. The world discarded Judas with his weakness still in effect.

The war is still raging. Satan is continually bargaining with people to get them to betray Jesus. Will they end up being rejected and hating the price they got? Many people are following Jesus at a distance. Will they turn to Jesus, be accepted, and become disciples? Or, will they be like Judas? Let us be responsive to the Holy Spirit and respond as Peter did.

Prayer – Dear Father, thank You that I see mercy and compassion when I look at You.

March 23   Forgive

Jeremiah 31:34c *For I will forgive their iniquity, and their sin I will remember NO more.*

Our iniquity is a state of being. Our sins are the result of our iniquity.

NO means never.

Q Can God forget?

Today's verse says, "*I will remember no more*" understood to mean that our sins will not be remembered <u>against</u> us. God doesn't think about them, neither should we.

This is where the saying, Forgive and forget came from. In God's grace, forgiveness is as if it never happened. When we are pure in Christ, there is nothing that needs to be remembered (1 John 3:3).

The worse that the offense of another hurts, the more we need to thank God for forgiving <u>us</u>. When we remember an offense, we should not re-member it, giving it new arms and legs. We should send it to the cross along with our own sin. We thank God for forgiving us and we extend forgiveness to our offender. Then we need to think about good things. Windshields are bigger than rearview mirrors for a reason.

When we have the mind of Christ we will forgive as He forgives. Jesus allowed that these people could be forgiven because they didn't know what they were doing (Luke 23:34). Some didn't know because they had just joined the mob, as people do today, with no idea of what was going on. Others had motive but did not realize they were crucifying the Christ of God. Even though they were forgiven, they did not accept the forgiveness so it was of no avail. Do we know what we are doing? Does it seem reasonable to sin against ourselves, others and against God?

Jesus knew what He was doing. He was bearing our sin in His body through death, that we might have life in Him. By Christ's redeeming action, God forgave us and doesn't re-member our sins against us.

Prayer – Dear Father, thank You for doing all that was necessary that I might have a perfect relationship with You.

March 24   Gain

Matthew 18:15-18 *Moreover if your brother sins against you, GO and tell him his fault between you and him alone. If he hears you, you have gained your brother. But if he will not hear, take with you one or two more, that by the mouth of two or three witnesses every word may be established. And if he refuses to hear them, tell it to the Church. But if he refuses even to hear the church, let him be to you like a heathen ...*

GO means you make the move to your brother just as Christ takes the initiative with us.

Q How do we deal with those who sin against us?

God has given us a procedure for reconciliation or rejection. One on one, two or three on one, the church on one, and, if he refuses – stop fellowship, because he has chosen to be a heathen. If this procedure isn't followed, the alternatives may be a festering wound weakening our witness, or a split in the church. This has happened all too many times.

This isn't payback. All of this is done with the goal of brotherhood and fellowship. The assumption is that you are not at fault and have been offended by a member of the Body of Christ. If a person who is not a "brother" sins against us, that is to be expected and we are to wash our hands of the situation and leave it to God.

1.Go and face the issue. Don't let it fester. Every time we re-member an offense, a flash-back, we rip the scab off the wound, deprive it of healing, and may even allow it to be infected with other germs of discontent. 2.Take witnesses who will testify of the interaction. When you share your grievance with them, they will correct you if necessary. 3.Inform the Church so that all will know and try to help the person repent. Again, the church as a body must agree that the offense needs correction. 4.To break fellowship is an attempt to motivate him to repent.

If we have an abscess or infection in our body, it will compromise our energy or even kill us. See 1 Corinthians 11:27-30 for the effects, when not confronted, of actions that make the church less effective, *sick*, and less attractive in and to the world. Know that this is serious business but it should be done. Satan wants churches to die from infection. The good news is that we have a procedure to deal with dissensions in the Body.

Prayer – Dear Father, help me to lovingly deal with any offense that may occur.

March 25   Forgive

<u>Matthew 18:21</u> *Then Peter came to Him and said, "Lord, how often shall my brother sin against me, and I forgive him, UP to seven times?" Jesus said, "... UP to seventy times seven."*

<u>Luke 17:4</u> *And if he sins against you seven times in a day and seven times in a day returns to you, saying, "I repent," you shall forgive him.*

<u>We look at these verses again because the need for forgiveness arises every day of our lives.</u>

Q What is a general rule about how many times we should forgive? Seventy time seven.

Q How many times are we to forgive someone who wrongs us if they repent?

Seven times. in Luke's account, the offender is repentant. This sheds a different light on the matter. *Seven times* deals with forgiveness after repentance by the offender. This is the case where the sinner owns the sin and asks for forgiveness. God will give us grace to extend grace to others so we don't have to wear the "hair shirt" (constant prickly irritation) of resentment that prolongs a festering wound.

Peter was struggling with a centuries old directive about offenses. In Exodus 21:24, Moses stipulated what seems to be a reverse of the Golden Rule, "Whatever a person does to you, do back to them in kind".

We don't want to forgive because that seems to make the offense of no account. It is as if we don't really matter. We think it lets them off the hook. We may think, "It hurts! It continues to hurt! He/she should hurt like I do, or worse".

Ask Jesus what He wants you to do. Even when we forgive, the offender is still on God's hook for He is fair in His treatment of all people (Revelation 19:2). We need to give the process of judgment to God and relieve ourselves of painful memories.

We are to forgive as we are forgiven (Luke 11:4), and in a parallel thought, we are to comfort as we are comforted (2 Corinthians 1:4). Seven times? Seventy times seven? 490 was considered to be a perfect number. God goes way beyond any number in His forgiveness for us.

Prayer – Dear Father, help me relieve myself of the burden of holding grudges.

March 26   Enter

<u>Matthew 7:13</u> *Enter by the narrow gate; for wide is the gate and broad is the way that leads to destruction, and there are many who GO in by it.*

GO means enter.

Q How do we avoid the gate that leads to destruction?

Go through the narrow gate.

The way to destruction is called broad because there are so many choices for evil. The gate that is called narrow is one path - Jesus (John 14:6). The world gives many wrong choices. Jesus is the way to and through the narrow gate. If the way seems difficult, it is because we make it difficult by coming up with rules for acceptance and with the assumption that in Christ we lose out on activities that seem to be fun. Actually, what God says is wrong is harmful to us.

The wide and broad way is the path of the crowd and is littered with all sorts of sin - broken promises, broken relationships, broken lives, and ends with a payoff of death. Two verses speak of death as an end to man's doing: the payoff for a life of sin (Romans 6:23), and the result of trying to find a way in life without God (Proverbs 14:12). The death written about here is much more than physical death, it is eternity without God.

The narrow way is the way of truth and life. It is a clear path through the field of the world's garbage. It is the way of following Jesus' commandments that keep us safely on the path. The end of this path is eternal life. We find directions to this path in the Bible. *Your word is a lamp to my feet and a light to my path* <u>Psalm 119:105</u>. When all else fails, read and follow instructions.

Prayer – Dear Father, thank you for showing me the way and helping me along the path to life.

March 27   Gird

1 Peter 1:13a *Therefore, gird UP the loins of your mind ...*

Gird UP is to prepare for action.

In Biblical times men wore long robes that could tangle with the feet. To *gird up* was to tuck the bottom fringe of the robe into a belt to free the feet for movement. An example is given in Ephesians 6:14 where we are to free up truth so we can keep from getting tangled up in Satan's lies.

Q Why the mind?

The metaphor is that we won't get tripped up with stinking thinking concerning laws and works. The human brain is estimated to have in excess of ten billion, TEN BILLION, cells with countless interconnections. When we look back at yesterday's meditation, we see the genius of God giving us one straightforward way to have relationship with Him.

Peter started this letter writing about trials and salvation – deep subjects investigated by many over the centuries. In order to understand the concept of grace presented in his letter, he recommended they ready their minds for truth. To summarize what he wrote: You have overcome trials, you have joy, you have faith, your salvation is secure through grace. Therefore, rest fully in grace. The message he wanted them to hear is, "Don't get tangled up in laws and works."

Paul echoed the thought in Galatians 5:1 – Be firm in your Christ given freedom. Don't leave any loose ends that can be used to drag you back into the slavery of sin.

We are saved by grace through a secure faith given to us by God so that we know it is a sufficient work. Our life in Christ is a response to grace. We need to focus on, and live in, grace, grace, and only grace.

Prayer – Dear Father, help me to have a tangle-free mind to ward off the lies of Satan.

March 28   Deny

Mark 8:34 *Whomever desires to come after Me, let him deny himself, and take UP his cross and follow Me.*

UP shows acceptance.

Q What must be done to follow Jesus?

We know that God is good and loving. He wants us to avoid pain and gain peace. Therefore, *deny yourself*, and *take up your cross*, must be good things. To deny oneself is to set our wishes and works aside and accept His guidance and grace. Grace is so much better than a do-it-yourself project. The cross has to do with forgiveness, so taking up a cross is to live a life free from the shackles of painful memories.

It should become our desire to follow Jesus. Satan is becoming more and more open in his methods and efforts to woo us away from God. We see all kinds of TV shows that don't show the true results of sin. As our boys were growing up we would often pause a TV show and discuss what they thought would really happen as a result of the decisions actors were portrayed as making. We encouraged them to think through to the results of the ideas that came to them.

After church a boy had a confused look on his face. When his father asked him what the problem was, the boy said, "Why would they sing 'I've half decided to follow Jesus'"? Many people almost believe. They are like Agrippa – almost persuaded (Acts 26:28). Almost doesn't cut it. That's like almost breathing.

We are to forsake, deny, any negative choices and stop literally "playing with fire." How often have we said to others, "Make up your mind!" or "Get off the fence." We need to take on those activities that are couched in grace and truth. We need to live a life in the cross, forgiving and being forgiven. Regardless of any suffering we may endure, we will follow and imitate God's loving act on the cross. It may be a crucifixion of worldly pursuits, leading to life, or the crucifixion of resentments that keep us from the joy and peace God wants us to have but we know the cross is love.

When Jesus says, "*Come after Me*," He means we are to accept His grace and live a life of forgiveness. While this seems to a narrow way it sure beats the path to destruction.

Prayer – Dear Father, I deny self and my desires; I have fully decided to follow You.

March 29   Receive

Mark 10:29 *So Jesus answered, "... there is NO one who has left house or brothers or sisters or father or mother or wife or children or lands, for My sake ... who shall not receive a hundredfold."*

> Sake – cause or purpose.

> NO one – all are included.

Q What should we hold on to in this life?

> Nothing, except Jesus Christ.

> Do you get the idea that there isn't anybody or anything more important or valuable than a relationship with Jesus Christ? Many missionaries have used this verse as a springboard for the entrance to their life's work. It can be a springboard for us.

> Earlier in Mark's gospel, it was mentioned that the disciples had *immediately* dropped whatever they were doing and followed after Jesus. Peter had just remarked that the disciples had left all to follow Jesus and Jesus gave the following summary: No one who has left buildings, family, or property for My purpose on earth will be left without a much greater reward (Mark 10:29).

> Today's verse is important because there are those who forsake their relationship with God for some immediate, earthly reward. With an earthly reward, all you get is all you got. When we leave all to follow Jesus, the rewards are infinite and eternal.

> The seed that bore a hundredfold was the seed that fell on fertile soil, devoid of negative influences (Mark 4:8). This promise was in effect then and has passed down through the centuries to receptive faithful followers, and to us today, all of whom are *good ground.*

> Don't think of what you may be leaving,

> think of what you are receiving.

Prayer – Dear Father, thanks for the hundredful (wonderful) return you give for a life in You!

March 30   Contend

Proverbs 29:9 If *a wise man contends with a foolish man, whether the fool rages or laughs, there is NO peace.*

Contends – debates – fool doesn't mean low mental ability.

NO means there is no peaceful way to argue with a foolish man.

Q Is it wise to contend with a fool?

NO. The fool starts out wrong because he has a heartfelt belief that God doesn't exist (Psalm 14:1). He will simply try to justify his ignorance with anger or stupidity. Paul enlarges on the Psalm by including impotent minds coupled with foolish hearts made dark by polluted thinking. They think they are so right but they are so wrong (Romans 1:21b-22).

If you try to contend with a foolish man you will get a foolish response. The fool may argue vehemently (*rage*), or get defensive and throw hissy fits. He may pull the skunk routine and try to drive you away with stinking thinking. Or, he may make jokes to make dark of the situation.

In any case there is no peace between the two of you (nor should there be) because you cannot reach resolution or agreement. The peace of God comes only from the God of peace (Philippians 4:6-9), and the fool will not have peace because his mindset is that God does not exist.

Don't waste your time arguing with a fool. Instead of wasting time on fools, there are plenty of valuable things God has for you to do with your time and the gifts He gives you. For instance, (1 Peter 3:15), be instantly ready to share your faith with anyone who sincerely asks.

Prayer – Dear Father, lead me to, or bring to me, those who desire to know You. Thank You for the peace that passes understanding.

March 31   Boldness

Acts 4:29 *Now, Lord, look ON their threats, and grant to Your servants that with all boldness they may speak Your word ...*

ON means to consider.

Q How do we deal with threats to our faith actions?

We appeal to God to grant boldness.

<u>Who</u>? The Lord Who has power. The rulers, elders, and scribes were actually the ones who felt threatened. The witnesses who spoke of and for God were bold.

<u>What</u>? consider their threats.

<u>Why</u>? That we may speak God's message.

<u>How</u>? With granted boldness.

<u>When</u>? Now, after the threats - *But so that it spreads no further among the people, let us severely threaten them that from now on they speak to no man in this name* Acts 4:17. Satan directs his agents to prevent the spread of the Good News. In today's world it seems anything goes except Christianity.

<u>Where</u>? At the place of the threat.

Have you ever been threatened because of acting out for Christ? Once we were with another couple in a restaurant and were giving thanks to God for our meal. An irate person came charging at us and demanded that we not impose our faith on him in a public place. He didn't seem to worry about his imposition on us. Listen to the news to find out how fools are trying to rid the world of evidence of God.

It was God's message. The disciples didn't make it up. They were following orders. The disciple's actions spoke as loudly as their words. A lot of social communication is nonverbal so we can be threatened for actions as well as words that proclaim our love and obedience to God.

Prayer – Dear Father, grant me boldness to proclaim the Gospel by my actions and words.

APRIL

IS

Meditation Aids

IS is a verb - that makes IS an action word.

IS may be a state of being, make a statement, ask a question, or give a command or direction.

IS shows balance or equality, as in an equation: $(6 + 4) = (12 - 2)$

Or one half of 11 IS 1.

This IS That.

Example:

God IS love (1 John 4:16b).

In this case, IS is a state of being.

The Personification of love.

It is often helpful to think of IS an equal sign. God = love. Mentally substitute an equal sign for is when you are reading a passage.

April 1   Fool   April fool's day.

Psalm 14:1 *The fool says in his heart, there IS no God.*

Fool says IS no God.

Q What does the Bible say about atheists (Those who say there is no God)?

They are fools.

Don't be a fool today or any day.

They are fools because the Bible defines them as fools. Accusing someone of being a fool is serious business placing a person in danger of *hellfire (*Matthew 5:22c). We need to be very careful about whom we designate as a fool. That is why these verses are so remarkable. Those who claim to be agnostic (no knowledge) are also foolish because the evidence of God is everywhere (Romans 1:20).

A person does not have to declare him/herself to be an atheist to be an atheist. If it walks like a duck, and quacks like a duck, and looks like a duck, it probably is a duck - as with atheists. If a person says there is a God, but doesn't live as if there is a God, it is as if they are an atheist.

The heart, as the wellspring of emotions, is not credited with the power of intellectual reasoning but it often controls our thoughts and actions. We are told that evil thoughts come from the heart and then proceed from the mouth and defile a man (Matthew 15:19-20b). Out of the heart comes the thought *there is no God.* This thought defiles a man from the get-go.

Once in a while we need to think of the importance of a word. If we are thinking, or acting in such a way as to deny God, the love of God, or the existence of God, *fool* is one of those words.

Prayer – Dear Father, I see You everywhere, I feel Your presence in my every thought and move. You ARE!

In the Hebrew of the Old Testament there were no vowels. The atheist would translate GDSNWHR as GoD iS No WHeRe while the theist says it means GoD iS NoW HeRe.

April 2   Message

1 Corinthians 1:18 *For the message of the cross IS foolishness to those who are perishing, but to us who are being saved, it IS the power of God.*

Message IS foolishness. To the perishing is the critical thought here.

Q What is the message of the cross?

The message of the cross is that we need saving and it took an incredible act of God to make our salvation possible. To those of us who are saved *it IS the power of God* giving us relationship with Him.

If we read this verse to consider contrasts, the word *foolishness* is contrasted with *power*. Those who try to live a life without God live a life without power over sin and death. They have unproductive thoughts, darkness shrouds their hearts, and part of their foolishness is they proclaim to be wise (Romans 1:21-22). Boy, do we see that today!

We learned yesterday that being a fool, or being called a fool, is a terrible thing. Today we begin to see why. We see how a fool is involved with foolishness. The actions of a fool are to deny God and to deny the message of the cross – to deny our need for the cleansing which is made possible by the sacrifice of Christ. But, in His love for us, God is constantly working to bring us into relationship with Him.

The Holy Spirit uses the message of the cross to lead us to salvation which is LIFE in Christ. It behooves us to heed the message. If you have been a fool long enough, quit being a fool - today is a good day for salvation. Satan urges some people to believe they are so terrible that God can't forgive them. Don't worry, the cross has enough power, even for you.

Prayer – Dear Father, thank you for the wisdom of *the message of the cross* and how You used the cross to give me relationship with You.

April 3   Way

Proverbs 14:12 *There IS a way that seems right to a man, but its end IS the way of death.*

Man's way IS death. Man's reasonable (??) way = death.

Q What if our ideas differ from God's ideas?

If we disagree with God, we are on the pathway to death. One more glance at being a fool. The way that *seems right* is a lie prompted by Satan. Satan puts pretty wrappings and a bow on garbage - sin. Note: it *SEEMS right* but it is WRONG – it ends in death (Romans 6:23).

The wages of sin, that is the wages of foolishness, is death. WAKE UP PILGRIM. This isn't a slap on the wrist. It's not like stealing a cookie from Grandma's cookie jar. We need to be serious about the seriousness of sin. Sin separates us from God. Redeeming us from sin required the death of Christ on the cross. Now, wages are deserved and earned while the gift of God is undeserved but given. We deserve death but are given life!

The way of God is the way of salvation. We all need salvation.

Everyone has sin that causes them to miss out on God's purposes and gifts (Romans 3:23). There may be two types of transgression listed here. (1) We have all sinned and (2) we have all fallen short of the glory of God. We have all transgressed in some manner and, given the nicest person on earth, that person falls short of the glory of God.

Salvation comes through grace. Paul's letters don't start, "Works and Peace"; they say *"Grace and peace,"* or *"Grace, mercy, and peace."* Don't waste time trying to justify yourself by good works. Instead, know that we can and must experience salvation which means – believe, confess, and receive God's gift of eternal life.

There is a clear separation between life and death. The direction we go is a matter of choice. It definitely is not God's will that anyone experience eternal separation from Him. However, if a person thinks outside of the guidance of the Holy Spirit, those thoughts lead to death.

Prayer - Dear Father, thank You for whatever process led me to faith in You and to accepting Your gift of eternal life.

April 4   Wisdom

Proverbs 9:10 *The beginning of wisdom IS the fear of the Lord.*

> Other meanings of the Hebrew word for *fear* can be awe or respect. If we don't stand in awe before God, or respect Him, we for sure need to *fear* Him.

Q What is the *beginning of wisdom*?

> The beginning of wisdom IS the fear, awe, and respect *of the Lord.*

> To begin with, it is not wise to say there is no God. Atheists don't even begin to have wisdom. They think they have the answers apart from God. A person doesn't fear someone they say doesn't exist. Maybe that is why they claim God doesn't exist.

> An agnostic denies that there is Godly wisdom. They think that excuses their wrong choices. Think again! It is difficult to believe that someone with ten billion plus brain cells could not believe in a loving, forgiving Creator.

> Knowledge is what we know; wisdom is what we do with what we know. We can have seven Ph. D.'s and fail to have wisdom if we don't have respect for God. Godly wisdom is readily and easily available.

> All we have to do is ask God for wisdom and He will give it generously and without criticism (James 1:5). The foundation of all we think and do should be with wisdom in awe of the Lord. However, we can't get wisdom if we don't believe in the Giver of wisdom.

> Whenever we accumulate any knowledge about ANY subject, we should present it to God and ask for wisdom in how we should use it. We need to make sure it agrees with the Holy Spirit, the Bible and with the experience of possessing Christians, past and present.

> It is helpful to know what is helpful. Solomon, reputed to be the wisest person in history, prayed to know how to understand how to judge people by knowing the difference between *good and evil* (1 Kings 4:9). We definitely need to know the difference *between* good and evil! It is good to respect God.

Prayer – Dear Father, grant me wisdom, so that everything in my life is directed by You.

April 5   Head

Ephesians 1:22-23 *And He put all things under His feet, and gave Him to be head over all things to the church, which IS His body, the fullness of Him who fills all in all.*

The importance of a concept is noted by the number of different words that describe it. For instance Eskimos have many words for snow. There are many words that describe the presence of Christ in the world.

Q How are the followers of Christ described? As:

1. Christians -   (Acts 11:26)   followers of Christ.
2. Body -   (Ephesians 1:23)   for Christ's work.
3. Church-   (Colossians 1:24b)   for belonging.
4. Family -   (Ephesians 3:15)   for living.
5. Building -   (1 Corinthians 3:9)   for business.
6. Fellow workers -   (1 Corinthians 3:9)   for working.
7. Field -   (1 Corinthians 3:9)   for fruit.
8. House -   (Hebrews 3:6)   for indwelling.
9. Temple -   (1 Corinthians 6:19)   for worship.
10. Kingdom -   (Luke 17:21b)   for power.

For all of this, Christ is the *Foundation* (1 Corinthians 3:11). Upon Him stand the descriptors of Jesus' followers – the church, the building, the house, and the temple. It is helpful to mediate on each of the descriptors to see how they function in our lives. You may want to make sticky notes.

The main descriptor of Christ in the world is that the followers of Christ are His *body* and He is the *Head* (1 Corinthians 12:27). As members of His body, we are His hands, feet, eyes, ears, mouth, etc. to perform His work. Christians are members of Christ's Body and function under His direction.

Prayer - Dear Father, help me to be a faithful member of Your Body.

April 6   Will

1 Thessalonians 4:3 *For this IS the will of God, your sanctification…*

Our sanctification IS God's will.

Q What is God's will in our lives?

That we be sanctified which means to be separate.

Sanctification is separation from sinful thoughts and actions and separation to dedication to all things of Christ and the Holy Spirit.

The question becomes, "How are we sanctified?" The answer is, we are sanctified by God's word which is the truth (John 17:17). The word/Word is Jesus, Who is the Truth, and/or the Bible which gives us the truth. We need to be in Christ and to get into the word with daily study and meditation. A set time and place is most beneficial. There may be interruptions from time to time but we must not let that disrupt our schedule.

This is when the conflict with Satan gets more serious. Satan will try to refute all the benefits of the Spirit. First of all, Satan tries to involve people in all kinds of sin before they even think of God. Then, once the Holy Spirit convicts us, Satan tries to make Christ and Christianity look stupid or constrictive. Then, once we know Christ and have accepted Him and His gifts, Satan does everything he can to subvert the power, gifts, and fruit of the Spirit. Spiritual warfare increases in intensity as we increase in Christ.

For the flesh lusts against the Spirit, and the Spirit against the flesh; and these are contrary to one another so that you do not do the things that you wish Galatians 5:17. You can always tell when something good is going to happen because someone or something will interfere and will try to steal your love, joy, and/or peace.

The thing to remember is that Jesus has overcome the world and we are safe in His care (John 16:33).

Prayer – Dear Father, saturate me with Your word that I may fulfill your will and be sanctified in Christ.

April 7   Victory

1 John 5:4-5 *For whatever IS born of God overcomes the world. And this IS the victory that has overcome the world - our faith. Who IS he who overcomes the world, but he who believes that Jesus IS the Son of God?*

Believing IS overcoming.

Q What gives us victory over the world?

Believing that Jesus Christ is the Son of God and being born of Him through faith.

We need victory over the world because the world is Satan's battlefield where spiritual warfare is constantly going on. There are three weapons suggested here that help us gain victory.

1. Being *born of God* gives us victory over the world and gives us entry into God's kingdom (John 3:3b). When we are born again, we begin life in Christ.
2. *Faith* gives us victory over the world. God has given us this faith so it is perfect, an incredibly strong faith capable of overcoming any threat. If we use our faith in the face of adversity we will find that it never fails.
3. Those who *believe that Jesus is the Son of God* overcome the world. When we believe and receive Jesus, we overcome. The writers of Scripture assumed that believing meant responding accordingly.

With all these weapons against evil we need to give ourselves totally over to God. In so doing we will have strength and resolve to stand firm against Satan and cause him to run away from us (James 4:7).

If, at any time or in any circumstance, you feel you are losing the battle, claim this three pronged weapon – claim your new birth – trust your *faith* – say, "*Jesus is the Son of God*" and know that you have victory.

These things I have spoken to you, that in Me you may have peace. In the world you will have tribulation; but be of good cheer, I have overcome the world John 16:33.

Prayer – Dear Father, thank You for the gift of faith that empowers us to overcome any of Satan's attacks.

April 8   Word

Psalm 119:105 *Your word IS a lamp to my feet and a light to my path.*

Word IS lamp/light

Q How can I use the *word* to light my path?

I can meditate in it day and night. We are told that we should meditate in the word day and night so we will do what is written (Joshua 1:8). When I meditate on God's laws, whatever I say or do can be directed by Him.

(Meditate - to consider with careful thought. The word of God is a gift and deserves our diligent consideration. Meditation is to the soul what medication is to the body or mind.)

Remember to make an easy road for your travels so that no weakness can lead to breakage (Hebrews 12:13). When the path is straight and level the lamp shows where my feet are at the present time and the light shows the way ahead.

We have help on our road because God, in His grace, has given us Christ and the Holy Spirit to keep us upright and steady (Jude 24). Jude uses the word *stumbling*. This is a nice way of describing unintentional sin. *Stumbling* will be less likely if we meditate on the word and

walk in its light,

day and night.

These verses give rich material for personal and group meditation. They tell us how important it is to have a reality check for our daily walk. Once I was rabbit hunting in a swamp. I took a step and was up to my waist in icy water. I learned to watch my feet and my path. Don't take your weight off your back foot until you know your lead foot is secure. Don't step into a chancy situation without the ability to make a quick retreat. Be careful; let God's word light your way.

Prayer - Dear Father, thank You for the lamp of Your word that lights my path.

April 9   Blasphemy

<u>Romans 2:24</u> *For the name of God IS blasphemed among the Gentiles because of you.*

Blasphemy is any word or action that goes against God, Christ, or the Holy Spirit.

Q What is the consequence if we claim to be Christian but don't walk the walk?

The name of God is blasphemed – degraded, spoken evil of. Remember, a large part of communication is nonverbal. The look on our face, the tone of voice, and our gestures can show contempt or appreciation. It is not a good thing when something about us causes a person to think poorly of God or the church

The name of God is His nature. God is love – loving. God is holy. God justifies us through Jesus Christ. God empowers us through the working of the Holy Spirit. When we think of all that God has done for us – His grace, mercy, and peace - how can we but respond with the wholeness of our being. We become witnesses of His truth for all peoples.

To deny any of God's truth, God's power, or God's blessings is to blaspheme Him. To live without any of His gifts is to die without any of His promises (Matthew 12:31-32). What a tragedy this is. Blaspheming God falls right into the plans and goal of Satan. Even our behavior can cause unbelievers to speak ill of God. It is their blasphemy but we should not encourage it.

The word *Gentiles* lumps in all unbelievers. We are to be a light to the Gentiles instead of pushing them into greater darkness. *For so the Lord has commanded us: "I have set you as a light to the Gentiles, that you should be for salvation to the ends of the earth"* <u>Acts 13:47</u> (Quoted from <u>Isaiah 49:6</u>).

Let our response to the nature of God be that He is praised among all with whom we come in contact.

Prayer – Dear Father, May my life never give another person the thought that You are less than Holy. I pray that this accusation may never be directed at me.

April 10   Acceptance

<u>1 Timothy 1:15</u> *This IS a faithful saying and worthy of all acceptance that Jesus Christ came into the world to save sinners.*

Faithful saying IS to save.

Q Why did God send Jesus into the world?

Jesus came to save sinners.

The fact of salvation is greater than the fact of sin.

This saying is *faithful*. It is to be trusted and accepted as being true. We can apply it first to ourselves and then to all others. This is GOOD NEWS for those who recognize the purpose of God and seek to find that purpose in their lives.

This saying is worthy of *all acceptance*. This isn't just a headline that can be read and discarded as yesterday's news flash. Salvation is an active force that is to be appropriated into our lives. Not only that, it is not a half-hearted endeavor, it is worthy of *ALL* acceptance. We need All of Christ in ALL of our life.

1.   He came to save me.
2.   He came to save my family
3.   He came to save anyone who believes and receives Him.

Remember, we all fit the description of *sinners*. Everyone – (Romans 3:23). Jesus Christ deserves our FULL acceptance because we are desperately in need of being saved. Salvation is our greatest need.

If we leave this life without salvation -

We have missed the point of creation -

And a life of exultation.

Prayer – Dear Father, thank you for meeting us at the point of our greatest need and opening up all that we have in Christ and Your Holy Spirit.

April 11   Longsuffering

<u>2 Peter 3:9</u> *The Lord IS not slack concerning His promise ... but IS longsuffering toward us, not willing that any should perish but that all should come to repentance.*

God IS longsuffering.

Q Why is God letting this strange world go on?

He is not *willing that anyone should perish.*

LET IT BE WELL KNOWN – God does not condemn anybody to hell which is eternity without Him. If people choose to live this life without God, they choose to live eternally without Him. Our eternal existence is <u>our</u> choice.

God *is not slack concerning His promise: ... scoffers will come in the last days ... saying, "Where is the promise of His coming ... all things continue as they were from the beginning of creation"* <u>vs3-4</u>. God does not wait in order to give us a chance to continue in sin. INSTANT REPLAY - God does not wait because He wants to give us a chance to continue in sin. Pause, and think about that. Instead, He waits to give us a chance to enter His kingdom. It is not because He lacks control of when and how He will return.

There are those who reject God because they can't see eternal judgment as the choice of a loving God. In reality, God allows people to choose. Again - If people choose to live this life without God, they choose to live eternally without Him. God is not hidden; He is obvious to anyone who has not chosen to be blind. He has come to us in Christ. He has given us a totally simple and wonderful way to have eternal life (John 3:16). We now need to respond to Him.

This requires that we make a 180 degree turn and go towards God instead of away from Him. Don't take a 360, that puts you back in the way you were going.

Life in Christ is so great,

why would anyone wait.

Prayer – Dear Father, thank You for suffering long enough for me to come to my senses and choose You.

April 12   Good

James 4:17 *Therefore, to him who knows to do good, and does not do it, to him it IS sin.*

Romans 14:23 *... whatever IS not from faith IS sin.*

These two verses go at sin from opposite directions. There are sins of omission and sins of commission.

Q What is sin?

Sin is anything contrary to God's will. Since God is love, then anything that doesn't fit the description of love is sin. Sin is whatever is in the realm of Satan's work.

Many people claim to be righteous because they have their own definition of sin. They say, "It's all relative". However, whether the sin is one of omission or of commission, the Bible teaches that ALL have sinned. The good news is, Jesus cleanses us from ALL sin.

Sins of omission are debts – things we should do that we don't do – unpaid financial or moral obligations, sometimes described as missing the mark – not hitting the target.

Sins of commission are actions that we do that we should not do – breaking the law, trespassing – walking on the property or feelings of others, breaking the ten, and other clear commandments in the Bible.

Q How can we avoid sinning?

We are to take God's word into the innermost part of our being and let it guide and control our actions so that we avoid sinning against Him (Psalm 119:11).

Starve a baby and it will die. Starve sin and it will die. Just don't starve the Holy Spirit; feed on God's promises.

We need

To feed

Prayer – Dear Father, may I study Your word to know what not to do and what to do that I might not sin against You.

April 13   Slave

John 8:34 *Most assuredly, I say to you, "Whoever commits sin IS a slave of sin."*

Q Is sin addictive? People can be addicted to, and be slaves of, sin.

Their sin "owns" them instead of them owning the sin and having control over it. There is often an adrenalin rush to sin but, with use, sin becomes jaded and takes on that tired look of a person who has been abused for decades. "Rode hard and put away wet," as they say out West.

> Many people, who are depressed, commit a sin such as adultery because the adrenalin brought on by the forbidden fruit pumps them up. They get kicks from the fix. It is difficult to break an addiction. People will return again and again to a sinful act even though they know it is wrong. Quite often they try to recapture the feeling they had at the first experience. There is truth in the saying that a criminal will return to the scene of his/her crime (like dogs and pigs 2 Peter 2:22). It is even true in crimes against oneself. We may keep returning to thoughts of our sin or someone's sin against us. Re-member.
>
> Actually, adrenalin is also created by positive things such as joy and exercise. It is God's puppy upper for us. We are to be filled with the Spirit not some manmade concoction (Ephesians 5:18-20). The exercise of the fruit of the Spirit gives us a wonderful, controlled state of contentment (Galatians 5:22-23).
>
> Sin is not only an offense against God, it is a violation of the self, for we are created in the image of God. Sin is a direction away from the self. People think they have made a rational decision when really they have succumbed to the seduction of Satan.
>
> Our society promotes dissatisfaction with ourselves and our situation in life. The whole advertising industry attempts to make us believe that life without their product is inadequate. The truth is, there is no amount of goods or services that will fill the God-sized hole in our hearts. INSTANT REPLAY - There is no amount of goods or services that will fill the God-sized hole in our hearts. Thank God, He fills us to the uttermost.

Prayer – Dear Father, I choose to be Your slave, Your bond servant, finding contentment in You.

April 14   Greater

1 John 4:4b ... *because He who IS in you IS greater than he who IS in the world.*

>John is discussing God's Spirit vs. Satan's spirit. Each is known by its activity and its results – life or death.   Jesus IS greater.

Q How is He Who is in us superior to Satan? Because we, in Him, overcome evil.

>We are to test, and not fear, the spirit(s) of the antichrist because Christ is greater, and no matter how horrible or terrible an attack of Satan appears, we are victorious in Christ.

>We are Christ's possessions, bought with the price of His life. That makes us precious to Him and God is not about to hand us over to Satan. God not only adopted us as His children, He abides in us and transforms us so that we can abide in Him.

>*And the glory which You gave Me I have given them, that they may be one just as We are one; I in them, and You in Me; that they may be made perfect in one ...* John 17:22-23. This is the genius and the mystery of Christianity that makes it separate from the religions of the world. Christ is IN us in the Person of the Holy Spirit. IN HIM we have all His power, gifts, and fruit. When we are filled with the Holy Spirit, there is no room for Satan. Religions are a set of exterior laws and Satan can sneak around them.

>If there ever is a time we feel the world is closing in on us and testing or tempting us beyond our ability to endure or resist, we need to know that we are in Him and He is IN us. We have the promise of His strength and victory over sin.

>We will have troubles as long as we are in the world, but we can rejoice in the fact that Jesus, Whose word is true, and Who is in us, has overpowered the world. Therefore we need to remember that as long as we are in Christ, we have peace (John 16:33 and Philippians 4:6-7).

>Rest in Him for He abides in you.

Prayer – Dear Father, fill me with Your Spirit and don't let the world pollute anything about me.

April 15   Sufficient

2 Corinthians 12:9-10 *And He said to me, "My grace IS sufficient for you for My strength IS made perfect in weakness. Therefore I take pleasure in infirmities, in reproaches, in needs, in persecutions, in distresses, for Christ's sake. For when I am weak, then I am strong".*

Grace IS sufficient - - - strength IS perfect. Grace = sufficiency.

Q Why is God's grace sufficient?

Because His strength is made perfect in us when we recognize our weakness and call on Him. Link the word sufficient with the word perfect. That which is perfect is sufficient.

Paul prayed three times for the *thorn in the flesh* to go away. It didn't go away. Then he saw the thorn as a gift that turned him from the temptation to *boast* of his spiritual condition, (vs5-7), to that of taking pleasure in difficulties.

There are those who mistakenly say that people who aren't healed must be sinning. The truth is, God often shows His grace through our ability to rejoice in illness. Which do you think is a greater witness, to be healed, or to rejoice in infirmity? God certainly heals in some circumstances but His action is always for the greater good. His will be done.

When we realize our weakness and call upon God, we are then mentally and spiritually ready to receive His strength. As long as we feel we can do it by ourselves, we will let pride get in the way of His sufficient grace.

Rule # 1: God's grace IS sufficient. Rule # 2: If at any time it seems His grace isn't sufficient, see Rule # 1.

There is debate about what the *thorn* is. There may be a reason for the ambiguity. It could be that whatever may cause you to think His grace isn't sufficient is a "thorn". Take your eyes off the thorn and focus on the FACT OF GRACE.

Prayer – Dear Father, help me, in all circumstances, to focus on Your sufficient grace. Thank You!!

April 16   Foundation

1 Corinthians 3:11 *For no other foundation can anyone lay than that which IS laid, which IS Jesus Christ.*

Our foundation IS Jesus.

Q What is the foundation for life?

Simply, the foundation for life is faith in Jesus Christ.

When buying a house it is essential to check the foundation for cracks, settling, and shoddy material. If the foundation is faulty, the rest is not worth fixing. When we check Jesus as the foundation for our faith and life, we find no imperfections. With Jesus, we have a perfect foundation.

Christ is the foundation and He has placed us, as His house, on Himself, a firm and unshakable base for our lives. Go through each room in your house. Think of how that room is a metaphor of our activities. The kitchen has to do with our food and drink intake. The living room has to do with our life and entertainment. The closets have to do with what we wear. The basement has to do with what we have stored up for occasional use. Take the time to recognize the metaphors of God's decoration and furnishings. Take a sticky note for each room and note how it has received God's fingerprint and how it can be used to glorify Him.

We are His house (Hebrews 3:6). Christ is the foundation, an absolutely secure base against all odds.

Prayer – Dear Father, thank you that I can trust that nothing can shake the foundation upon which my life in Christ is built.

April 17   Purpose

John 12:27 *Now My soul IS troubled, and what shall I say? "Father save Me from this hour?" But for this purpose I came to this hour. Father, glorify Your name.*

> Soul IS troubled.

Q Are troubles (tribulations) supposed to be a problem for us?

> No, we are to look for God's purpose in allowing the circumstance.

> No matter what the circumstance; be thankful. Bring what you think you need to God in prayer, accept His answer, and His peace, without our even having to understand how it works, will work through the guardianship of Jesus (Philippians 4:6).

> In everything – not for everything. Look for God's purpose, without resentment, and you will have peace.

> Is your soul troubled by anything at this time? What shall you say? Save me? Release me from this trouble? Or should we ask if God has a purpose. Consider Romans 8:28 - *And we know that all things work together for good to those who love God, to those who are the called according to His purpose.* God wants us to grow: our troubles are carefully measured to ensure proper growth (Matthew 6:34b).

> *All things*? Really? ... Really? ... Really! God said so. We need to take our eyes off the thorn and focus on His perfect grace (2 Corinthians 12:9). We need to take our eyes off the test and focus on the way of escape (1 Corinthians 10:13). We need to say, "Okay, Lord, how are you going to use me in this situation?"

> We are God's. We are precious to Him. He paid a great price for us. Even a mud-bogger wouldn't let his/her most precious possession stay stuck in a slime pit. God loves us and is always preparing us to be our ultimate best – each experience, no matter how messy or challenging, leads us to greater growth. Therefore, when He has a purpose for us in a troubling time, we know that He will equip us with whatever we need for the battle and we will win.

Prayer – Dear Father, forgive me for wallowing in self-pity instead of looking for how I can glorify Your name through victory in Jesus.

April 18   Defile

Mark 7:15 *There IS nothing that enters a man from outside which can defile him; but the things which come out of him; those are the things that defile a man.*

> To defile is to pollute, spoil, and make unclean.
>
> Come out IS what defiles

Q What defiles us?   Things that come out of us.

> Rats! You mean I can't blame someone else, or the weather, or, or, or … Nope, nothing that enters from the outside can defile me. According to several Bible passages the things that defile me come out from my own heart and mind. That is why the heart and mind have to be transformed.
>
> The heart and mind are often linked together in the Scriptures, as we have considered and will consider in several devotions. The heart is not physically capable of generating emotions but is thought to be the source of strong emotion because it races with adrenalin. When the heart dies, emotion ceases. The mind is the source of thought which is the other engine that directs the train. When the mind dies, thought dies.
>
> Heart - What we hold dear in our hearts will produce an effect on our lives and the lives of others, good produces good and bad produces bad (Matthew 12:35). It's as simple as that. So, the evil that I treasure in my heart defiles me whereas the good that I treasure builds me up.
>
> Mind/spirit – The ungodly thoughts of my unredeemed mind are neither God's thoughts nor His ways; it is my thoughts that defile me.
>
> The good news is that if I pray and ask God, I can have *a* new heart and a new spirit. *Create in me a clean heart, O God, and renew a steadfast spirit within me* Psalm 51:10. WOW! Now what comes out can glorify God and edify the Church.

Prayer – Dear Father, continually repurpose my heart, my mind, and my spirit so that Your ways become my ways and give me the strong desire and intelligence to walk in your paths.

April 19   With

<u>Matthew 12:30</u> *He who IS not with Me IS against Me ...*

　　　With Me IS for Me

Q Who is *with* Christ?

　　　Those who are with Christ desire to see God's will become actuality.

　　　What does it mean to be *with* Jesus? It means we agree with Him realizing that we are sometimes going to share in His suffering (1 Peter 4:1b). If we think that Christianity means a life without challenges, that is growth experiences, we aren't thinking as He thinks and we are *against* Him. As we see in other devotions, we are with Christ when we understand that God's will is that we should have eternal life, that we should be sanctified, that *we* should rejoice always, pray without ceasing, and in everything give thanks.

　　　There is no gray area, no middle zone. Those who deny that Christ is the necessary and sufficient gift of God for salvation are against Him.

　　　If we are not with Christ, that is, if we are against Him, we are part of what John calls the antichrist (1 John 2:22). But, we have made the choice to be with Christ. To be with Him is to be in Him and have His power, gifts, and fruit. When we are with Christ, instead of regrets and sorrows, we have love, joy, and peace. Easy choice.

　　　Some people try to live in the middle, jumping one way or the other, whatever is convenient at the time. Now we know that isn't possible. So choose – there is one of two choices. We are either for Christ or against Him. Make your choice and verbally admit to it. If you are against God, have the guts to say so. INSTANT REPLAY - If you are against God, have the guts to say so.

　　　We who are with Christ have read the last chapter and we win. Read it!

Prayer – Dear Father, I choose to be with You, up front in thought, word, and deed.

April 20   Liberty

2 Corinthians 3:17 *Where the Spirit of the Lord IS, there IS liberty.*

Spirit IS Liberty - freedom – liberation. In Christ we are free from the captivity and penalty of sin.

Q Where do we find liberty?

We find liberty *where the Spirit of the Lord is.*

The Spirit of the Lord is in us (John 14:16). Therefore the liberty exists within ourselves. We do not have to retain or bind ourselves with our sin because Jesus has removed all sin from us and taken it upon Himself. Christ hasn't released us from sin so we would be bound by sin (Galatians 5:1). That doesn't even make sense. We are new creations in Christ. Our sins are forgiven. We are to live as free people. Hey fish, swim.

The Spirit of the Lord is unique to Christianity. So many people feel Christianity is restrictive. They do not see how God's instructions and commandments save us from tons of grief. They do not recognize the oppression and penalty we have when sinning. When we were in sin, we were under the direction of a thief, a killer, and a destroyer (John 10:10). When working for Satan, we are in bondage to death, sometimes a living death. But, when we are in Christ, we have the Spirit of Christ with all of the benefits, one of which is liberation from sin.

Don't believe Satan's lies. Jesus hasn't placed us in bondage; He has set us free from bondage. This should be noticeable so others see us as liberated from sin. We do not have to, nor do we want to, sin any more. Positive changes are obvious.

We can paraphrase Patrick Henry, "Give me liberty" - freedom from oppression, or give me LIBERTY – freedom from death!

Prayer – Dear Father, thank You for setting us free from sin and placing Your Spirit within us where we have constant access to Him.

April 21   Rest

<u>Matthew 11:28-30</u> *Come to Me all you who labor and are heavy laden and I will give you rest ... For My yoke IS easy and My burden IS light.*

Yoke/burden IS easy/light - Jesus isn't talking about our jobs.

Q Where do we find rest?

We find rest in life in Christ. Jesus is the oasis in the desert of life.

Come to Me - The invitation is to those who are struggling with labor and heavy burdens. The labor is the attempt at self-justification. The burdens refer to consequences of sin. Think of the work we make for ourselves when we live apart from Him. Much of our burden is self-imposed by wrong choices that seemed reasonable at the time. Look at the consequences the world is getting for misguided choices.

To have labor and to be heavy laden are references to the emotional strain of trying to find peace in world worries, false thinking about the benefits of money, and worthless longing for things, thinking these dead end desires bring lasting comfort (Mark 4:19).

Jesus gives us rest because His yoke is easy and his burden is light. All we have to do is accept the faith He gives us and, through this gift of faith, find salvation. There are two yokes to consider, the easy yoke of the grace of Jesus or the yoke of bondage of trying to be justified by works (Galatians 5:1).

When we are in Christ, the yoke is on us. Ha! But seriously - we are out of the rat race and into His perfect peace. It sounds like an oxymoron but the yoke of Jesus frees us.

Prayer – Dear Father, thank You for giving me rest in You and rest from the consequences of evil.

April 22   Kingdom

Luke 17:21b *For indeed, the kingdom of God IS within you.*

Kingdom IS within.

Q Where is the kingdom of God?

The kingdom of God is within us.

The kingdom of God is Christ in you and you in Christ (John 17:23). The kingdom of God is the Holy Spirit in you (John 14:17).

Where? Within us, you and me.

What is the kingdom of God like? Even now, in our present condition in Christ, we find love and forgiveness, and faith that we will eventually dwell in the eternal kingdom.

How? do we enter the kingdom of God? We need to earnestly look out for, and find, *the kingdom of God* and the purity that comes only from Christ. Then, and only then will the resources of His kingdom come to us (Matthew 6:33).

Who does all this? God.

Why? Because He loves us.

When is the kingdom of God within us? When we ask the Holy Spirit to come into our lives. It is when His will is manifested in us.

Right here, right now, at this time, the kingdom of God can be ours to enjoy, so enjoy.

Prayer – Dear Father, thank You for placing Your Spirit in such a convenient, accessible place - in me.

April 23   Kingdom

Romans 14:17 ... *for the kingdom of God IS not eating and drinking, but righteousness and peace and joy in the Holy Spirit.*

Kingdom IS righteousness, peace, and joy

Q What is the kingdom of God?

> The kingdom of God is only that which is of *righteousness, peace, and joy.* Note the order - without righteousness, there is neither peace nor joy.

> Yesterday we reviewed Jesus' teaching that the kingdom of God is within us. Today we see that Paul stated the kingdom of God is *righteousness, peace, and joy in the Holy Spirit.* Therefore, it follows that righteousness, peace, and joy are within us through the activity of the Holy Spirit.

> The kingdom is not a disputable matter. Apparently, the Romans had been caught up in arguments about things that were not clearly defined in Scripture (Romans 14:1b) and had lost the essence of their faith. Having been saved by grace through faith they were reverting to rules about days and food. Sound familiar? Those disputes are still going on today. Rules about food and drink don't secure our position in the kingdom of God.

> That which is within us, righteousness, peace, and joy, is the kingdom of God.

> Is it possible, in this world of sin, war, and sadness, that we have righteousness, peace and joy? The answer is YES! – in and through the activity of the Holy Spirit.

> When we are *in the Holy Spirit,* we have the fruit of the Spirit and we are His righteousness (Galatians 5:22 and 2 Corinthians 5:21). If you haven't done so, invite Him into your life now. He wants to dwell in you.

Prayer – Dear Father, constantly remind me that I rest in Your grace, love, joy, and peace, not rules and regulations. Thank You that I can enjoy Your gifts.

April 24   Confess

Romans 10:9-10 ... *that if you confess with your mouth the Lord Jesus and believe in your heart that God has raised Him from the dead, you will be saved. For with the heart one believes unto righteousness, and with the mouth confession IS made unto salvation.*

Confession leads to salvation.

Q What does God desire for the world to say about Jesus?

He wants every person to confess and accept Jesus as Lord.

When does this come about? It may only happen in the final judgment that every person will have this realization. However,

confessing that Christ IS Lord

does not necessarily mean you accept Him as Lord.

What? Simply put, paying lip service to God doesn't cut it. Our lives have to give evidence to what we say (Matthew 7:21-23). The heart, mind, and actions must all be involved.

Whether or not a person accepts Christ as spiritual Lord and Savior, Jesus is the Lord over all creation. Jesus is the salve of salvation that heals the scars of our sin.

In Philippians 2:11, we have two of the separate activities of the triune God – God in Christ as Savior, and God as Father. When we accept Christ as Savior we bring glory to God. The glory of God is His work in the world: (1) justifying us through the sacrifice of Christ so that we would be pure and could have relationship with Him, and (2) sanctifying us through the work of the Holy Spirit so that we can grow in grace and become as like Him as humanly possible.

Prayer – Dear Father, I want to glorify You by accepting Christ as my Savior and Lord, and by living my life under the direction of Your Holy Spirit.

April 25   Commandments

*Mark 12:29-31 Jesus answered him, "The first of all the commandments IS:
Hear O Israel, the Lord our God, the Lord IS one. And you shall love the Lord
your God with all your heart, with all your soul, with all your mind, and with all
your strength. This IS the first commandment. And the second, like it, IS this:
You shall love your neighbor as yourself: There IS no other commandment
greater than these.'"*

Commandment IS to love God and others

Q What are the most important commandments?

Jesus sums up the commandments by quoting Scripture based on
Deuteronomy 6:4-5 and Leviticus 19:18.

First: Love the only one God with all your heart, soul, mind and
strength – the basis of monotheism

Second: ... *love your neighbor as yourself –* the extension of love for
God is love for humans.

Jesus concludes that these are the greatest commandments.

The SPICE of life: The expansion of how we should love God and
keep the commandments presents four elements of human nature –
heart, soul, mind, and strength. In order to make these elements
easy to remember, the second commandment is added to make the
acronym SPICE. All your Soul – Spiritual, All your strength –
Physical, All your mind – Intellectual, Your neighbor as yourself –
Community, and All your heart – Emotions.

SPICE stands for – Spiritual, Physical, Intellectual, Community,
Emotions. Any psychological study of humans that leaves out any of
these characteristics, especially the spiritual, is deficient. The
commandments of God take into account every aspect of our being
and ministers completely to each of them. As we consider a check list
for daily application of the commandments to our lives, thinking of the
items in SPICE can be helpful.

Prayer – Dear Father, may the words of my mouth, the emotions of my heart,
the actions of my body and the thoughts of my mind be delightful in Your
sight.

April 26   Salvation

<u>Romans 1:16</u> *I am not ashamed of the gospel of Christ for it IS the power of God to salvation for everyone who believes.*

Gospel IS *power*

Q What should be our attitude concerning the Gospel of Christ? We are to glory in the Gospel.

What is the Gospel? The Gospel of Christ is the good news that He is our Savior; it is He Who justifies us before God. The Gospel *is the power of God to salvation* and relationship with Him. Think of the power it takes to elevate us from being an enemy of God to being His beloved children. With this power we are adopted into the family of God

Believers - what does being a believer mean? Belief leads to action. If I believe I'm going to get hit by a truck coming at me, I MOVE! In James 2:19, we are told, demons believe but only shake in their boots. They don't benefit because they don't respond with obedience to God's instructions and commandments. We are to glory in the Gospel. Those who are ashamed disqualify themselves from God's promises.

This wicked world, immersed in sexual and other sinful activities puts a lot of pressure on Christians to live and speak their faith. Be it known, if the world means so much to us that we are ashamed of Christ, that shame will be reflected in Christ's attitude towards us when we come into His presence during His return or at the time of our death (Mark 8:38). What an ugly thought that we would act in such a way that Christ would be ashamed of us.

Those who are ashamed of Jesus have allowed themselves to be judged by Satan's adulterous and sinful minions. I have guilt, but guilt is for what I have done; shame is for who I am. Know this! There is no shame for being in Christ.

The Bible does not use the word "proud" as an opposite of ashamed. Pride is one of the seven deadly sins. We are to go beyond pride to glorying in the Gospel.

Prayer – Dear Father, I glory in the Gospel and I glory in Your power to grant salvation to those who believe.

April 27   Return

Joel 2:13b ... *Return to the Lord your God, for He IS gracious and merciful, slow to anger, and of great kindness ...*

The Lord IS gracious.

Q Why can we return (or turn) to God?

Because *He IS gracious and merciful.*

It is interesting that grace and mercy, so often used by Paul in the introduction to his letters, was introduced way back by Joel. Remember, grace is getting what we don't deserve and mercy is not getting what we do deserve.

God is *slow to anger*, He is longsuffering and really, truly, does not WANT anyone to die without Christ so they spend eternity outside of His kingdom (2 Peter 3:9).

God has *great kindness*. That is, He has compassion, gentleness, and thoughtfulness. His kindness is something we can depend on. Kindness doesn't cost us anything. It is a feel good activity. Kindness is its own reward. Kindness is becoming more rare in this stressful world. We should pay ahead, making the recipient more likely to pay ahead ... Pete and repeat ...

As we return/turn to the Lord we enter through the way of Christ. As you consider the 360 degrees of the compass, people are going all sorts of ways. The single degree of the way to God is through Christ.

Why look for another way? Why, in heaven's name, would we even bother to look?

Turn or return – come to the Lord!

Prayer – Dear Father,- thank You that Your grace and mercy has existed for thousands of years and exists for us today.

April 28   Risen

1 Corinthians 15:20 *But now Christ IS risen from the dead, and has become the first fruits of those who have fallen asleep.*

IS – A positive statement of the resurrection of Jesus. *Christ IS risen!*

The chief priests and Pharisees gathered together with Pilate and, without knowing that they were going to guarantee the truth about the resurrection, used their memory of Jesus' claim that He would rise after three days, and asked that the tomb would be securely sealed and guarded. They were so mindset against the truth of Christ, they thought the disciples would steal the body and give a false claim of resurrection. They claimed this would be a double deception, the theft being worse than Jesus' claim (Matthew 27:62b-65). The chief priests and Pharisees didn't realize that the disciples were confused and lacking faith in the whole scheme of things.

Q How did they try to say the resurrection was a lie?

Special attention and investigation should be given to the resurrection of Jesus. The resurrection of Jesus is the lynch pin of Christianity. Without the resurrection, Christianity is just another ism.

The chief priests and Pharisees did not believe Jesus would rise from the dead, nor did they want Him to. Pilate bought into their hatred of Jesus. Pilate then thought Jesus' claim was a deception and if the body were stolen, that would be a second deception. Pilate gave the command to secure the tomb and it was secured by round-the-clock shifts of Roman soldiers (vs65-66). This event is one of the salient proofs that Christ IS risen! (See devotions for February 3 and June 10.)

For today's Christians, Satan still says the resurrection of Christ is a deception and Satan will do everything he can to destroy our faith. Those who want to disprove Christianity must disprove the resurrection. INSTANT REPLAY - Those who want to disprove Christianity must disprove the resurrection.

Thankfully, we have the indwelling Holy Spirit, Who convinces us of Jesus' resurrection presence.

Prayer – Dear Father, thank you for the truth of the resurrection of Jesus Christ as proven by His indwelling presence in my life.

April 29   Shepherd

Psalms 23:1 *The Lord IS My shepherd …*

> *Lord IS shepherd.*

> When meditating, it is often helpful to highlight each word in a verse separately.

Q How does God's activity as a shepherd work in our lives??

> *THE Lord not* "A" Lord but THE only God, all else are man-made idols, objects, religions.

> *The LORD* - Creator, Master, Lover, Savior, Sustainer, Guide.

> *The Lord IS* - Not was, not will be, but IS, now in every present moment.

> *The Lord is MY* - Not others, leaving me to my own devices, universal yet personal.

> SHEPHERD: In the tenth chapter of the Gospel of John, verses 4-14, we find Jesus is the fulfillment of Psalm 23. He is the door and the good Shepherd. He knows and cares for His sheep. He gives His sheep abundant life.

> *I have come that they may have life, and that they may have it more abundantly (John* 10:10b).

> He knows us, we know Him. He is in us, we are in Him. Thus we have salvation and life.

Prayer – Dear Father, thank You for the good Shepherd, Who is Jesus. I gratefully take my place as one of His sheep.

April 30   Stone

John 8:7b *He who IS without sin among you, let him throw a stone at her first.*

Without sin IS permission to throw.

Q Who is qualified to accuse others of sin?

The stoners can be those who are without sin.

Jesus was talking to a group who wanted to stone a woman who had been caught in adultery.

But, … The Bible says everyone sins and doesn't live up to God's glory (Romans 3:23). You haven't? Good for you! Hope you have good aim.

A lot of people have "comparative sin." "My sin is less than other's sins." Or, "I have a good excuse for what I do (did)." Or, "I'm basically a good person." Funny thing is, in the lists of sins in the Bible, not one of them is capitalized. In James 2:10, we find, *"For whoever shall keep the whole law, and yet stumble in one point, he is guilty of all."* OUCH!

In today's news we see that people are literally looking under rocks to find stones to throw at each other. Some even rejoice if they think they have found even a pebble to use as a projectile. So much of what is happening is the opposite of the description of love given in 1 Corinthians 13:4-10. We should know that love, amongst other things, is courteous, thinks of good, and doesn't take pleasure in other's mistakes.

When accusing others, we put them on the defensive and create a no-win war of words.

Accusation is contagious!

Kindness is katchy!

Prayer – Dear Father, help me to act in love towards others, and to pray for them, especially those who despitefully use me.

MAY

SO

Meditation aids

SO is an adverb; An adverb usually is a word used before another word, often a verb, to form a phrase that modifies (qualifies, describes, or limits) some aspect of the sentence. The object of the adverb could be a word or a phrase. Check the objects of the adverb to understand its impact.

SO is a powerful and versatile adverb. It may specify, clarify, amplify, qualify, or emphasize an action.

Uses of SO – thus – therefore - as a result, if/then, because of, from, part of, concerning.

Example:

For God SO loved the world ... <u>John 3:16</u>.

SO *loved* is a verb phrase.

SO emphasizes how much God loves the world – us, you, and me.

May 1   Edification

<u>1 Corinthians 14:12</u> *Even SO you, since you are zealous for spiritual gifts, let it be for the edification of the church that you seek to excel.*

SO - here, means *let it be.*

Q What is the purpose of spiritual gifts?

The purpose is Body building.

Paul had just finished an explanation of the use of tongues and had emphasized how they, and other gifts, were to be used. Some groups feel we need to have a gift, or a certain gift, in order to be qualified as a Christian. This verse teaches us that spiritual gifts are for edification, not qualification. INSTANT REPLAY – spiritual gifts are for edification, not qualification. According to 1Corinthians 12:7, spiritual gifts are given by the Holy Spirit, not by man's desires or dictates.

Don't ask, "What is my gift?" Ask, "Is there a gift You want me to receive for Your purpose at this time." God will give you the gift He wants you to have for that moment for whatever builds up the Church. You may have it for life or you may never have it again.

THEY ARE GIFTS!

We should be aware of what the gifts are so we can recognize them and be open for them. Gifts are listed in 1 Corinthians 12, Romans 12, 1 Peter 4, Ephesians 4, and various other places.

We are to be *zealous for spiritual gifts*, not for self aggrandizement but for the edification of the church. The gifts are NOT something required to validate our being a Christian. Note the rhetorical questions (1 Corinthians 12:29-30). The implied answer is, "No." We need to be open for any gift that God wills to give at any time for His appointed goal.

Prayer – Dear Father, Help me to be open for whatever gift You choose to give me, at any given time, for Your purpose.

May 2   Pleasing

1 Thessalonians 2:4 ... *even SO we speak, not as pleasing men, but God, Who tests our hearts.*

SO clarifies how we speak - to please God.

Q Who should be pleased with our speech?

God.

As Christians, we don't speak to tickle the ears of human listeners. Our listeners may want to hear or there may be times they are not receptive of the truth. They may cover their ears and run away babbling. When we speak to them, we should let God test our hearts, the wellspring of our thoughts and emotions, and speak to please Him. We need to check with the Holy Spirit to see if we have any "speech impediment" or "action impediment" in our verbal or nonverbal communication.

There are many ways to get a message across. Humans have the unique ability to verbalize thousands of words. Interestingly enough, other than in writing or texting, a large percentage of communication is non-verbal. An expression, a tone of voice, or a gesture will often convey an entirely different message from what is said. We should strive to make our body language give a true but gentle and pleasant message. As the saying goes, Our actions speak so loudly that people can't hear what we are saying, and, thankfully, that is also true of positive actions even without words.

Our talks with others should be considerate of their needs, with unearned favor and free from pollution. These properties, which guide our understanding, help us give answers to people (Colossians 4:6). The people may be someone inside or outside the Body of Christ.

Our speech should not be bland, but be that which preserves, has zest, and gives a delightful flavor to life.

Prayer – Dear Father, please help me know when to speak with my mouth and when to be silent, when and how to speak with my actions and when to walk away.

May 3   Body

Romans 12:5 *SO we, being many, are one body in Christ, and individually members of one another.*

SO - means we are to be a close family, one in the body of Christ.

Q Should there be divisions in the body of Christ? No, just individual members of *one body.*

These two linked concepts, many but one, are critical in presenting Christ to the world. One of Satan's major tools in undermining Christianity in the eyes of the world is division in the Body and competing denominations. This is not a new problem. Paul addressed the problem of church divisions in 1 Corinthians 3:3-9. He ended his argument there saying we are to work together.

The world may think there is no sure way to know the truth when they see hundreds of denominations and hundreds of subgroups in a single denomination. One aim of Christianity is to spread the Gospel. Divisions in the body don't help meet this goal. We should not emphasize a sub-doctrine that promotes division.

Being *one Body* is a super goal. Being In Christ is the unifying factor and should be the goal that dominates all doctrinal differences. There should be *one body in Christ.* We are saved by grace through faith for works (Ephesians 2:9-10). INSTANT REPLAY - We are saved <u>by</u> grace <u>through</u> faith <u>for</u> works. All else is subject to this unifying factor.

Paul uses the human body as a metaphor for the church. Each part of the body needs to work together for the good of the whole body. One of the parts can't deny being part of the whole. That doesn't make sense (1 Corinthians 12:12-17). The lesson for us today is that there are no groups or denominations that should believe, or try to operate, as if they are separate from the Body of Christ. However, if they deviate from the basic truths of Christianity, they should not claim to be part of the Body.

We are one in Christ but we don't lose our individuality. However, even as individuals, we make our wills and intents subject to oneness in Christ. SO, have compassion and understanding with forgiveness, following the example of the forgiveness we have received from God through Christ (Ephesians 4:32).

Prayer – Dear Father, help me, with all my differences, to be part of the one Body of Christ.

May 4   Boldness

1 John 4:17-18 *Love has been perfected among us in this: that we may have boldness in the day of judgment; because as He is, SO are we in this world. There is no fear in love; but perfect love casts out fear.*

SO clarifies how we are to be like Jesus.

Q How are we like Christ?

We are to be loving and bold because we are in Christ.

We are *as He is* because *everyone who has this hope in Him purifies himself, just as He is pure* 1 John 3:3. Grace, grace, marvelous grace!

When we really, truly love others, we will tell them of God's love for them. Jesus really, truly loves us and, through His sacrifice, has made us perfect.

The most important way that we can show love for our friends is to give up any thoughts we have for our own needs or emotions and tell them the good news about Jesus. We show our love for Christ by following His commandments (John 15:13). We have boldness but with utmost purity, humility, and gratitude.

This is an *us* and *we* thing. *Among us*, that is, in the body of Christ, we will *have boldness in the day of judgment* but we can also have boldness at all times. We are in Satan's realm which means we will be challenged by events and, sometimes, people. There may be times that our faith comes to the fore and nonbelievers will take actions to have us be quiet. They may even become hostile.

Love is among us so we can have *boldness*. Did you know that boldness is a product of love? Think about that. Think of what mothers will do for their children. An energized human mother makes Mama Bear look like a cream puff.

His love is so perfect in us that we can face any judgment without fear. Therefore we not only speak with boldness, we live with boldness.

Prayer – Dear Father, thank you that I can face judgment with boldness. May I also face the daily judgments of the world with a love for Jesus that erases any lack of boldness for Him.

May 5   Victory

<u>1 Corinthians 15:54</u> *SO when this corruptible has put on incorruption, and this mortal has put on immortality, then shall be brought to pass the saying that is written: "Death is swallowed up in victory."*

SO clarifies what is to happen and when it is to happen.

Q What is the victory?

Corruptible changes to purity. Mortal changes to eternal life. Death is consumed by victory. No wonder the Holy Spirit is credited with power.

The victory is that *death is swallowed up*. Now, if death becomes a victorious event, there must be something beyond death. We do not die the second death. Instead of going from death to death, we go from death to life everlasting.

When the fulfillment of the promises of God through Christ make us incorruptible and immortal, the prophesy of Isaiah becomes true – that death would be swallowed up *forever* (Isaiah 25:8).

We who were corrupted can no longer be corrupted. Life which was confined to the body is released for eternal life. The written promise is fulfilled. That which is mortal will live forever because: all these promises are gifts to us, founded on the gift of faith given through God's grace (Ephesians 2:8). The promises are based on a valid faith that can be trusted.

Faith is given by God and overcomes death so we know faith makes us incorruptible, immortal, and victorious.

Prayer – Dear Father, thank you for the faith that gives us victory in Jesus.

May 6   Attributes

Romans 1:20 ... *His invisible attributes are clearly seen ... SO that they are without excuse.*

SO – here means there is no excuse.

Q Do atheists have an excuse for not believing in God?

No, their pride makes them want to make up their own rules.

The atheist says, "There is no God". My wife says to them, "No what?" The atheist adopts a mindset that there is no God and then fabricates "evidence" to support it. Some of their fabrications are ludicrous.

No thing comes from nothing. A Creator God makes more sense than something coming from nothing. Something comes from God. God always was.

Those who do not believe in God assume a lot more than those of us who do. Think about the imagination of a person who tries to convince himself that all that there is and all that we are "just happened".

We can't see God in Person, but we know of Him by His appearance in Jesus Christ and the Holy Spirit and Their effects on our life (John 14:9b).

His attributes are clearly seen in humans (Romans 1:20). We are created in His image with abilities: physical, emotional, and verbal. Also, there is incredible color, beauty, majesty, variety, and awesome power in the universe. If God's attributes are not enough, He has spoken to us in the Living Word – Jesus.

Fuel supplies, that are called fossil fuels, as if they came from ancient life, are now known to be of such quantity that no amount of life could account for them. The variety of metals and precious stones defy the imagination. We continue to find vast quantities of materials that God has provided for us. The only excuse anyone can have to deny the existence of God is a terrible mindset leading to a horrible end.

Prayer – Dear Father, thank you for the very visible attributes that declare your majesty, power, and presentation of beauty and materials for our use.

May 7   Time

Esther 4:14-16 *Yet who knows whether you have come to the kingdom for such a time as this ... And SO I will go to the king, which is against the law, and if I perish, I perish!*

SO means therefore, because of *such a time.*

Q How do we know when it is *such a time*?

We don't.

At all times we need to ask God. There may be times we have to go against prevailing wisdom and do what should be done. Esther simply said, *"If I perish, I perish!"* Hopefully, it won't come to that. Paul may have been thinking of this passage when he said there was no law against the fruit of the Spirit (Galatians 5:23). He may have felt that the items listed, love, joy, and peace, etc. (Galatians 5:22) should not offend anybody. It would be nice if love, joy, and peace were not offensive but the way these attributes are obtained is certainly vilified in many circles.

There is a parallel passage in Peter's experience. *Now, Lord, look on their threats, and grant to Your servants that with all boldness they may speak Your word ...* Acts 4:29. We have learned that love gives boldness.

We may not know for sure if we have been placed in a certain place for a certain time. We don't always know what another's need is. If we are going to err, we should err on the side of grace. We don't want to look back and regret not following the prompting of the Holy Spirit. Sometimes a seemingly simple word or act can have a positive eternal impact. To mix a metaphor, we can put our toe in the water and take one step at a time.

We live in a world where it seems that the message of Christ breaks an unwritten law. Practically any other expression of faith can be publicly promoted except Christianity. Christianity is not politically correct. We need to know that the laws of God overrule the laws of man. We are to be subject to authority but if the authority is clearly contrary to God's commands and Jesus' teaching, if there are consequences, so be it.

Prayer – Dear Father, even in the face of danger or ridicule, I will do your will when the time is right.

May 8   Magnified

Philippians 1:20 ... *according to my earnest expectation and hope ... SO now also Christ will be magnified in my body, whether by life or by death.*

SO, as a result, Christ *will be magnified.*

Q Do you want a win/win situation?

Whether by the way we live or by the way we die, we will magnify Christ.

Too many people look at Christ through the wrong end of the binoculars. We need to magnify the image of Christ through our lives so that even the spiritually visually challenged can see Him in us.

Expectation and hope are tied together here. Earnest expectations are very strong. If I expect something to happen, it is my best thinking at the time that it will happen. If I hope something will happen, it is what I want to happen but there is a measure of doubt. For example - "I expect it is going to rain." vs. "I hope it will rain."

We have to be cautious about where we place our reasonable expectations. In Satan's realm, it isn't reasonable to be reasonable. We have to get realistic. However, in God's domain, we can have reasonable and realistic expectations.

SO now also Christ will be magnified is a verb phrase followed by *in my body,* a prepositional phrase, both of which support *my earnest expectation and hope.* Let Christ's love shine through your looks and actions.

The phrase *in my body* emphasizes the <u>importance of body language</u> and will communicate the magnification of Christ by the way I live <u>and</u> by the way I die. So often we can tell by a person's facial expression or body language that what they are saying is not what they mean. We want our total communication to tell people the great good news of life and death in Christ. Death in Christ is really life in Christ.

Prayer – Dear Father, it is my earnest expectation and sincere hope, that whatever happens in life or death, my actions will magnify Christ.

May 9   Faith

<u>Romans 10:14-17</u> *And how shall they believe in Him of whom they have not heard? ... SO then faith comes by hearing, and hearing by the word of God.*

SO tells us faith comes from hearing the word of God.

Q How do we acquire faith?

Again, faith comes by hearing the word of God.

Isaiah becomes poetic when he talks about *beautiful feet* on the mountains of those who bring good news of *peace, good things,* and *salvation* (Isaiah 52:7). The word of God says it becomes our joy to tell, by our actions and our words, the great good news of Jesus. Tell people, "Your sins are forgiven. The Spirit of God is available with power, gifts, and fruit." Tell people, "We have salvation through God's grace, we don't have to work for it" (Ephesians 2:8). We tell others all kinds of simple stuff that happens to us. Shouldn't we tell them about Jesus and how we received the greatest gift of all?   Who told you?   Love gives boldness.

Amongst other things, we are God's trumpet, heralding the good news. We can be sure of the message so we can speak with boldness. If our words have an uncertain sound, others may not respond to what we say (1 Corinthians 14:8).

One day my mother had one foot in the boat and another on the dock. The boat drifted. I thought the result was hilarious. She didn't. When we have one foot in Christ and the other in the world, subject to Satan's ridicule, the results are not funny. We need to have both feet in the boat.

Speaking of boats, we are like an ocean liner leaving port. First obvious mooring lines are cast off, but when we are a short distance from the dock, others appear out of the water. We cast them off and go farther out. Then ropes crusted with barnacles appear. Eventually, through the work of Christ and the Holy Spirit, all our ties to the dock are loosed and we sail victoriously on God's ocean.

Prayer – Dear Father, may the words of my mouth and the actions of my body give a clear, unashamed message to those You bring to hear.

May 10   Fear

<u>Matthew 14:28-30-31</u> *And Peter answered Him and said, "Lord, if it is You, command me to come to You on the water." SO Jesus said, "Come"... But when Peter saw that the wind was boisterous, he was afraid; and beginning to sink, he cried out, saying, "Lord, save me!" And immediately Jesus stretched out His hand and caught him*

SO, because of Peter's request.

Q What happens when faith wavers in the sea of life?

Jesus reaches out to us

After the feeding of the 5000, Jesus sent the disciples on their way and He went off by Himself to pray. Then began two living parables to demonstrate Jesus' power. First, He walked on water to show His power over nature. Then, the event with Peter showed His ability to help in life's crises. Peter saw Jesus coming, and being impeteruous, he wanted to share the moment. Jesus said, "*Come,*" as He does today in times of challenge. Peter started out well, as we often do, then Peter took his eyes off Jesus, looked at the impossibility of what he was doing, and began to sink. Jesus then reached out, as He does for us today, and helped Peter get into the boat.

When we see an impossibility that Christ can make possible, we need to step out in faith and keep our eyes on Him. We may start out in faith but then look at the "*water*" and become fearful. Sometimes we step out in faith and begin to tell someone the good news and then the winds of Satan become *boisterous*, causing us to sink. If we start to sink, we need to look back at Jesus in trust and say, "*Lord, save me.*" If we keep our eyes on Him we can know, because of our faith in Him, He will save us from sinking. Are you sinking? Reach out –

Prayer – Dear Father, help me ignore the stormy waters of life and keep my eyes on You.

May 11   Salvation

Hebrews 3 ... *how shall we escape if we neglect SO great a salvation ...?*

Not just great, SO great - amplifying greatness.

Q How shall we escape?

We can't.

Why would anyone want to neglect this great salvation? Pride is one reason. Some people are total do-it-yourself projects - SELF-MADE-LOSERS. They are too arrogant to admit their emptiness and they try to fill their "God-sized hole" with man-sized solutions.

Some people think today's verse is a directive and begin to look for other means of salvation, such as works. They often say, "I'm basically a good person." Others claim to read the Bible, pray, even tithe. However, if they treat Christianity as a religion, based on works, they may waste many years only to find out that works are not sufficient. Only being in Christ gives us the efficacy and sufficiency of grace.

Why on earth, or in heaven's name, should we want to escape from this great salvation? This salvation is so great because it is based on God's loving gift of grace and, therefore, absolutely fulfills the attributes mentioned by Paul in Philippians 4:8; true, noble, just, pure, lovely, of good report, with virtue and praiseworthy results - pure descriptors of the message of John 3:16.

It is so easy, how can we miss the obvious? It is simple enough for those who are challenged and so profound that the wisest cannot plumb its depths. It is available to all.

Are you trying to escape? Why? If so, stop! Stop relying on your own efforts and decide to accept this *great salvation*. There is nothing for us to do except to accept.

Prayer – Dear Father, thank You for finding me, convicting me of righteousness, and for justifying me – my search is over in You.

May 12   Joy

Acts 20:24 ... *SO that I may finish my race with joy ...*

SO means finish with joy.

Q What will be our emotion at the end of our races?

If we are in Christ - joy.

The question then becomes, "How can I live so that my life ends with joy?"

Live in and through the Holy Spirit. Avoid evil! -- *Rejoice always, pray without ceasing, in everything give thanks, for this is the will of God in Christ Jesus for you. Do not quench the Spirit ... hold fast what is good. Abstain from every form of evil* 1 Thessalonians 5:16-22. Follow the commandments of God.

As joy is part of the fruit of the Spirit (Galatians 5:22), pray continually to be filled with the Spirit and you will have His joy. Jesus told the disciples if they kept His commandments they would live in His love, His joy would be with them, and their joy would be full (John 15:10-11). A follows B follows C. Keep, live, rejoice!

An old saying goes, "The only sure things are death and taxes." Really, the only sure thing is death. SO, we need to have death assurance. INSTANT REPLAY - we need to have death assurance. Christ is our eternal life insurance. His joy is with us through life and at the finish line.

Good news! Spiritual death is optional. We only have to die once – a physical death. If we are only born once, a physical birth, we die twice, physically and spiritually. If we are born physically and born again, spiritually, we only die once, physically. It follows that if we are born twice, we will see the kingdom of God (John 3:3).

Our faith makes up for the lack of sight so we have glorious joy that is beyond words. Our sure salvation is the result of our faith, a nice circular transaction (1 Peter 1:8b-9).

Prayer – Dear Father, help me to live in such a way that my physical death will be a joyful entrance into your presence.

May 13   Repent

Acts 3:19 *Repent therefore, and be converted, that your sins may be blotted out, SO that times of refreshing may come from the presence of the Lord.*

SO – conversion enables times of refreshing.

Q What is one result of life in Christ?

Times of refreshing – a lifetime of happy hours.

There are two requirements: Repent,

be converted.

To repent is to turn 180 degrees – changing from going away from God to going towards God. True remorse starts us on the road to salvation, the only requirement is that we repent of our sin(s) (2 Corinthians 7:10). Many people go 360 degrees - right back where they started. After remorse, there is need for confession, acceptance, and right living.

There are two results: our sins are blotted out.

there are times of refreshing.

Our sins are blotted out as an ink blotter leaves a paper without a trace of a smudge - not just covered over like with correction products, but removed. Think of a potentially wonderful message written on a piece of paper with spills, smudges and splatters all over the page. This is our story outside of Christ. Then He comes into our lives, blots away, and the print comes sharp and clear. Times of refreshing come. Times, plural, refreshing again and again and again. Those times come because we have peace and joy in the *presence of the Lord.*

If we don't repent, our sins don't get blotted out. When we do repent, blotting out and conversion occur. They are the activities that allow blotting so that refreshing may come as the Lord enters our life.

Have your sins been blotted out? Blots away! Yay!

Prayer – Dear Father, thank you for constantly blotting out my sin and refreshing me as I live in Your presence.

May 14   Belief

<u>John 3:16</u> *God SO loved the world that He gave His only begotten son that whosoever believes in Him should not perish but have everlasting life.*

SO emphasizes how much He loves us!!

Q Do you really know how much God loves you?

He loves us SO much that He sacrificially gave His only begotten Son, the only Son by way of a human mother, so that *EVERlasting life* would be <u>given</u> to believers.

Try leaving out the word SO: God ___ loved the world ... Not nearly the impact. Quite often, omitting a word shows its impact.

<u>Who</u> does He love? – the world – all of mankind – me - you.

<u>What</u> is love? – there are so many definitions, here, love is giving.

<u>Why</u> did He love? – so believers would have eternal life.

<u>How</u> did He love? – SO much He gave His only Son.

<u>When</u> does this love become active? Instantly when we believe and receive (John 1:12).

<u>Where</u> does it become active? In our lives - right here, right now (Romans 10:9).

John 3:16 tells us what God's primary purpose is – that believers should have eternal life. He gave Christ for the world, every race and creed, that *whosoever believes* may have eternal life. When we receive Him, when our mouths and hearts testify to Him, we have eternal life.

God's love has always been there for us but it only works into and through us when we believe and accept it. The key word is believe. Meditate on the word – believe each of these verses.

Prayer – Dear Father, thank You that because you loved me so much, and gave me perfect faith, I have eternal life.

May 15   Shine

Matthew 5:16 *Let your light SO shine before men, that they may see your good works and glorify your Father in heaven.*

SO is the result that enables people to see, and glorify God.

Q How can people *see* our faith?

By letting our *light shine* by way of *good works.*

We do this, not to bring glory to ourselves, but to give glory to God.

Who – Those who look at Christians.

What – see good works.

Why – that God be glorified.

How – let your light SO shine.

When - always.

Where – in the dark, the world can be a dark place at times.

The action is to let our light shine. The purpose is that God might be glorified. We need to take advantage of dark places. Never waste a dark place. INSTANT REPLAY - Never waste a dark place. Thanking God for them releases Jesus' joy and peace as power that generates light. There are times a dark place allows the light to shine brighter. The darker it is, the more our little light shines. Let our light be so bright and compelling that it doesn't go in one eye and out the other of those who *see our faith.* When it seems darkest, people see our light to be brightest. We don't know bright without dark.

Jesus has transformed us from being darkness to being light. Now we need to understand that we don't cover our light with any fears or actions (Matthew 5:14-15).

People in the dark have to look in the dark but we let our light shine in their darkness. When they see the light shining in our lives, they will be led by the Spirit to look there.   *Let your light SO shine ...*

Prayer – Dear Father, help me not to curse the darkness or to belittle my light, but to rejoice in the darkness where I can let my light shine.

May 16   Love

1 Corinthians 13:2 ... *though I have all faith, SO that I could remove mountains, but have not love, I am nothing.*

SO that we should have love.

Q How important is love?

We are *nothing* without love. Therefore, God is everything (1John 4:8).

It doesn't say we are going to remove mountains, it just means even if I had that much faith, and have not love, I've missed the point.

Faith without love is nothing giving us an equation: $F - L = 0$ Faith, take away love, leaves nothing. Do you know any unloving church people? Look into people's eyes. Check their "unbody" language – that which undermines the Body.

What is love? The love of God is manifested in giving: The gifts of first, Christ, and second, the Holy Spirit are generated by the love of God (John 3:16, 14:16). There is a list of characteristics of brotherly love in 1 Corinthians 13. *And now abide faith, hope, and love, these three; but the greatest of these is love* v13. We can see, it should be clear, let love guide your life.

How do we get love? First, believe and receive the love of God by accepting Christ as your Savior, then accept the Holy Spirit as your Helper. Once we are filled with the Spirit, we have the power, gifts, and fruit of the Spirit, part of which is love (Galatians 5:22). Again, It is the Spirit of God Who gives us power, gifts, and fruit. Thank You Lord!

Prayer – Dear Father, may my interactions with people show Your love through me.

May 17   Grace

<u>Galatians 1:6</u> *I marvel that you are turning away SO soon from Him who called you in the grace of Christ.*

SO means a very short time.

Q How soon did the Galatians turn from salvation by grace to works?

A very short time - SO soon.

Why did they turn away? The Galatians had trouble believing that they were justified by grace alone. They may have been trapped in pride. They did fall prey to promoters of the law. Others may fall away because they give control to the temptation of the moment and return to vomit and wallow (2 Peter 2:22), Yuk, and lose sight of the free gifts of help in this life and life eternal through the Holy Spirit and Christ Jesus.

The parable of the sower sheds some light on the subject. In the explanation of the parable of the sower (Matthew 13:18-22), some seed was not understood – some fell on hard ground, some had no root, and some were choked by busyness and the false lure of money and possessions. The insights into human nature are obvious.

The benefits of salvation by grace are so apparent to Paul that he is amazed that the Galatians were reverting to works to try to gain favor with God. Whatever causes people to lose confidence in justification by faith in Christ, we need to be assured that amazing grace really is true. We can believe it and live in grace. Continue in grace!

It does seem that it doesn't take much to cause some people to deviate from God's clear path. Sometimes we get so busy with the cares of the world that we take our eyes off Christ. We have to be careful and take advice from the writer of Hebrews. Cast off any burden or any ties that are so tempting, waiting to lure us into some sinful trap (Hebrews 12:1b).

We need to look beyond cares and temptations and keep on following Him who called us. I urge you to remain in the grace of Christ and not go off on any wild demon chase. Let us keep our eyes on the goal.

Prayer – Dear Father, help me overcome the constant chipping and chirping of Satan so I can endure to the end.

May 18   Fulfill

<u>Galatians 6:2</u> *Bear one another's burdens and SO fulfill the law of Christ.*
(Love)

SO means thus fulfill.

Q How can we help *fulfill the law of Christ?*

By bearing *one another's burdens.*

The implication is that everyone has burdens. We need to be available to give help and to receive help. Check your SPICE. Our needs may be Spiritual, Physical, Intellectual, Community, or Emotional. Whatever our need, God will provide. As we admit our needs to others, they are more likely to share their needs with us.

You help me help you help me help you help me help you, etc. By helping others we bring to fruition the ultimate relationship for which we were united with God through His gift of redemption in Christ.

The law of Christ: If you really fulfill the royal law according to the Scripture, "You shall love your neighbor as yourself," you do well ... <u>James 2:8</u>. Apparently this phrase was so important to early Christians, they had a special term for it – The Royal Law. It is often called The Golden Rule.

Sometimes we need to give the gift of receiving. Don't let your pride, or self-sufficiency, deprive another of the joy of giving. If we refuse to receive help, we deprive others of their fulfillment of the Royal Law.

First and foremost, <u>we</u> have to receive the Gift and the gifts that God gives to us.

Prayer – Dear Father, first let me accept that you love me, then, let me love myself as you love me, and then may I love my neighbor as myself.

Tomorrow we apply this law to marriage.

May 19   Love

<u>Ephesians 5:22-33</u> *Let each one of you in particular SO love his own wife as himself ...*

SO means equality of love.

Q How shall husbands love their wives?

As they love themselves! "*... just as Christ al<u>so</u> loved the church ...* This applies to wives as well. This verse might be called the Golden Rule of marriage because it applies the second commandment, the Royal Law, to marriage. It is interesting to note that in the Ephesians passage, Paul gives more directions to husbands than to wives. Our English language is impoverished when it comes to expressing love. We refer to making love as having sex when we should be making love 24/7/365 - just as we love God 24/7/365.

The love here discussed is marital love, shared between husband and wife. Marital love is precious as seen by the fact that marital love is compared to the relationship between Christ and His body, the church (v23-24). Leave out the word SO – *Let each one of you love his own wife ...* It loses some punch. Traditional marriage vows say, "Keep myself only unto you."

No sane person hates himself. Instead he cares for his physical and emotional needs similar to the way that Jesus cares for His Body the Church (Ephesians 5:29). Show me a man who mistreats his wife and you will see a man who hates himself, and others.

Today's Scripture encourages husbands, and wives for that matter, to show love by nourishing and cherishing the other, and then to forgive our self, and our spouse, instantly and constantly when we fail. This verse applies to *each* individual. Don't return to the scene of any forgiven crime.

To nourish is to provide physical and emotional needs. To cherish is to hold in high esteem. This is to be done regardless of the behavior of the spouse. We are to act in Christ, not react to the behavior of our spouse. More than anywhere else in human relationships, in marriage don't do anything you think you might have to lie about. A spouse who loves <u>selfishly</u> impoverishes the self, the other, and the marriage. The spouse who loves <u>selflessly</u> enriches both parties, and the marriage.

Prayer – Dear Father, may I, as a husband, or wife, love myself as God loves me and may I extend that same love to my spouse.

May 20   Example

Philippians 3:17 ... *follow my example, and note those who SO walk as you have us for a pattern.*

SO clarifies how we should walk.

Q Why is our example so important?

SO other Christians will know how to act. Walk as I walk, follow my *pattern.* And, SO non-Christians will be attracted to Christ.

Note: we are to notice others and know that others are noticing us. This is to be a joy, not a burden. If it seems to be a burden remember all that we have in Christ and think of what Christ endured for us. Live a life that is a joyful fragrant offering to God; one that is a pattern for others to follow (Philippians 4:9).

This is not like the old comedy routine - "Walk this way." This is a joyous walk in a way that is the way Jesus meant when He said He is the way, truth, and light (John 14:6). A walk in the way of the Spirit is a walk of love, joy, and peace ... Think of the joy of a child learning to take steps and the joy of the parents as the child toddles to them.

Don't live as if life is drudgery, as some do, indicated by their, "I'm suffering for Christ" look or a "Woe is me" testimony. Some people brag about their problems and enjoy poor health.

In Christ we can view each day, with its rewards and opportunities for growth, as a day with the Holy Spirit. Don't leave home without Him, or stay home without Him.

We need to live as people who have been included in the family of God. We need to consider all things joy. God loves a cheerful liver (word intended). Whatever the condition of my life, I have learned a lesson – be content regardless of circumstances (Philippians 4:11b). In order to do that, Paul must have rested in the conclusion that God only allowed in his life what God intended to use for His purposes.

Prayer – Dear Father, may my walk be an example and a pattern for others. May my words, emotions, actions, and thoughts be acceptable in their sight as well as Yours.

May 21   Forgive

<u>Colossians 3:13</u> ... *even as Christ forgave you, SO you also must do.*

SO clarifies the manner of forgiveness - as Christ forgives us.

Q How can we be sure of forgiveness?

We can be sure of our purity in Christ because of His characteristics of faithfulness and justice.

Q How must we forgive?

Even as Christ forgave, making the forgiven, including ourselves, pure in our eyes, as if it never happened. INSTANT REPLAY - as if it never happened. THIS WE *MUST DO!* Because He makes sure there is not a smidgen that keeps us from a total relationship with them, and us, in Him. We are to live as if other Christians are pure in Christ - because they are. Forgiveness is not optional.

Relieve yourself of the curse of not forgiving. Imagine the ugliest thing you can, - think of it as a grudge - hold on to that grudge – working, eating, sleeping, everything you do - it will compromise your life. It will be a cancer that eats away at your peace. Ask Jesus what He wants you to do with this grudge – and any other grudges you may have.

Now we know that Christ always makes intercession for us while Satan continually lies, steals, and attempts to destroy us. We also know that Christ is the over-comer. Forgiveness should be initiated often because opportunities for resentment occur every day. We should imitate Christ and make intercession for those who may sin against us.

We are new creations in Him. We can forget what is behind us. Forgiveness is the key to relationship with God, others, and self. If you don't feel and accept forgiveness, the river of your joy and peace is blocked, or dries up. Windshields are bigger than rearview mirrors.

Prayer – Dear Father, may I realize the magnitude of Christ's forgiveness so I can forgive others and have a pure relationship with them and You.

May 22   Abound

Colossians 2:6 *As you therefore have received Christ Jesus the Lord, SO walk in Him, rooted and built up in Him ... abounding in it* (faith) *with thanksgiving.* (faith inserted).

SO means therefore.

Q What should we do after receiving Christ?

Walk in Him.

Q How should we walk?

Abounding – with leaps of joy - with heaps of thanksgiving.

We don't need to worry that we will leap into danger because we are rooted and built up in Him.

RECEIVE - We have received Him (John 1:12).

ROOTED - We have become rooted in Christ. This is a given right, not an earned privilege. There is no better soil. *For no other foundation can anyone lay than that which is laid, which is Jesus Christ* 1 Corinthians 3:11. When a tree is transplanted, there is a necessary ritual to the process to make sure the roots extend into the surrounding soil so the roots can absorb nutrients and so the tree can stand against the wind.

BUILT UP – And we can be built up in and on Him because Jesus is the best possible foundation (1 Corinthians 3:11). Grow up, don't just receive and vegetate.

ABOUNDING - Joyously, with thanksgiving abounding in Him. We can imitate young animals, leaping around for the pure joy of living. We can abound in Him, like a time-lapsed film of a flower going from seed to vibrant life.

Prayer – Dear Father I delightfully bounce in my walk with You.

May 23   Greatest

Luke 22:24-27 *Now there was also a dispute among them as to which of them should be considered greatest ... Jesus said, "Not SO among you ...". "Yet I am among you as the One who serves."*

SO means not like that.

Q Should there be debates about status?

No.

Q Who is to be the greatest in the kingdom?

He who serves.

There was a dispute - - sound familiar?

Even James and John's mother got into the act. She wanted to promote her boys by having Jesus make them His right and left hand men when He took over His realm (Matthew 20:20b-21).

Which of us should be considered greatest? There are those who hang on to a position even when someone else can do a better job. Some people insist on keeping a position when it is no longer needed. There seems to be an inherent drive in some people to compete, to be Alpha Dog. However, in God's kingdom there is no differentiation. Paul was against being high-minded (Romans 12:3).

In our Scripture, Jesus said, *"Not so ..."*

It is a joy to know that we are serving Jesus when we serve others, whether great or small. There is no one so insignificant in the body of Christ such that he/she isn't worthy of care (Matthew 25:40c). Remember, even toenails perform a necessary service.

Prayer – Dear Father, help me join Christ as one who serves.

May 24   Day

1 Thessalonians 5:2 ... *the day of the Lord SO comes as a thief in the night.*

SO clarifies how Jesus will come.

Q How will Christ return?

Like a *thief in the night.*

The reference to his coming is a metaphor of being unknown, not that something is stolen from us. The return of Christ should not be a threat. Nor should we put off our response to Him because the time of His return is unknown. Life in Christ begins when we receive Him and is so wonderful that an immediate response to the urging of the Holy Spirit to receive Him is the thing to do.

Q When will Christ return?

Jesus said neither he nor angels knew that time and date. He told His followers that only God knew that bit of information (Mark 13:32). So there is no misunderstanding, Jesus said even He didn't know. INSTANT REPLAY - Jesus said even He didn't know. Beware of those who claim they know what Jesus didn't know.

Those who predict an actual time of Christ's return, whether to scare people into the kingdom, to make themselves feel important, or to gather a following, are in violation of clear Bible teaching. For now, it is enough to know that we live in Christ and gain when we die in Him (Philippians 1:21).

The day refers to His return. He will return physically some day because He said He would. In the meantime, He is with us now, so there is no need to worry. We are secure in Him so whether we live or whether we die we are the Lord's. When Christ is in you, as He promised He would be when we believe and accept Him, then He has, for all intents and purposes, returned as a forerunner of His physical return.

Prayer – Dear Father, thank you that Christ has returned in me and that His kingdom is in me already.

May 25   Slaves

Romans 6:19b ... *for just as you presented your members as slaves of uncleanness, and of lawlessness leading to more lawlessness, SO now, present your members as slaves of righteousness for holiness.*

Holiness is a good thing and simply means practicing right living.

SO means at this time.

Q What is to be our attitude about holiness?

We should present ourselves as willing *slaves of righteousness for holiness.*

I beseech you therefore, brethren, by the mercies of God, that you present your bodies a living sacrifice, holy, acceptable to God, which is your reasonable service Romans 12:1. Note: this is possible because of God's mercy, not our merit, and it is the *reasonable* thing to do.

Holiness is not a common word today in most churches, but it should be because of clear instruction in Scripture (Hebrews 12:14).

Holiness is not a bad word but Satan has used some Christian behaviors to dissuade people from faith in Christ. The terms "holy rollers" and "holier than thou" are used by some to downgrade the body of Christ.

Being a slave to righteousness means that lawlessness, breaking a commandment, isn't even a consideration. Slaves just don't do that. The marvelous thing about being a slave of Christ is that we choose to accept that position in life. The curious thing about being a slave of Christ is that in Him we have perfect freedom. We even become His siblings (Romans 8:16-17). KISS – Keep It Simple Slave.

Now, instead of being slaves of sin, we are *slaves of righteousness for holiness.* Our *members* are the usable parts of the body: eyes, ears, mouth, arms, legs, etc. Every activity of any member of our body should be an act of holiness, that is God-like-ness.

Prayer – Dear Father, it is my desire to be holy in all my conduct.

May 26   Give

<u>2 Corinthians 9:7</u>   *SO let each one give as he purposes in his heart, not grudgingly or of necessity, for God loves a cheerful giver.*

SO – means give cheerfully.

Q What should be our attitude when giving?

Cheerful.

Not grudgingly - If this is our emotion when giving, our gift is not pleasing to God. We are not to give resentfully. My grandfather was putting a dime, a <u>dime</u>, in the collection plate at church. It fell to the wooden floor with a recognizable clunk. He whispered loudly to my hard-of-hearing grandmother, "The d--- thing stuck to my fingers". Really. The congregation laughed but it was really sad.

Not of necessity – giving is to be a response to grace, not some legalistic work to earn favor. Those who feel they are Christians because they tithe have missed the message of grace.

As he purposes in his heart - the purpose should be to extend the Gospel through the work or by meeting the needs of others. Good man – good heart – good treasure – good things (Matthew 12:35). It is a given that we give, not to gain but as a response to grace. It doesn't make sense that a person would plant just a few seeds and then expect a great harvest.

God loves a cheerful giver, not as a matter of course but part of the joy of relationship with God and siblings. I remember, as we planted corn in our garden chanting, "One for the black bird, one for the crow, one for the mole, and two to grow.

God so loved that He gave, and we become like Him in relationship when we copy His attitude of giving. All this is also true in a marriage. Give to your spouse joyfully, because you want to, from a loving cheerful heart.

Prayer – Dear Father, it is my delight to respond to Your grace by sharing what You have given me with those who need to hear the Gospel, or who have physical needs.

May 27   Begin

<u>Galatians 3:3</u> *Are you SO foolish? Having begun in the Spirit, are you now being made perfect by the flesh?*

SO means THAT foolish!

Q Are we capable of perfecting ourselves?   No.

Can the flesh, that is our own efforts, make us perfect? (Another rhetorical question.) Paul calls this idea foolishness.

The Galatians were slipping into the error of thinking they could be worthy through their own efforts because they were listening to legalists and considering works as a basis for salvation. The crucifixion of Christ is unnecessary if we can gain salvation on our own merit (Galatians 2:21b). They were operating partially through the influence of pride and partially out of a lack of understanding of the total efficacy of grace.

Remember the seriousness of being a fool. There are so many that know they are saved by grace, but then forget grace, and labor as if they were saved by worry and works instead of gladness and giving their lives as a response to God's grace.

We begin in the Spirit because it is the Spirit who has convicted us of sin and righteousness. We continue in the Spirit because He continues to work in us in the process of sanctification. When we are in the Spirit, we are free of laws and motivated by grace.

God's children follow God's Spirit. In so doing they are released from fear to peace (Romans 8:14). The spirit of bondage is based on law which brings fear of whether or not we satisfy the requirements for salvation and eternal life. But we have the Spirit of freedom and never again need to be snarled up in bondage (Galatians 5:1).

If we live in laws and works, we live in the anxiety of whether or not we qualify to be in the family of God. Instead of hoping we are good enough because of our own efforts, we should be in the Spirit and know we are made good enough because of Christ's sacrifice.

Prayer – Dear Father, thank You for beginning me in the Spirit and continuing to perfect me through sanctification, led by Your Spirit.

May 28   Bring

1 Thessalonians 4:14 *For if we believe that Jesus died and rose again, even SO God will bring with Him those who sleep in Jesus.*

SO means in like manner.

Q Who will God bring with Him?

Those who believe in Jesus' death and resurrection will be brought along with those who have died while being in Christ. To bring with Him is to bring in the same way or to bring to be in the same place.

Today's Scripture is based on the premise … *if we believe that Jesus died and rose again.* Without belief, there is no promise of eternal life with Christ. Even so, regardless of whether we believe it or not, Jesus died and rose again. We shall die and rise again to be with Him or to be separated from Him. God will bring us with Him, that is with Jesus. Those who have died in Christ have a win/win situation - life in Christ in the world and life in death over the world to come – life all the way around (Philippians 1:21).

The word sleep is used for death because death sounds so final. Our experience in Christ is simply a transition, a passing. There are varying theories as to how this will occur; the critical fact is that it will occur. Actually, what is called death, is for Christians the reality of life. There may be times that someone may want to prevent a Christian's death, when, in reality, they are delaying the person's life.

A person who *sleeps in Jesus* is like a child who falls asleep on the living room floor and wakes up in bed. Without knowing it, the child was carried by a parent as God carries us.

Prayer – Dear Father, thank You for the promise that when I experience physical death, You will take me to be with You.

May 29   Straight

Hebrews 12:13 ... *and make straight paths for your feet, SO that what is lame may not be dislocated, but rather be healed.*

SO means healing can occur.

Q Why *make straight paths for your feet?*

So there is healing instead of crippling.

What is *lame* is a physical metaphor for a spiritual condition. If we are spiritually dislocated, movement in our faith is difficult if not impossible. What is lame may refer to an element of our beliefs or to the beliefs of those around us. We have a-path-y (no path).

The question becomes, "How do we find this *straight path?*" Scripture is loaded with answers. We aren't left to our own devices in this task. We are told that God provides light for our journey (Psalm 119:105). Be in the word.

We are blessed when we don't follow ungodly advice (Psalms 1:1). We often get into trouble because we intentionally follow bad advice, or accidentally get off the path. Be on THE path.

In Romans 14 we find that some people, having questions about diet and days, are called weak in the faith. Part of our walk is so others aren't dislocated in their walk. Be strong in the faith but don't injure others.

How beautiful upon the mountains are the feet of him who brings good news, who proclaims peace, who brings glad tidings of good things, who proclaims salvation ... Who brings the Gospel of peace Isaiah 52:7. Proclaim the word.

We can check ourselves with each of these verses to strengthen our walk in Christ.

Prayer – Dear Father, let me walk according to Your word so that my path is the path of righteousness.

May 30   Received

Acts 17:11 *These were more fair-minded that those in Thessalonica in that they received the word with all readiness, and searched the Scriptures daily to find out whether these things were SO.*

SO means are they true.

Q What is one important thing about Scripture?

Scriptural prophecy, that is clearly fulfilled, gives evidence to the truth of Christ.

These are the people of Berea who were more *fair-minded* then some of the Thessalonians. In Thessalonica some envious people gathered a mob and caused a riot. As a result, some brethren sent Paul and Silas to Berea where the word was received *with all readiness.*

The Bereans were careful even though they received the word gladly. They *searched the Scriptures daily to* find if the great good news of the grace of God was SO. And it was! The Lord said let's figure this out together. Even if your sins are as red as blood, they will become as white as snow (Isaiah 1:18). (We should follow their example and search to see that any information we receive is backed by Scripture.)

They probably found many of the passages Jesus told about on the road to Emmaus (Luke 24:13). One particularly obvious passage was *… He was wounded for our transgressions, He was bruised for our iniquities; the chastisement for our peace was upon Him and by His stripes we are healed* Isaiah 53:5.

Our acceptance of the word (Word) and our knowledge of the Scriptures are being used by God to further His kingdom in us and others through us. The word of God is wonderful, keeping us in Him, and He in us. It also helps us to be His evangelists.

Prayer – Dear Father, I joyfully and thankfully receive Your word and continue to search daily to appreciate the SO-ness of the Gospel.

May 31   Come

<u>Revelation 22:20</u> *Amen. Even SO, come, Lord Jesus!*

SO means let it happen.

Q Why *Amen. Even so*? when they both mean the same thing?

Following the practice of early writing, when there was no punctuation mark for exclamation (!) to show emphasis, a word or phrase was repeated two, and sometimes three times. The emphasis in this sentence is because the return of the *Lord Jesus* will be a BIG EVENT!

Come, Lord Jesus is a translation of the Greek word Maranatha. It can be an expression of greeting and encouragement as well as a shout of triumphant faith

In 1Corinthians 16:22b, Maranatha is translated *O Lord, come.* Through the years, the immanent coming of Christ has dimmed in the minds of Christians. However, the truth of His coming is still in effect, in God's time, and we can still share this phrase with siblings in Christ.

Both John and Paul, in the closing words of these respective books, used the term *Maranatha*. It was a powerful crescendo to the powerful message of God's work of redemption. It was a final statement but leads to a wonderful beginning of all that eternal life is to bring.

Can we joyously, whole heartedly say, with John and Paul, "*Come, Lord Jesus*"? Do we joyously anticipate His return? We can use this phrase, not only when He returns to <u>take</u> the world unto Himself, but each day as He <u>keeps</u> us unto Himself.

Maranatha!

Prayer – Dear Father, thank you for Christ in us now and Christ to come in future glory at the end of this age.

JUNE

WE US

Meditation Aids

WE and US are pronouns referring to people and are used as substitutes for nouns. The two are considered together in this month because of their commonality.

Uses of WE and US - actions or recipients of actions by individuals or groups. The context of the verse will help explain who WE or US are and what is happening.

Examples:

... that which WE have seen and heard WE declare to you ... that your joy may be full

1 John 1:3-4.

John and his group saw and heard joyful information about life in Christ.

... thanks be to God Who gives US the victory through our Lord Jesus Christ.

1 Corinthians 15:56.

Christians receive victory through Jesus.

And forgive US our debts as WE forgive our debtors.

Matthew 6:12.

Christians are to forgive as they have been forgiven.

June 1   Burn

Luke 24:32 *Did not our hearts burn within US while He talked with US on the road, and while He opened the Scriptures to US?*

US means the two people on the road.

Q How do we know a Scripture is significant?

Our hearts burn within us.

It is like connecting two electrical wires together so current flows. We have a noticeable reaction – joy – peace – tears. Our hearts burning within us can be our *burning bush* (Exodus 3:2) as God speaks to us. In order for the Spirit to work within us, we have to invite Him to do that. The Holy Spirit is with us on our road every step of the way and He will open the Scriptures to us. We have to read the Bible and listen to Spirit led sermons for that to happen. INSTANT REPLAY We have to read the Bible and listen to Spirit led sermons for that to happen.

The Holy Spirit is the guide to *all truth* (John 16:13). The Holy Spirit interprets the world and the word to meet our growth ability at any given time. As time passes, a verse may take on deeper meaning because we have had some experience that readies us for it.

In the case of today's verse, two of Jesus' followers were walking to Emmaus, perhaps going back to their old way of life (Luke 24:13-20). Jesus joined them and showed them how He had fulfilled prophesy. They recognized Him when He broke bread – a powerful witness to the need to celebrate communion. If we attend to His word and obey His directives, we too, will feel the fire of the Holy Spirit.

We have to know the truth about the Holy Spirit, acknowledge Him, accept Him, and allow Him to work within us. Then God's messages will *burn within us.*

Prayer – Dear Father, thank You for the Spirit's witness to Your truth.

June 2   Victory

<u>1 Corinthians 15:56</u> *The sting of death is sin, and the strength of sin is the law. But, thanks be to God Who gives US the victory through our Lord Jesus Christ.*

US means all Christians.

Q How do we gain victory over the sting of death?

We have victory over death through the life and work of Jesus.

<u>We have a problem</u>:

1. The payoff of a life in sin is death. If we fall for Satan's lies, it seems like we are getting paid but it turns out to be a sting and the result is death. Police often set up a situation that looks good to a criminal. "You have won two tickets to a Tiger game. Come to 555 Sucker Street at 8:00 pm to collect them". Bait in a trap. This is called a sting.

2. Even with the grace of Christ, the laws of God are still in effect (Deuteronomy 27:26). Jesus said he had not *come to destroy* the law but to *fulfill* the law (Matthew 5:17).

<u>We have a solution to the problem</u>:

3. We are no longer under the penalty of the law because of the grace gift of Christ (Ephesians 2:8-9).

4. We are a come-as-you-are project for God. We don't have to "pretty ourselves up" to be accepted by Him (Romans 5:8). He comes to us in the quicksand of our hopeless condition, and

5. He gives us victory through Christ. Our faith in Christ gives us victory over anything the world may throw at us (1 John 5:4b).

Prayer – Dear Father, thank You for Your grace that gives me victory over sin and death through my Lord Jesus Christ.

June 3   Forgive

<u>Matthew 6:12</u> *And forgive US our debts as WE forgive our debtors.* (sins. trespasses.)

> Three different words are used in what is called The Lord's Prayer or the Our Father. <u>Debts</u> are what we owe. <u>Trespasses</u> are treading on other's emotions, rights or property. <u>Sins</u> are lawlessness, that which is against God's commandments.
>
> WE/US means all people.

Q Why is it important to forgive?

For if you forgive men their trespasses, your heavenly Father will also forgive you. But if you do not forgive men their trespasses, neither will your Father forgive your trespasses <u>Matthew 6:14-15</u>.

That seems clear. I cringe when I hear someone say, "That is unforgivable.," or "I'll never forgive him." I know some offenses can be excruciating but we need to forgive so we don't keep re-membering (giving life to) an offense. We need to trust God's judgment to be true and righteous. It is impossible to forget but we just have to stop feeding the old stray cat that keeps meowing at our door. Don't feed him, don't pet him, and don't chase him around with a broom. Take your eyes off the offense and focus on God's forgiveness.

There are two ways that this verse can be taken: (1) forgive us in the same way we forgive others thus disqualifying ourselves from grace if we don't forgive and/or (2) forgive us along the way <u>as</u> we are forgiving others.

Forgiveness is essential for relationship. God forgave us by having Christ take the penalty for our debts, sins, trespasses so we could have fellowship with Him - likewise, with others. It is difficult to love those whom we hate. Forgiveness is sometimes excruciating and difficult to give. We may need to experience in our bodies the *afflictions of Christ* who was crucified because of our sins (Colossians 1:24).

No matter how hideous the offense, as we forgive, so we are forgiven. God has already forgiven their sins but the forgiveness may not have been accepted. God will make a way for you to forgive. Ask Him.

Prayer – Dear Father, relieve me of the burden of vengeance and help me realize all sin is forgiven. Then help me accept and live in forgiveness.

June 4   Daily

<u>Matthew 6:11</u> *Give US this day our daily bread.*

US means all people.

Q When do we need *daily bread*?

Each day.

Live in this moment. Each split second is all we really have. We can dedicate individual seconds to God or to Satan. We make thousands of decisions every day, most of them unconsciously or by habit. We need to make sure our habits are developed in Christ so when we look back we can think of it as a Godly succession of moments. The joys and tribulations of each day are sufficient for that day. God gives us measured joys and tribulations to grow on so we can develop immunities to temptations and sin (Matthew 6:34b, 1 Corinthians 10:13).

God is the Giver. Today's bread is the gift. We recognize that gifts of food and experiences come from God. He gives us <u>physical</u> sustenance for strength for physical battles and He gives us <u>emotional</u> sustenance for strength for spiritual battles

Physical - Flash back to the wilderness when the Israelites were given bread for one day at a time. God gave this directive, I'll give them bread each day, and only for that day. There is a test involved. If they only take what I prescribed, they will prove their faithfulness to My laws (Exodus 16:4) – <u>a condition based on works</u>. They were given bread so they would have strength to walk in God's ways.

Emotional – God gave bread for a day at a time. Jesus gives a better type of bread – spiritual bread – that lasts for eternity (John 6:48) <u>a condition based on grace</u>. We are given spiritual bread in order to have eternal life.

We need and appreciate the physical, but above and beyond the physical, we need spiritual food so the physical food is not wasted.

Prayer – Dear Father, thank You for providing what I need, both joy and tribulation, for this day,

June 5   Demonstrates

Romans 5:8 *But God demonstrates His own love toward US, in that while WE were still sinners, Christ died for US.*

WE/US means all people.

Q What is the most significant way God shows His love for us?

He sent His Son to die for us.

Paul didn't have John 3:16 but he expressed the same intent and purpose of John's message.

Who – *God.* Our greatest and most basic desire should be oneness with our Creator. Let the desire that God places in you manifest itself in seeking and receiving Him.

What – His *own* love is available!! Through His love we move into relationship with Him. But there is what my wife calls "The available more." We learn what relationship with God has to offer. Call it holiness, sanctification, second work, whatever. In Christ there is a beginning and a continuation.

Why – We can't accomplish our salvation by our own strength. But it's not a lost cause. No matter what our sin, we can have life in Christ.

How – He takes the lid of garbage off from our hearts and minds so that joy can well up within us. Believe it is possible. Ask for His grace. Receive His grace. Know you have His grace. Live in His grace.

When –The first time, and every time thereafter that we might not sin - when we first receive His grace, and every time we fall, He picks us up to continue in Him.

Where – He paid the price on the cross and sealed our life in Him – in every circumstance and in eternal life.

Prayer – Dear Father, thank You for coming to me as I was, so I could come to You as you are, that I might be perfected in Christ. WOW!

June 6   Love

<u>1 John 4:10-19</u> *In this is love, not that WE loved God, but that He loved US and sent His Son to be the propitiation for our sins. WE love Him because He first loved US.*

WE/US means all Christians. Propitiation means to make favorably inclined.

Q Who started our love relationship with God?   God did.

John ends his letter with the exultant message that God came to us before we came to Him. Paul wrote, towards the beginning of his letter to the Romans, that God showed His love for us by Christ's sacrifice while we were still estranged from Him in sin (Romans 5:8). As we read in yesterday's devotional, the two leaders were in complete agreement about God's intent in sending Christ into the world.

God initiated the relationship by convicting us of our sin and His righteousness (John 16:8). Part of our understanding of the ugly wretchedness of sin is what it took for God to redirect His wrath from our sin to His love. This was shown by offering salvation through our acceptance of Jesus. Most of us seldom think of the awfulness of sin because we live in the midst of it. We must not become immune to the abhorrence of sin. <u>Satan inoculates us with seemingly benign sins so we would tolerate worse sin.</u> Think of what used to shock us that we now take for granted.

Before we knew God, we did not know how to love. God made it possible for us to know because He loves us. As we see how He loves us, we learn how to love Him and beyond that to love each other. *This is love.* He loves us more. He loves us most.

He made it possible for us to come forth from our sin like Lazarus who came out of death to be set free from bandage (intended - bands of bondage) by his friends (John 11:44).

We did not love Him before, but now, in accepting Jesus' sacrifice and redeeming work, we know His love and how to love Him. Now, in loving Him, we should not hesitate to live by His commandments and lay down our lives for Him.

Prayer – Dear Father, thank You for showing me what love it so I can love You and others.

June 7   Intercession

Romans 8:26b *For WE do not know what WE should pray for as WE ought, but the Spirit Himself makes intercession for US with groanings which cannot be uttered.* Jesus also makes intercession for us (v34).

Hebrews 7:25 *Therefore, He is also able to save to the uttermost, those who come to God through Him, since He always lives to make intercession for them.* (Jesus for US)

WE/US means all Christians. Intercession is pleading for one in trouble.

Q How do Jesus and the Holy Spirit continually support us? With intercession.

> We don't always know what for or how we should pray. The Holy Spirit prays for us about things we don't even know or think about. There are things we never know about that we avoid, or that are brought into our lives, by the Spirit of God.

> It is not too often that we groan with such intensity when we pray. The Spirit's groanings are beyond human emotion. It reminds us of Jesus' prayer in the Garden of Gethsemane. Jesus' prayer is described as agonizing, causing an intense physical reaction. His sweat was a representation of the blood of the covenant we celebrate in the sacrament of communion (Luke 22:44). Jesus, Who is able to save us completely because He is alive and active in our lives, was in agony for us. We need to realize the intensity and cost of our salvation that brings us into relationship with God.

Have you had a Gethsemane? Have you, in a desperate battle with Satan over your soul, said, "*Not my will, but Yours be done"?* Luke 22:42. Jesus' experience is an indication of the intensity of our own conversion event.

> We have the greatest powers in the universe in agreement praying for us. INSTANT REPLAY We have the greatest powers in the universe in agreement praying for us. Whether it is the Holy Spirit and us on earth, or the Holy Spirit and Jesus in God's kingdom, our prayers are to be in the nature of Christ. It is an absolute joy to know that both Jesus and the Holy Spirit are negotiating for you and me. How can we but be awestruck by the extent of the Love of God which He extends to us!

Prayer – Dear Father, I thank you with my life!

June 8   Followers

<u>1 Thessalonians 1:6</u> *And you became followers of US ...*

US means Paul and his companions.

Q How can we help others follow us to Christ? By being righteous people.

For your benefit, It wasn't just what we said, but with evidence of the Spirit's power for good measure, that you could see *what kind of men we* were when we were with you (1 Thessalonians 1:5). A person's faith is a three step process: people have faith in us, then they copy our faith, then they develop a faith of their own. The progress is much like growing from being a baby to a teen to an adult.

It is truly unfortunate that there are many servants of Satan, some in churches, who intentionally, or unknowingly, are leading people astray. Many children are in great trouble today because their parents are not Spirit led. Whether it be our biological or spiritual children, our most important task, and greatest pleasure in life, is to lead them <u>to</u> Christ and then, lead them <u>in</u> Christ. If we lead, it is more probable that they will follow. An old adage, "Like father, like son," has much truth to it.

Paul gives a model of winsome Christian behavior in Philippians 4:9.

What you find out about me from other people's observations, what you have received from me in written messages, the words that I have spoken to you, and the message that my life has shown to you, you should imitate and you will have the peace of God.

Leading others to Christ is an *US* thing. It takes a church. When an individual brings someone in, the rest must be welcoming and supportive. There are many in the body of Christ that are leading, some towards God, some away from Him. While I can't control the witness of another person, I can strive to be worthy of being followed, as in Paul's example.

We need to realize that people are watching and listening. Where are we leading people? Who does our witness support, God or Satan? Let's make it a rule to lead towards God.

Prayer – Dear Father, may the words of my mouth, the emotions of my heart, the actions of my body, and the thoughts of my mind help lead others to You.

June 9   Redeemed

Galatians 3:13 *Christ has redeemed US from the curse of the law, having become a curse for US ... that WE might receive the promise of the Spirit through Him.*

To redeem is to pay off a debt, like at a pawn shop – to release upon payment.

> WE/US means Christians.

Q How did Jesus redeem us?

> He became a curse.

> Salvation, justification, redemption, deliverance, release, liberation, emancipation: all are words that express what it means to be transformed from a person outside of God to being a person in Christ - from the curse of the law to the promise of the Spirit! WOW!

> When I was a child, we saved S&H Green Stamps and sent them in to a redemption center to exchange the stamps for items in the Green Stamp Catalog. That was a big deal and required a lot of thought to make the best choice. God has credited us with extreme value. He has redeemed us with the cost of the sacrifice of His Son.

> Who? Christ, Who was the price that was paid.

> What? Redemption – through His death on the cross

> How? He became a curse for us. Jesus became our sin so that we could become His righteousness (2 Corinthians 5:21). This verse spells out an interesting price of redemption – the perfect for the imperfect.

> Why? So we could receive the promises God made of the Spirit with all His power, gifts, and fruit.

> When and Where? Right now, right here!

> WE should try as hard as we can to let the Spirit work in us, and be instantly and constantly giving and forgiving, of self and others. This is love.

Prayer – Dear Father, thank You for Your Spirit and all that He brings to us.

June 10   If

<u>1 Corinthians 15:32</u> *If the dead do not rise, "Let US eat and drink, for tomorrow WE die!"* (From Isaiah 22:13).

WE/US means all Christians.

Q What if there is no life after death? We die – It's, "Turn off the light when you leave". "Or not, who cares?"

If there is no life after death, then some would say we should live it up and take whatever we can get, whatever the cost. Whoever has the gold, rules. It would mean that laws and morality are meaningless. Life would have no value except what someone could do for me.

Solomon also recommended that, unless we fear God, we live a life of fun because there was nothing better to do than party (Ecclesiastes 8:15). There are those who proof text this verse to excuse their negative behaviors. If someone wants to excuse sin, they say, "There is no God, no law, no life after death." They may not say that out loud but that would be their motto if that is what their behavior says.

Some religions attempt to explain some continuation of life but they don't have Christ and the Holy Spirit for redemption and guidance.

In 1 Corinthians 15:19-20, we find a thought provoking argument. If Christ didn't rise from the dead we are pitiful having wasted our lives on a grave dream. But, BUT, He did rise and He became the forerunner of all who have believed in the grace of His resurrection. That includes you and me. This is the hugest <u>IF</u> in the human language. If Christ did not rise, then any intent to do good is foolish and futile.

However, there is good news, as Paul proclaims it, *"Christ is risen"*. Tell people if they are going to take a chance on eternal separation from God, they would need to disprove the resurrection of Jesus Christ.

Who wants to escape salvation?

Prayer – Dear Father, thank You for so great a salvation and for spiritual life now and after physical death.

June 11   Children

1 John 3:1 *Behold what manner of love the Father has bestowed on US, that WE should be called children of God. Therefore the world does not know US, because it did not know Him.*

> WE/US are all Christians.

Q What is the significance of God's love? The incredible fact that we are called His children.

> In today's Scripture the word *Behold* means you are about to learn of a big deal! The love of God is so incredible! He loves us so much that He sacrificed His only perfect Son so He could have relationship with us. Jesus is God's greatest gift to us. This gift is not deserved by right of birth, earned by our efforts, nor by anyone else's effort, only as we personally believe and receive (John 1:13).

> Are you ready for the big deal? It is *that we should be called children of God*! WOW!

Q Why are we misunderstood by the world?

> Because they don't know God. They have selective spiritual blindness. Therefore, it follows that they don't know us because they don't know God. They can look Him in the face of the things He has made and not see Him (Romans 1:20). What they see goes in one eye and out the other. To know something is to acknowledge, recognize, and give meaning to an idea or a person that exists. *Therefore the world does not know us, b*ecause they do *not know Him.* I wouldn't have seen it if I hadn't believed it. When we know Christ, we recognize Him in ourselves and in His other children. So many times we meet a sibling in Christ and it seems we have been friends forever. It is like looking into a spiritual mirror. Two wires connect.

> Satan is totally evil and he will try to steal your spiritual birth right (John 10:10). Don't let an unbeliever's lack of recognition make you feel you aren't God's child. If you have confessed with your mouth and believed in your heart, YOU ARE GOD'S CHILD!

Prayer – Dear Father, thank You that You love me enough to make me Your child so that I can call You Father.

June 12   Children

<u>Romans 8:14, 16</u> *For as many as are led by the Spirit of God, these are sons of God ... The Spirit Himself bears witness with our spirit that WE are children of God.*

WE means all Christians.

Q How do we know we are sons of God?

Here, the emphasis in on those of us who are led. We are led by the most credible witness in the universe, the Spirit of God Who bears witness with our spirit.

The children of God follow God. The servants of Christ are with Him. It doesn't make sense that they would be off doing their own thing or following and serving someone else (John 12:26). We need to choose to be led by God. INSTANT REPLAY - We need to <u>choose</u> to be led by God.

When I was a counselor in a boy's correctional facility, we would go on 50 mile hikes. Each day a different boy was to follow a compass and lead the rest to that day's destination. We went through swamps, creeks, and dense brush so thick that we had to crawl because they often didn't trust, or ignored, the compass.

There is agreement between our spirit and the Holy Spirit. One-to-one correspondence for you math students – congruence.

Consider yourself giving testimony in a courtroom and someone questions your statement. Then, a person with impeccable reputation says, "Yes, what this witness says is true." What a verification!

The testimony of the Spirit is that we are children of God and being His children we are also heirs along with Christ. We qualify by sharing in His suffering and, therefore, in His glorification (Romans 8:17).

This is true for those who follow the Spirit. We have inside information, an interior compass.

Prayer – Dear Father, thank You for the witness of Your Spirit in me. I choose to follow you.

June 13   Deceive

<u>1 John 1:8</u> *If WE say that WE have no sin, WE deceive ourselves, and the truth is not in US.*

WE/US means any who deny being sinful.

Q Can we deceive ourselves?   Yes, if we say we have no sin.

If a lie is told often enough, it takes on a semblance of truth. If we deny and do not confess our sin(s) often enough, we deceive ourselves. This is a terrible if-then lie. If we want to, we can justify almost any act or thought. However, if we try to justify sin we receive its wages which is death. We may become experts at fooling ourselves but it is foolish trickery. *If we say we have no sin* we call God a liar. We need to move away from a sinful activity before it becomes a habit.

Every lie requires a flock of supporting lies. Denial is a tool of Satan who, amongst other things, begets all lies (John 8:44). In following him we deceive ourselves. We follow pride to destruction, ... *the truth is not in us.* Therefore, Christ is not in us because He is the truth.

We need to accept the fact that every single person has committed sin and that causes them to fail to demonstrate God's intended glory in His creations (Romans 3:23).

This verse could be taken in two ways. The most common is that in sinning we fall short of God's glory. The second is to split into two types of sin - that (1) All have sinned, and (2) All people fall short of God's glory. In the second thought, there may be those who have never broken a commandment, are totally right in their own and other's eyes, but aren't equivalent to God in glory. They need Christ just as much as the rest of us.

Some people deny sin and won't face the truth because they are afraid of the consequences. They don't realize that Jesus has already taken their consequences which is death - the wages of their sin. The truth is, the only way to get rid of sin and guilt is to confess and accept God's forgiveness. We can't consider 1 John 1:9 often enough. We are forgiven of ALL sin, Yes ALL! Anything we have done or not done, and anything Satan is accusing us of doing or not doing.

Prayer – Dear Father, I confess my sinfulness and sins because I long for Your forgiveness and for relationship with You.

June 14   Receive

Romans 8:15 ... *but you received the Spirit of adoption by whom WE cry out,* *"Abba, Father."*

Abba is an affectionate word for father.

WE means all Christians.

Q What allows us to be so bold as to call God "Abba"?

By the abiding assurance of the indwelling Holy Spirit testifying with our spirits that we are His children.

What do we receive? We receive a gift. What is the gift? The gift is adoption into the family of God attested by the Holy Spirit. The Holy Spirit is not wages paid for service. He is not earned nor deserved. The Spirit of God is a gift. As indicated in John 14:16-17, Jesus asked God to give us His Spirit as a helper who leads us in truth.

God is a loving heavenly Father and He enables us to recognize that by the inspiration of the Holy Spirit. Therefore, we can run to God as little children, with our arms out, and joyfully shout, "Abba!"

Children react to adoption in differing ways ranging from anger at their birth parents to total appreciation that someone wants them and cares for them. What many people fail to realize is that, as Christians, we are all adopted. We are adopted children of God. Regardless of what we think of our birth parents, our Adoptive Parent cares for us with inexpressible love.

Instead of thinking we have to toe some impossible mark to satisfy a harsh master, we come to God Who loves us beyond description. Jesus took the wages of sin; we are given the gift of life.

When we look into the eyes of love, we see ourselves in an entirely different light – as lovable. When we look at people, what do they see in our eyes?

Prayer – Dear Father, thank You for making me part of Your family.

June 15   Purify

Titus 2:14 … *Jesus Christ, Who gave Himself for US, that He might redeem US from every lawless deed and purify for Himself His own special people, zealous for good works.*

US means *His own special people.*

Q Why did Christ give Himself for us?

To *redeem us* from sin and to *purify us for good works.*

Jesus gave Himself for us. His gift was the excruciating death by crucifixion, which brought about the joy of our redemption. His life was an incredible gift, and in the economy of God, no other price was adequate.

In today's Scripture we see that He paid the price, He took the penalty for all our lawless deeds. He literally saved us from the penalty of death by cleaning up and clearing away all our sinful messes (1 John 1:9c). Satan hocks us for much less than our value. Think of the cheap return we get for the price of sin. Jesus redeems us at an incredible price! When we are redeemed by Christ and have redemption through Him, we are imputed with the purity of Christ (1 John 3:3). We must have remorse, confess, receive, and then live as people who have been redeemed.

When we hope in Him, our purity is equal to His. INSTANT REPLAY - When we hope in Him, our purity is equal to His (1 John 3:3).

You and I are special to Jesus. We are redeemed and purified. Who is special and precious to you? We are more special than that to Him.

We are to be zealous, joyfully diligent, active in good works. God has jobs for us to do. He has to-do lists for everyone. And, He has created us and gifted us for the specific tasks each of us can do (Ephesians 2:10). Note: We are created for good works; we are not accepted because of good works.

Jesus' work was to give His life for us; our work is to live our lives in and for Him.

Prayer – Dear Father, I accept Your gifts of redemption and purity. As Your special person, open my eyes to the good work You want me to do.

June 16   Hope

1 Peter 1:3 *Jesus Christ ... has begotten US again to a living hope through the resurrection ...*

US means all Christians.

Q What has given us a *living hope*?

The resurrection of Jesus Christ from death gives us a living hope!

What is a *living hope*? It is not a wish or Pie in the sky by and by. It is a living hope that has vitality, it is full of action. A *living hope* is an inner feeling that expresses itself in a loving, joyful, and peaceful life. *Living hope* is given to us by a living Christ.

Who – Jesus, not available in any other person, place, or thing.

What – He has given us new birth.

Why – to give us a living hope. Because we were dead in our sins (Ephesians 2:1).

How – His resurrection shows His power over death and guarantees our eternal life.

When – when He guaranteed us victory by rising from the dead.

Where – The empty tomb.

We have been begotten! Rule # 1 - He is alive! We are ALIVE! Rule # 2 - If ever you feel dead, down and out, see Rule # 1. Claim it and thank God for it. Live in it!

Prayer – Dear Father, thank You for a hope that is alive and well and active in energizing my life for You.

June 17   Separate

Romans 8:35-36 *Who shall separate US from the love of Christ? Shall tribulation, or distress, or persecution, or famine, or nakedness, or peril, or sword?*

US means all Christians.

Q What can *separate us from the love of Christ?*

Nothing! No event or physical hardship can separate us.

Why is this a rhetorical question? Because the answer is obvious. No thing from the outside can separate us *from the love of Christ.*

Who can? Nobody, with the exception of ourselves, with our permission.

It is interesting to tie this verse to the Parable of the Sower (seeds, soils) *Afterward, when tribulation or persecution arises for the word's sake, immediately they stumble* Mark 4:17b. Hard ground, shallow soil, and thorns are things that, with our permission, can separate us from Jesus' love. Paul lists some "thorns":

Tribulation - Some people let troubles destroy their self-generated faith. They need the faith that only God gives (Ephesians 2:8).

Distress – Anxiety – We are told not to be anxious about anything (Philippians 4:6-7).

Persecution – The weakness I feel when I experience persecution makes me rely on strength in Christ.

Famine/Nakedness/Peril – *... in perils ... in fastings ... in nakedness ...* 2 Corinthians 11:26-27. All these are things Paul experienced and thanked God for.

God gives us the faith that will endure all forces because He either gives ways to handle any problem or else provides an escape route (Corinthians 10:13b).

Prayer – Dear Father, thank You for the faith that there is no thing that can separate me from Jesus' love.

See tomorrow for a different list.

June 18   Persuaded

<u>Romans 8:39</u> *For I am persuaded that neither death nor life, nor angels nor principalities nor powers, nor things present nor things to come, nor height nor depth, nor any other created thing, shall be able to separate US from the love of God which is in Christ Jesus our Lord.*

Persuaded is being convinced by logical argument.

Yesterday we learned that no physical hardship can separate us from the love of God. Today we see the same is true for spiritual threats.

US means all Christians.

Q How is Paul persuaded?

By evidence as written in Romans 8:31-34: God loves us, justifies us, and intercedes for us proved by the death and resurrection of His Son.

Nothing can *separate us*:

Neither death nor life – In Christ we have a win-win situation (Philippians 1:21).

Nor angels nor principalities nor powers – God gives us an impenetrable suit of armor so we can withstand any adversary (Ephesians 6:12-13).

Nor things present nor things to come – He promised He would never leave us. (Hebrews 13:5b quoted from Deuteronomy 31:6).

Nor height nor depth – Heaven or hell, wherever our dwelling place, He is with us (Psalm 139:8).

Nor any other created thing - *shall be able to separate US from the love of God which is in Christ Jesus our Lord.*

If all this cannot separate us, what can? Just us - No other thing or power can separate us from God. Let us accept His persuasion and rest in Him as He is in us.

Prayer – Dear Father, thank You for Your Spirit Who convinces us of your love that endures all things. I choose to abide in You.

June 19   Multiplied

<u>2 Peter 1:2-4</u> *Grace and peace be multiplied to you in the knowledge of God and of Jesus our Lord ... by which have been given to US exceedingly great and precious promises, that through these you may be partakers of the divine nature ...*

US means all Christians.

Q How do we receive *exceedingly great and precious promises*?

They are given to us.

Grace comes before peace. Without grace, there is no peace because we are beset with guilt and shame. It is remarkable what people will do to try to escape their negative emotions – all kinds of negative addictions and behaviors. They try to fill a God sized hole with a self-sized idea. But God multiplies, not just adds, but multiplies grace and peace – adequate grace that is beyond our comprehension (2 Corinthians 12:9, Philippians 4:7). He also gives power over addictions (Ephesians 4:22-24).

If you don't have peace, you haven't understood grace. Even then, we don't need understanding; we simply need to accept the gifts. We don't need to do anything except to accept.

As today's Scripture tells us, grace and peace will be multiplied *in the knowledge of God and of Jesus our Lord. K*nowledge is what we know. We learn not from just reading, but meditating on the word and listening to God-filled preaching.

Also, in addition to the gifts of Christ (John 3:16), and our Helper, the Holy Spirit (John 14:16), He has promised that we will share in the *nature* of Christ through His redeeming action. We can depend on God's promises. It is through the redeeming act of Christ and the power, gifts, and fruit of the Spirit that we become *partakers of the divine nature ...*

Let us choose to live in *grace and peace – knowledge - and precious promises,* so that we may be like Him.

Prayer – Dear Father, thank You for giving us avenues that we might become partakers of Your divine nature.

June 20   Reconciliation

2 Corinthians 5:18 *Now all things are of God, Who has reconciled US to Himself through Jesus Christ, and has given US the ministry of reconciliation, that is that God was in Christ reconciling the world to Himself ...*

US means all Christians.

Q What has God done and why did He do it?

He reconciled us and gave us a ministry of reconciliation so we could bring others to reconciliation with Him. Take the word reconciliation apart. Re – again, con – with, cilia – accomplish motion. Reconciliation moves us into relationship with God. Neat, huh?

First off, there is a difference between forgiveness and reconciliation. Forgiveness is a one way street. The forgiven one may not even accept forgiveness nor feel they need to be forgiven. However, we are asked to forgive so our lives are not muddied up with resentment. Remember, what we won't forget we can't forgive, or is it what we can't forgive, we won't forget? It is probably both. Anyhow, relationship doesn't necessarily occur.

Reconciliation is a two way street. Both people have to forgive and forget. Sometimes we need to reconcile with ourselves. We need to accept God's gift of reconciliation. Reconciliation restores relationship. Relationship with God, with our self, and with our siblings in Christ, is what Christianity is all about. We have a double barreled activity of God – what He did and how He did it.

Who? God. What? Reconciliation - He moved us into relationship with Him.

How? *Through Jesus Christ. - But He was wounded for our transgressions, He was bruised for our iniquities; the chastisement for our peace was upon Him, and by His stripes we are healed* Isaiah 53:5. Isaiah knew that way back when.

Why? So we can tell others about reconciliation. WE are to move people towards relationship with God. WE become the who, what, and how. The same way He did it - *through Jesus Christ.* WE are to tell others the great, good Gospel news that God wants to reconcile us unto Himself and that the Way to Him is through Jesus.

Prayer – Dear Father, may I pass forward Your reconciliation to those prepared to receive it.

June 21   Righteousness

<u>2 Corinthians 5:21</u> *For He made Him Who knew no sin to be sin for US, that WE might become the righteousness of God in Him.*

<u>2 Peter 1:1b</u> *To those who have obtained like precious faith with US by the righteousness of our God and Savior Jesus Christ.*

> Righteousness is a right relationship with God and results in living in the right way.

> WE/US means all Christians.

Q How do we become the righteousness of God?

We become His righteousness through the righteous action of our God and Savior Jesus Christ. Sometimes it helps to use Scripture to explain Scripture.

> Jesus' righteousness was that He became sin for us. The righteousness of Christ makes us the righteousness of God. What? In other words, the righteousness of God is that He makes us righteous through Christ's righteousness. The process is circular.

> The words in 2 Peter are so winsome. We can have that same precious faith! INSTANT REPLAY We can have that same precious faith! How do we gain *like precious faith* obtained by Peter and his group? It is through understanding and accepting the righteous action of Christ. We don't need to do anything except to accept.

Becoming God's righteousness means that we fulfill the purpose of His love.

> Righteousness is a descriptive term. Righteousness describes God's character. We are to become righteous so that we might become holy because holiness is one of the characteristics of God (Leviticus 11:44).

> We don't have to work for it. God has done the work for us through Jesus. We just need to accept the gift of Him in us and let His righteousness work through us.

Prayer – Dear Father, as awful as it is, thank You making Jesus sin for me, so that as precious as it is, I have Your righteousness.

June 22   Glory

Romans 8:18 *For I consider that the sufferings of this present time are not worthy to be compared with the glory which shall be revealed in US.*

US means all Christians.

Q What makes sufferings of small comparison?

Today's Scripture indicates it is God's glory *revealed in us*

The glory revealed in us causes sufferings to shrink by comparison.

For I consider (con – side, with sides) - there are two sides to the story, *sufferings* and *glory*.

The word consider implies that Paul had given the matter a lot of thought. We can accept the results of his thinking and we can add our own time and meditation to it. It might be helpful to compare your own suffering to the end result – like having a baby.

Peter adds this insight: We may have experienced grief in different trials for a short time, but the promises given make it all cause for great rejoicing for all time (1 Peter 1:3-6). In the meantime, let our victory in suffering produce glory in us.

Further, *Of this present time* … Our present time is not so different. The same problems beset us as beset Paul's *present time*. This time's suffering is small potatoes compared to the glory that shows in us.

Prayer – Dear Father, help me to focus on the glory so the sufferings shrink proportionately and can be seen as Your exercise program to build my faith.

June 23   Ambassadors

2 Corinthians 5:20 *Now, then, WE are ambassadors for Christ, as though God were pleading through US ...*

An ambassador is a representative of an authority. In this case, the authority is God, who sends someone to plead, that is to earnestly persuade, a cause.

WE/US means all Christians.

Q How in heaven's name can WE, in our humanity, become God's voice?

He pleads through us.

When *now* is used, we need to look back, in this case to verse seventeen. We are new creations, uniquely fitted to be Christ's ambassadors. *Now,* at this time, *then,* because we are new creations, we have the honor of representing God to those around us. We become an ambassador - the highest ranking official that is sent to a country.

God shows His intense longing for relationship through *us.* If we are to be a pipeline from others to God, it behooves us to keep our pipes clean. We need to have clean and unclogged lines of communication. There need to be daily inspections. Dear Lord, examine my innermost being, give me a thorough test, look at what makes me anxious, expose any evil in my life, and guide me in the way of eternal life (Psalm 139:23).

It is interesting that David mentioned anxieties. We will not be winsome ambassadors if we are anxious. We need to heed Paul's instruction not to be anxious (Philippians 4:6-7). When we are worry-worts, we announce to the world that God is not to be trusted and that we don't trust Him. Instead, we are to show that we know He measures our experiences for growth in Him. Then, we receive mind boggling peace through our thanksgiving for everything.

If anyone is in Christ, he is a new creation.

He has given us the ministry of reconciliation.

Prayer – Dear Father, may the words of my mouth, the emotions of my heart, the actions of my body, and the thoughts of my mind faithfully represent You wherever You send me.

June 24   Comfort

2 Corinthians 1:3-4 *Blessed be the God and Father of our Lord Jesus Christ, the Father of mercies and God of all comfort, who comforts US in all our tribulation, that WE may be able to comfort those who are in any trouble, with the comfort with which WE ourselves are comforted by God.*

WE/US means all Christians.

Q Why does God comfort us in tribulations?

So we can have comfort and be able to extend comfort to those who have any trouble. What if we refuse comfort? What if we are resentful and bitter? What if we rail against our circumstances? If someone comes for comfort from the uncomforted, they will hear a loud, "Don't ask ME!" We can't share what we don't have.

Why shouldn't we have tribulations? Jesus said we would have tribulations in this world (John 16:33). How can we comfort others if we haven't received comfort in similar circumstances. We need to know that each day's trouble is carefully measured out for our growth (Matthew 6:34b). We will never get more than we can handle. We just have to take our eyes off the tribulation and focus on the escape route (1Corinthians 10:13).

Remember, God is *the Father of mercies and God of all comfort.* Then, *WE may be able to comfort those who are in* any *trouble with the comfort* we received.

When Paul pleaded with the Lord THREE times about a vexing situation, the Lord told him that whatever he needed would be provided through His *sufficient grace* (2 Corinthians 12:9). Grace = whatever is needed. Paul then subjected himself to God and rejoiced in his discomfort, being strengthened by God. God's grace and mercy are the comforts that are sufficient for any problem we may have.

So we need to get rid of the arrogant idea that we know better than God what is best for His purposes. We need to junk the do-it-yourself mentality and accept His help, knowing that His concern and care for us exceeds our own thoughts, and that He will raise us up at appropriate times (1 Peter 5:6-7).

Rule # 1 – God cares for us --

Prayer – Dear Father, I am Yours to prepare for whatever use You have for me. Thank You for Your grace and mercy.

June 25   Go

<u>Luke 2:15b</u> ... *the shepherds said to one another, "Let US now go to Bethlehem and see this thing that has come to pass, which the Lord has made known to US."*

US means shepherds.   Christmas all year long.

Q Why did the angels come to shepherds? Because the shepherds were the lowest on the totem pole - they touched dead animals.

Jesus was born in the lowliest place, seen by the lowliest employment group, and spent His time with the lowliest people - tax collectors and sinners. There was no one for them to look down on. Obviously, anyone of higher class was welcome to join in but many of them were busy enjoying and defending their positions in society.

The shepherds said to one another, "Let us go now ..." - *Now!* They didn't form a discussion group, or send a delegation. They left the sheep! The message made them ignore all else. ... *I bring you good tidings of great joy ... there is born to you this day ... a Savior, who is Christ the Lord ... Glory to God in the highest ...* <u>Luke 2:10-14</u>.

Today's Scripture tells us the shepherds needed to go *and see this thing that has come to pass* - the historical event of God coming in human form in the body of Christ. He enters into our lives so that we can enter into eternal life. God has ambassadors for you to meet and heed. Christmas all year long! We need to remember each day that Christ was born and can be born in us.

There was *great joy* amongst the shepherds for what God had led them to see (Luke 2:20). There is greater joy in us when we ask Jesus to be born in our hearts and we come alive in Him and He in us

Shepherds and angels - Who was your angel? Mine was a co-worker on a construction site who had something that I didn't have. Whose angel are we supposed to be? We are to be angels with good news and to be shepherds who tend God's flock.

The joy of His birth is repeated in the life of each person who accepts Him.

Prayer – Dear Father, thank You for giving me the joyful message. May I return *glorifying and praising You*!

June 26   Seen and Heard

1John 1:3-4 ... *that which WE have seen and heard WE declare to you ...
that your joy may be full.*

WE means John and his group.

Q How authentic is the message that John gives?

Very! They were eye/ear witnesses to what they declared.

Who? John and his group of fellow believers.

What? They were eye witnesses and ear witnesses to the life and
message of Jesus Christ. What they heard didn't go in one ear and
out the other. What they saw didn't go in one eye and out the other.

How? *WE declare to you.* What they saw and heard came into their
eyes and ears and out of their mouths.

Why? *That your joy may be full.* They spoke to fulfill the message of
the angels, ... *good tidings of great joy* ... Part of the fruit of the Spirit
is *joy* (Galatians 5:22). If, in any circumstance, you lack joy, pray to
be filled with the Spirit and you will be filled with *joy.* Our faith gives
us insight that produces joy that can't be expressed in words, but that
fills us with supreme emotion (1 Peter 1:8b). John saw and heard
Jesus; we haven't seen Him, yet we believe, and so we can rejoice!

When? Right now!

Where? Right here!

People see us; people hear us. We live to share our joy and that their
joy might be full.

Prayer – Dear Father, fill me with *inexpressible* joy such that it overflows to
the point that others can see and hear in me what John saw and heard in
Christ.

June 27   Fragrance

2 Corinthians 2:15-16 *For WE are to God the fragrance of Christ among those who are being saved and among those who are perishing. To the one WE are the aroma of death leading to death, and to the other the aroma of life leading to life.*

WE means all Christians.

Q Are we "life fresheners" to those who are saved?

As the wise men presented frankincense to God at Jesus' birth, we celebrate our spiritual births by returning the fragrance of Christ to God. We present ourselves, our lives, as a fragrant offering. We want to make sure that there is no stink in our lives. We certainly don't want to present stench to Him.

For WE are to God - the offering of our lives is the return of the pleasant aroma of His offering to us in Christ. Christ in us enriches the atmosphere for all people around us.

The fragrance that is the essence or aura of Christ will be an attraction *among those who are being saved.* It should be part of His presence in us that wafts out to all those within sight, sound, and smell. It should increase their faith and their joy – their total well-being.

And our verse continues - the aroma of Christ is offensive to the non-Christian world. This should not stop our pleasant "smell". The actions of the Body of Christ should not be dictated by agents of Satan. INSTANT REPLAY - The actions of the Body of Christ should not be dictated by agents of Satan. Maybe the reason they don't like us is that we don't listen to them and join in their sinful actions. However, we should be an attractant like honeysuckle to humming birds. It should help them to know there is relief from the stench of their lives. They can hover around us and gain Christ's fragrance for themselves.

As far as I know, only skunks are attracted to skunks. Let us freshen up the atmosphere around us with love, joy, and peace.

Prayer – Dear Father, help me "smell good" to You and for others, regardless of their spiritual condition.

June 28   Judge

1 Corinthians 11:17-34 *For if WE would judge ourselves, WE would not be judged.*

WE means all Christians.

Q What is the importance of judging ourselves? That we would not be judged.

It is important to interpret this scripture in context. Paul is writing to the Corinthians in regard to their behavior and attitude towards the sacrament of communion. He is addressing a particular event, not final judgment. Apparently there was drunkenness and divisions among members of this community of believers. Paul speaks of the sacredness of the act of communion. He reminds the Corinthians, and us, that we are remembering the crucifixion of our Lord. By taking the elements of communion, they were testifying to the act of redemption on the cross – a very serious matter. Christ's death was what gave them life and they needed to respond in humble worship.

Once Paul established the sacredness of communion, he warned them - *Therefore whoever eats this bread or drinks this cup of the Lord in an unworthy manner will be guilty of the body and blood of the Lord* v27. When they, we, partake without sincerity of purpose, we become guilty, not cleansed, condemning ourselves and not considering the needs of the church. Instead of benefiting from the death of Christ, they became guilty of His death and of disrupting the fellowship (*body*). Treating communion with disrespect was having serious consequences – spiritual weakness, spiritual illness, and spiritual death (1Corinthians 11:30). That is, they are dead as far as Christ is concerned. We need to judge ourselves as needing the sacrifice of Christ.

Only you know whether or not you have repented of any sin of omission or commission. How do we judge ourselves? We need to hold our activities up to the light of Scripture. If we sincerely ask the Holy Spirit to expose anything that is improper, He will certainly do it. Watch to see if any excuses or rationalizations are being made. If we are trying to justify an activity, we are forfeiting justification by faith. Once our conscience is clear, we can proceed to celebrate communion, our with-union in Christ.

Prayer – Dear Father, help me to know the meaning and value of communion and when I take the elements may I take stock of my life to be sure I take communion in a worthy manner.

June 29   Live

<u>Romans 14:8</u> *For If WE live, WE live to the Lord and if WE die, WE die to the Lord.*

WE means all Christians.

Q What if we live?

We live to the Lord.

Speaking of <u>life</u> - And *you He made alive who were dead in trespasses and sins* ... Ephesians 2:1. We <u>were</u> dead in sin but now we <u>are</u> alive in Christ.

We are in Christ. His Spirit lives in us. We have the power, gifts, and fruit of the Spirit. We have a win-win situation. And we have a message for those who think Christianity is for losers. We are always ready to give a humble yet powerful defense for the hope that is in us (1Peter 3:15). The message is - In Christ, there is life!

Q What if we die?

We die to the Lord.

Speaking of <u>physical death</u> - Those who die when they are in Christ are blessed (Revelation 14:13b).

It is not a problem to repeat things over and over again. When I taught math to middle school students, there would be times, after repeating a concept several times, when someone would say, "Now I get it!" Others would chide them, but I would tell them, "No matter how many times you hear something, you don't HEAR it until you GET it, until you understand." Just because something is said doesn't mean it is "heard," that it is understood, accepted, and put into practice.

Have we HEARD? Have we understood, accepted, and put our faith into practice? YES! We are ALIVE! WOW! *For me, to live is Christ, and to die is gain* <u>Philippians 1:21</u>.

Prayer – Dear Father, thank You for giving us victory over every circumstance.

June 30   Chastening

Hebrews 12:7-9 *If you endure chastening, God deals with you as with sons, for what son is there whom a father does not chasten? ... Shall WE not much more readily be in subjection to the Father of spirits and live?*

>Chasten means discipline with intent to instruct, correct, and improve behavior.

>WE means God's children.

Q What should be our attitude towards what others call bad things in our lives?

>We place ourselves in subjection to God. The citizens in a kingdom are subject to the will of the king. If we *endure*, we *live*, else we die.

>I'm not sure how much I enjoyed the discipline my parents inflicted on me but most of it was deserved. Other times I would wonder if they were taking out their frustrations on me instead of raising me according to God's intent (Proverbs 22:6). We do know that God's chastening is intended for our greater joy and peace.

>Because God is the Father of our spirits, and we are His children, it is His joy to raise us up to be mature adults in Christ. Our response is to *endure chastening* with respect and obedience.

>When an institution doesn't correct its members, they lose respect for the institution. When parents don't correct their children when a child knows he/she is behaving badly, the child loses respect for the parent. If they don't respect their parents, they lose respect for all authority - teachers, police, etc. Then, they often go on to worse behavior. We see this happening at every level of society.

>Where are the parents today? If we are parents, may we prayerfully, with firm but calm intent, raise up our children unto God with love and appropriate discipline. As children of God, may we accept His correction and discipline that we may enjoy the ensuing benefits. Let us *be in subjection to the Father of spirits and live!*

Prayer – Dear Father, I want to live as Your child, please do whatever is necessary to shape me as Your child.

JULY

TO

Meditation Aids

TO is a preposition - A preposition is used to show the relation of a noun, or some other word, to some other word in the sentence. A preposition (pre – position) usually is a word used before a noun or pronoun to form a phrase that modifies (qualifies, describes, or limits) some aspect of the sentence. The object of the preposition could be a noun, a verb, or an adjective. Check the object of the preposition to understand its impact.

Uses of TO – toward - make happen – install – intent.

Example:

... for the Son of Man has come TO seek and TO save that which was lost Luke 19:10.

Seek and save are the objects of the preposition TO.

The prepositional phrases *TO seek* and *TO save* modify *that which was lost.*

July 1   Filled

<u>Acts 5:28</u> *Did we not strictly command you not TO teach in this name? And look, you have filled Jerusalem with your doctrine …*

TO shows action.

Q What were the Apostles ordered not to do?

They were ordered not to teach *in this name.*

The high priest couldn't even bring himself to say Jesus' name. Others could. Can we speak, in words and actions, His name and nature? Do our lives <u>fill</u> our town?

If you or I were ordered not to talk about Jesus, would we be resentful or relieved? Do we <u>have </u>to talk about Jesus, or do we <u>want</u> to talk about Jesus? Do we talk grudgingly or with rejoicing?

Q What did the Apostles do?

Just exactly what they were told <u>not</u> to do. And not only that, each day they taught and preached that Jesus was Christ (Acts 5:41-42). Do you think there was a resurrection? What else would make them so determined?

When we are asked, we are to be instant in defending our hope in Christ. We can do this if God has a distinct place in our inmost being. Even then, we witness with gentle respect (1 Peter 3:15). The Holy Spirit is constantly convicting people so we should always be ready to tell them the good news.

These days there are some things we don't want on our face book. But what if a new baby is born in good circumstances? What if a wonderful couple is engaged? Isn't this good news? Don't grandparents love to show pictures of their grandchildren? What if Christ has made it possible for us to have our sins forgiven and have a relationship with our Creator? Shouldn't we talk about it?

Realistically, we should love to tell others the good news of Jesus – and joyfully speak His name so that our lives fill our town.

Prayer - Dear Father, I am prepared, and I joyfully live, so that others will ask about Jesus' power in me; please give me words to speak.

July 2   Keep

Deuteronomy 11:22 *If you carefully keep all of these commandments which I command you TO do, TO love the Lord your God, TO walk in all His ways, and TO hold fast TO Him ...*

> This verse looks like a summation of the Ten Commandments given in Exodus 20, split three and seven, with an added requirement to *hold fast* to the Lord your God. TO requires action.

Q How do we keep the commandments?   *Carefully.*

> First, we delight in God's laws. Keeping them saves us from a world of hurt - unplanned pregnancies, social diseases, and more. There is appreciation for His guidance in keeping us from the consequences of evil and enabling us to receive His blessings. Secondly, each day we study, meditate, and act on His wise words (Psalm 1:2).

Love the Lord your God - (the first three commandments) - We are to have no other god, material or emotional. Anything made of substance or that brings about a negative emotion is rejected as not-God. We use His name reverently and with respect. We respond to Him appropriately.

> *Walk in all His ways* - (The next seven commandments) - We observe a day of worship, we honor our parents, we don't kill, commit adultery, steal, or lie about our neighbors. We don't covet anything belonging to our neighbor. Later on, in the New Testament, a summation of commandments was given: *You shall love the Lord your God with all your heart, with all your soul, with all your strength, and with all your mind, and your neighbor as yourself* Luke 10:27. SPICE!

Hold fast to Him - Paul instructed us to avoid, like the plague, anything that might come between us and God. We should Velcro ourselves to God, not allowing anything between us and Him (Romans 12:9).

> Part of our response to grace is keeping the commandments that God has given us. We need to stop, think, and understand that the commandments protect us from the consequences of evil. They are our safety belts in the journey of life. Buckle up!

Prayer - Dear Father, thank You for the commandments and the benefits of following them.

July 3   Believe

<u>1 John 5:13</u> *These things I have written TO you who believe in the name of the Son of God, that you may know that you have eternal life, and that you may continue TO believe in the name of the Son of God.*

> 1John is the *know* letter. The word *know* is used some 14 times. Samples: 3:16, 3:19, and 3:24.
>
> TO means towards those who actively believe.

Q Why do we have this message?

> To let us know that we have *eternal life* and that we *may continue to believe.*
>
> Who? *You who believe.*
>
> What? The whole letter of 1 John, especially John's eye and ear witness to the life and teachings of Jesus (1John 1:3).
>
> Why? *That you may know* and *continue to believe* that you *have eternal life.*
>
> How? By the words John has written.
>
> When? Now and forever more.
>
> Where? The message of Christ is effective wherever we may be found.
>
> Because John saw and heard the Person and Truth of Jesus, we can b*elieve, know,* and c*ontinue* to believe that we have eternal life in Christ. Take a few moments and meditate on each of these three words – believe – know - continue. Pause and let verses come to your mind. Meditation is medication for the soul.

Prayer - Dear Father, thank You for a compelling eye witness account that inspired John to write this helpful letter.

July 4   Liberty

In honor of July 4, consider Galatians 5:1b *For freedom Christ has set you free* ... (See September 8). In Christ we have the most meaningful freedom.

Galatians 5:13 *... you have been called TO liberty; only do not use liberty as an opportunity for the flesh.*

> TO means enter into liberty.

Q Can we do anything we want to because we are saved by grace?

> No!

> Liberty, in this case, speaks of freedom from laws in our relationship with God. Grace liberates us from the law (Galatians 5:1).

> Liberty is not license. We don't purposely sin and presume upon God's grace (Romans 6:1). Grace is not permission to do evil.

> God gives us liberty, set free from the tyranny of sinful actions. We are now freed to dedicate our lives to right living (Romans 6:18). We are all slaves of something - make it righteousness. (KISS - Keep It Simple Slave.)

> When we are following the leading of the Spirit we are not bound by laws (Galatians 5:18). But, our lesson today warns us - *Only do not use liberty as an opportunity for the flesh.* The flesh is anything that works against the Spirit. Expressing faith while indulging in fleshly lusts is a delusion and leads to slavery to sin.

> You may want to try the Corinthian's statement: Everything may be permissible for me to do, but it isn't necessarily beneficial (1Corinthians 6: 12). Those who are using Christianity as a pretense, who are involved in sinful behavior, do a great disservice to the Gospel of Christ. Those who want to use liberty for an excuse to do evil really haven't apprehended the essence of relationship with God. Those who are in Christ look for righteous actions. Those in Christ want to be helpful in the cause of the Gospel. They do not incorrectly use grace as an excuse to get away with evil.

Prayer - Dear Father, help me enjoy liberty unhampered by entanglements of the flesh.

July 5   Life

John 10:10 *The thief does not come except TO steal, and TO kill, and TO destroy. I have come that they may have life, and that they may have it more abundantly.*

> TO shows intent.

Q Why does Jesus come to us?   To give us abundant life.

Q Why does Satan come to us? TO *steal, kill, and destroy*. He isn't some comical red caricature with a forked tail.

First, compare why Satan and Christ appeared. Jesus gives us abundant life. Satan came to destroy that abundancy. Jesus and Satan represent opposing forces. We need to choose a side. The choice should be obvious. Accept the fact of spiritual warfare. Don't fall into Satan's trap of believing those who deny this reality. Many people deny the existence of Satan so they won't have to admit their allegiance to him.

In a sense John is answering Jeremiah's question about why the heart is so evil (Jeremiah 17:9). Now we know why humans *steal, kill, and destroy*. Satan never enters into a person for any good reason. When our hearts are Satan's territory, we become his agents in the world and do his bidding.

Satan has power over the world but he does not have power over us. We need to battle against him but we don't have to worry about the outcome of the battle. We don't have to fear those who may destroy our bodies because they have no control over our soul (Matthew 10:28).

We have armor made up of pieces that protect every part of our bodies and the emotional and spiritual aspects they represent (Ephesians 6:14-18). God has given us armor to put on for a battle, not an empty metal suit to put in a museum. And He, Jesus, has come, not to kill, but to give us life, and that *more abundantly*. Whatever you have without Him, you will have more with Him! Whatever troubles you have as a Christian, they are far less than those of the world. We have read the last chapter and WE WIN! We have life, and *that more abundantly*!

Prayer - Dear Father, help me to recognize Satan's ploys and to rest confidently in Christ.

July 6   Thoughts

<u>Jeremiah 29:11</u> *For I know the thoughts that I think toward you, says the Lord, thoughts of peace and not of evil, TO give you a future and a hope.*

TO shows intent.

Q What is God's desire for you?

Peace, a future, and a hope.

God does not have evil thoughts where we are concerned (1 Corinthians 13:5d).

God knows His mind and He spoke His mind. The thoughts that God has for us are put into words and action in and through Christ and the Holy Spirit.

Today's Scripture emphasizes *the thoughts I think toward you.* This is God speaking. Listen and know this is truth. These are the gifts that God gives to us in Christ. They are thoughts of:

<u>Peace</u> – When Jesus left the earth He left His peace with us as a continuing gift *(John 14:27). And a*

<u>Future</u> – We have a future. We are filled with the Holy Spirit for this life (Luke 11:13), and life in relationship with God for eternity (John 3:16b). And

<u>Hope</u> - Our hope is based on the unique characteristic of Christianity which is Christ living in us (Colossians 1:27).

We are promised a wonderful *future* filled with *peace* and *hope* - - <u>if we receive it</u>. INSTANT REPLAY - We are promised a wonderful *future* filled with *peace* and *hope* - - <u>if we receive it</u>. As He offers these wonderful gifts to us, let us accept them with an attitude of gratitude and praise.

Prayer - Dear Father, thank You for Your *peace, a future* in heaven, and *hope* fulfilled in Christ.

July 7   Captivity

2 Corinthians 10:5b ... *but mighty in God ... bringing every thought into captivity TO the obedience of Christ ...*

TO shows obedience.

Q How do we handle our thoughts?

We need to bring them *into captivity*.

The essence of this passage is one of necessary strength. We are at war and we need to have control over our thoughts. Every action stems from a thought. The first thought may belong to Satan. The second thought needs to be our choice, to make it obedient to Christ. It is our response-ability - using strength and weapons given by God in our response. Necessary armor is laid out in Ephesians 6:14-18. The *helmet of salvation* protects the mouth as well as the brain.

Our thoughts should agree with God's thoughts - *peace, hope, and a future* (From yesterday). When we don't capture our thoughts, something that seems to be the reasonable thing to do at the time, may lead to regrets. Thankfully, God gives us all the wisdom we need without scolding us for our lack of understanding (James 1:5).

In today's Scripture we are urged to capture every thought. This means we are to stop it before it becomes words or actions. We are to set up a guard tower that prevents bad things from getting into the compound of our lives. This calls for desire and effort on our part. God does not do this for us. He will warn us but if we allow a thought to run His stop signs, we own the results. As soon as we recognize an untamed thought, we need to confess it and accept God's forgiveness. INSTANT REPLAY - As soon as we recognize an untamed thought, we need to confess it and accept God's forgiveness. Then don't do it again. Quite often we need a reverse mouth guard to protect ourselves from injury from the inside.

Then, meditate on The Nice Juicy Plum, Lovely, Good, Very Purple. If we fill our minds with praise, there won't be room for garbage. See Philippians 4:8 if you don't remember.

Prayer - Dear Father, may the thoughts of my mind be delightful in Your sight.

July 8   Attention

1 Timothy 4:12-13 ... *give attention TO reading, TO exhortation, TO doctrine.*

To means read, lead, and feed.

Q How do we grow by *reading, exhortation, and doctrine*?

Give attention!

Feed a baby or it will die. Feed your soul or it will die.

Scripture is given, so *give attention,* undivided attention! Not in one eye and out the other, not just a passing where you read and not remember what you just read.

We need to read – Be accurate in your interpretation and use of the word (2 Timothy 2:15).

So many people and groups misrepresent different areas of the Bible. The Bible gives affirmation that rests in *grace, mercy, and peace.*

We need to exhort – We need to meet with fellow believers and encourage them (Hebrews 10:25). Exhortation is listed as a spiritual gift in Romans 12:8. This is a good gift to desire.

To exhort is to vigorously encourage each other. Our attendance in the corporate Body encourages others in their faith and practice.

We need to embrace doctrine - *All Scripture is given by inspiration of God, and is profitable for doctrine, for reproof, for correction, for instruction in righteousness, that the man of God may be complete, thoroughly equipped for every good work* 2 Timothy 3:16.

Doctrine refers to elements of the faith, a set of guidelines if you will, that are to be learned, taught, and put into practice.

If we obey this teaching, we will be strong in the faith and productive in our work.

Prayer - Dear Father, help me to store Your word in my heart and express it in my life.

There was a person who had read so much about sinful behavior that he decided to give up reading - bad idea.

July 9   Called

Romans 8:28 *And we know that all things work together for good TO those who love God, TO those who are called according TO His purpose.*

TO means toward.

Q What should our attitude be about *all things? That all things work together for good.*

God works for good in all things to bring about His intended purposes. Sometimes we have to look back to see what God intended as He looked forward. How do *we know all things work together for good?* God is in control. Nothing happens that doesn't pass His throne first. So why all the evil? One of the reasons is because the inner being, without the guidance of the Spirit, is extremely wicked (Jeremiah 17:9). Another is so we can make choices that strengthen our faith.

Don't focus on the moment of impact. Quite often the *good* result is not obvious at the time. We can't always see the whole picture until the whole picture is complete. That's where faith comes in. Don't get tired of your work in Christ. When the time is ripe we'll see results if we don't lose the courage of our convictions (Galatians 6:9). If we look to God for comfort, He gives comfort that we can share with others. If we don't feel comforted, we won't be useful to others in need (2 Corinthians 1:4). My parents divorced when I was nine. My father died when I was ten. I suffered a severe burn when I was ten and spent several weeks in the hospital. Been there, done that. I can have empathy and can comfort others. I may not have experienced your trials but you get the idea. When you consider your experiences, trust today's verse.

We must be in agreement with His purpose, which is bringing all people into relationship with Him. Trials are not meant to make us bitter and broken but to better us and bring us to Him for His strength and comfort. In some cases we can ask, "Why is this the best possible thing that can happen?" That gets us outside the pity party box and allows us to take a different perspective.

Today's verse seems foolish to those who do not *love God.* This directive is for those *who love God and are called according TO His purpose.* Seek to find God's purpose in good, and seemingly bad, events.

Prayer - Dear Father, help me find Your purpose in my *things.*

July 10   Forgiving

Ephesians 4:32 _And be kind TO one another, tender hearted, forgiving one another even as Christ forgave you._

TO means toward.

Q How are we to treat our Christian family?

We are to treat them with kindness and forgiveness as Christ has forgiven us.

Be kind - compassionate, understanding, sympathetic.

To one another, This is not, "I'll be kind to him so he will be kind to me." Nor, "If she isn't kind to me, I won't be kind to her." This should be a reciprocal, two-way activity. If not reciprocal, make it one-way on your part. Besides that, our kindness is our response-ability, regardless of how others act.

Tender hearted - gentle, sensitive to other's pain and needs.

This is the opposite of being hard-hearted, that is, lacking understanding and compassion. However, in some cases, there is a need for tough tenderness. We must not be taken in by Satan's wiles working in a person who is intentionally sloughing off.

Forgiving - make positive relationships possible, even as Christ forgave you. This is love.

"Who, me, forgive that?" "Yes, you, forgive that." Whatever! This is personal and sometimes flies in the face of worldly belief. Do we want forgiveness? Then forgive. See siblings in Christ as He sees them - as pure, the same way He sees us - as pure as He is (1John 3:3). If something seems unforgivable, give it to God. His judgments are without fault (Revelation 19:2). Trust that God will judge appropriately. This will relieve you of the burden of holding a grudge. Grudges can get really heavy.

Prayer - Dear Father, help me to forgive as I have been forgiven.

July 11   Armor

<u>Ephesians 6:13</u> *Therefore take up the whole armor of God, that you may be able TO withstand in the evil day, and having done all, TO stand.*

TO shows intent to stand.

What is the importance of spiritual armor?

We need *the whole armor* so we can withstand evil.

We are wrestling with powers of evil, some of which are very challenging (Ephesians 6:11-12).

WE need to avoid the mistake of denying that there is a perpetrator of evil, Satan. Denial allows him free entry into this confusing life. We need to put on *the whole armor of God*, with no chinks or cracks. We need *the whole* armor with pieces to protect us in every important area of our lives- *belt, breastplate, shoes, shield, helmet, sword, and prayer –* (belt, chest protector, spikes, catcher's mitt, face mask, bat) (v14-18). Not using every part leaves an opening for Satan. Do an inventory. Got it all? Use it all!

What is the evil day? Every day has the possibility and presence of evil. Be a cheerleader about armor for yourself and others! "Take it up. Put it on. Fight, fight, fight!" Don't leave it in the closet when you go out. If you forget it, or part of it, go back and get it. Don't leave home without it.

We need the ability to *stand* firm in the faith. As Peter encourages us – Be calm and alert: the enemy, Satan, is stalking Christians to see who he can destroy. When you detect his presence, be strong in your convictions and don't give him a chance to do his dirty work (1 Peter 5:8-9).

We need to do this anywhere and everywhere; any time and every time. There is good - God, and there is evil - Satan. The lines are drawn, there is no demilitarized zone.

Prayer - Dear Father, thank You for complete armor which fits me and fills my every need.

July 12   Grace

<u>1 Timothy 1:2</u> *TO Timothy, a true son in the faith: grace, mercy, and peace from God our Father and Jesus Christ our Lord.*

TO – means granted to.

Q How did Paul address Timothy? Paul addressed Timothy as *a true son.*

As far as we know Paul didn't have any biological children but he had offspring *in the faith.* Timothy was third generation - Father God, Paul, Timothy.

Q How should we greet fellow Christians?

As family - the entire family, the Body of Christ, is involved. We need them and they need us *in the faith.* We meet them with *grace, mercy, and peace.*

Grace - Remember, grace is getting what we don't deserve. We need to extend grace to our family even if we feel they don't deserve it. We may say, in error, "This is unforgivable." Or, "I can't", or "won't, forgive that." There is no unforgivable sin in the family of God. We give what we receive - forgiveness.   There is nothing we need to do except to accept.

Mercy is not getting what we do deserve. We don't give our abusers what they deserve; that is God's prerogative. All sin, for all time, is already forgiven. It is just that it hasn't been accepted and given to others. We don't retain our, or other's, sins.

Peace - The peace that God gives is the peace that defies human explanation (Philippians 4:7). As we grant grace and mercy to others, REALLY grant grace and mercy, a peace will come over us that defies explanation.

Note the order, after grace and mercy comes peace from God. The only source is Jesus Christ our Lord. It is through Jesus that *grace, mercy, and peace* come to us. All these virtues are sanctified by the sacrifice of Christ. They are given to us that we might share them with others.

Prayer - Dear Father, thank You for the peace that comes from Your grace and mercy.

July 13   Furtherance

Philippians 1:12 ... *things that have happened TO me have actually turned out for the furtherance of the gospel ...*

TO refers to *things that have happened* - Satan's attacks, allowed by God.

Q What can be the result of what seems to be a negative event? The Gospel can be furthered.

For a list of the *things* Paul has experienced see 2 Corinthians 11:23-27.

And, *Actually,* these things can be good? *Actually* - This may come as a surprise until we become familiar with God's workings. Maybe Paul didn't see what was coming but he knew God was at work. At an earlier time Paul and Silas were having a good time in jail, feet in stocks, praying and singing to God and ... other prisoners were listening (Acts 16:25). Imagine what would have happened if Paul and Silas were griping about their situation.

We find a similar situation with Joseph's experiences. Joseph went through all kinds of grief but, through it all, he was convinced that God was working towards a good goal. He was frank with his brothers letting them know he knew that they had evil intent, but he expressed his faith by telling them that God was able to turn their bad behavior into good results (Genesis 50:19-20). Joseph said he wasn't God Who would be their Judge. He just saw all that had happened to him as being God's prevenient grace to provide for his family.

Paul certainly knew of Joseph's story and, combining that with his experiences, wrote that when you love God, and are living in His plan, everything can be used for His purposes (Romans 8:28) Those who are alert to God's intentions can find good in everything. Sometimes we need to look under the lid of suffering to find His purpose.

What is your experience? Are you one of *the called*? People are watching and listening. The *furtherance of the Gospel* is what we really care about. Are you experiencing a hardship? Ask, "Why is this the best thing that could be happening?" Or else, simply pray, "Your will, not mine."

Prayer - Dear Father, help me not to be surprised when You *actually* take something "Bad" and bring about the increase of Your kingdom.

July 14   Pray

Luke 6:12 ... *He went out TO the mountain TO pray, and continued all night in prayer TO God.*

Jesus gave us the model prayer in Matthew 6:9-13.

TO shows direction and intent.

Q Did Jesus need times to talk things over with God?   Yes.

Luke 5:16 *So He Himself often withdrew into the wilderness and prayed.*

On one occasion Jesus had healed on the Sabbath and the scribes and Pharisees were enraged (Luke 6:6-11). At another time, great multitudes had come to Him for healing (Luke 5:15). Many times, Jesus needed to have communication with God.

Luke was emphatic about Jesus' prayer life. He wanted to give an accurate account of Jesus' life and actions so he felt it important to tell that Jesus set an example by meeting with God. Jesus *often withdrew.* He went by *Himself,* One on One with His Father.

He probably needed to ask how to deal with the scribes and Pharisees' opposition and the response of the crowd to miracles. He went by *Himself* because the disciples weren't ready for discussions like that at that time.

Jesus went often, at this time at least, continuing *all night in prayer.* These were serious, lengthy discussions. He probably discussed past, present, and future events. His life was a beehive of activity. He had much to talk about. (If you are awake all night worrying, switch to prayer.)

It is helpful to know that He found quiet places where He wasn't interrupted. During the day He was besieged with crowds. So He went *into the wilderness,* or to the solitude of *a mountain* - quiet places, no distractions.

We need to be in conversations with God. Talk to Him and listen for His responses. The Holy Spirit will remind you of Jesus' words. All the responses must agree with Scripture.

Prayer - Dear Father, in quiet times and during difficult times, I love to withdraw and spend time with You.

July 15   Riches

Philippians 4:19 *My God shall supply all your needs according TO His riches in glory by Christ Jesus.*

TO – His availability of riches.

Q Who will supply all our needs?

God.

Today's verse tells us - *My God* - as opposed to any other source. When it is God Who supplies, we have an unconditional guarantee of the perfect and eternal quality of that which is given. And, He shall *supply all your needs.* This does not necessarily mean He will supply all our wants. We have to be careful here. Satan will make a lot of wants seem attractive but they won't necessarily be glorious and may have negative results.

Furthermore, all of our needs are supplied according *to His riches* - He measures the supply generously and will not impoverish us. Take one of our needs, wisdom for instance: Just ask and God will freely give wisdom without giving you a hard time (James 1:5). Or, our need for growth – If you need to toughen up, He will give you just the right experience so you can grow in your spiritual life (Matthew 6:34b).

Then, God's supply brings *glory* to, and magnifies, His nature. Because it is *by Christ Jesus* these needs are supplied. Christ is our greatest need and that need has been fulfilled (John 3:16). The intensity with which He loves us is another indication of God's bountiful supply.

Be mindful that we have given our lives to God in a trust relationship. He knows our needs better than we do and He knows the purpose He has for our lives. We need to trust His word.

If ever we are in a spot where Jesus is all that we have, we find that He is all that we need. INSTANT REPLAY If ever we are in a spot where Jesus is all that we have, we find that He is all that we need.

Prayer - Dear Father, help me to define my needs accurately and to know, if what I think is a need is not supplied, it is not something I need.

July 16   Honor and Glory

1 Timothy 1:17 *Now TO the King eternal, immortal, invisible, TO God Who alone is wise, be honor and glory forever and ever. Amen!*

TO – means toward the King.

Q Who deserves our highest praise?

The King Who is God.

How interesting! - A closing doxology (a prayer of praise) in the middle of a letter. How often the pure joy of being in Christ bursts forth with a triumphant shout!

Now - why now? Always now, because each day is a new *now*. The King is forever to be praised for His attributes. The King is:

Eternal – God is forever. Backwards and forwards, He is God (Psalm 90:2c).

Immortal – God is alive and guarantees His care for us. He was never born and He will never die. God is always alive!

Invisible - Invisible yet clearly seen by eyes that see (Romans 1:20).

Who alone is wise - God's wisdom is the epitome of wisdom, making man's wisdom seem foolish by comparison.

Let us render unto Him *honor* - respect and esteem – *and*

glory - utmost praise

for ever and ever. AMEN!

Prayer - Dear Father, thank You for interludes of spontaneous praise to You for all that You are and all that You have given.

July 17   Faultless

<u>Jude 24-25</u> *Now TO Him Who is able TO keep you from stumbling and TO present you faultless before the presence of His glory with exceeding joy, TO God our Savior, Who alone is wise, be glory and majesty, dominion and power, both now and forever. Amen.*

TO – so that, toward.

Q Who keeps us and presents us faultless?

God - in and through Christ Jesus.

Speaking of praise statements, yesterday, 1Timothy 1:17 was the basis of our meditation. Today's benediction in Jude is one of the best, if not <u>the</u> best, ending statements to all spoken and written word. It begins in verse 21; ... *keep yourselves in the love of God, looking for the mercy of our Lord Jesus Christ unto eternal life.* Jude speaks of mercy, a blessed gift of God. And ends with the following – what I used for the benediction of every service I preached:

To Him Who is able to keep you from stumbling – God is omnipotent (all powerful) (Psalm 28:7-8).

And to present you faultless – He purifies us. Our hope in Christ gives us purity (1John 3:3).

before the presence of His glory with exceeding joy - YES! It is simply fantastic that God has great joy when we come before Him.

To God our Savior, Who alone is wise, be glory and majesty, dominion and power, both now and forever. Amen. There are many praise sections in the book of Revelation. See Revelation 5:12 as a wonderful example. Let us give glory to God!

Prayer - Dear Father, Now to <u>You</u> Who are able TO keep <u>me</u> from stumbling and TO present <u>me</u> faultless before the presence of <u>Your</u> glory with exceeding joy, To God <u>my</u> Savior, Who alone is wise, be glory and majesty, dominion and power, both now and forever. Amen. (Pronouns changed out of pure joy!)

July 18   Saw

Mark 2:5 *When Jesus saw their faith, He said TO the paralytic, "Son, your sins are forgiven you."*

TO – toward the paralytic.

Q Can faith be seen? Yes, when it is in action.

Jesus saw their faith. He watched four men lower their friend through a hole they had made in the roof. It is important to note that the friends were the ones whose faith could be seen.

Jesus saw their faith - a visual observation, and

said to the paralytic - a verbal forgiveness of sin.

When He saw, as opposed to hearing, He said, *"Son, your sins are forgiven."* Was some sin the cause of his paralysis? We don't know. What we do know is that forgiveness of sins is the most important transaction in our relationship with God.

Before texting became a frequent substitute for talking, a lot of communication was nonverbal – body language. Gestures, facial expressions, and/or tone of voice verified or negated our words. It is important that people "see" our faith. What we do lends power to what we say. Unfortunately a text is less powerful than a vocal statement backed up by action.

The paralytic had to switch from helplessness to hopefulness. What a joy it must have been to hear forgiveness given. But others, for some satanic reason, disputed. So, Jesus, probably by design, proved His authority to forgive sin by performing an undisputable miracle. A paralyzed man stood up and walked!

We can have faith that our faith will be rewarded. If we bring a friend to Jesus, they need to know that his/her sins are forgiven. Someone was friend enough to lead us to Christ. Are we being friendly to our friends? Think of a friend or family member who needs a divine introduction. Ask God for opportunities and words to speak.

Prayer - Dear Father, help others see my faith. May I be a walking textbook telling about You.

July 19   Rose and Came

Mark 10:46-52 *Be of good cheer, He is calling you ... and throwing away his cloak, he rose and came TO Jesus.*

> TO – toward Jesus.

Q Why should he be cheerful?

> Because Jesus was calling him.

Be cheerful - This should be the message given to all the world! Not just, "Be warm and well fed" (James 2:16). Bartimaeus had cried out, *"Jesus, Son of David, have mercy on me!"* Apparently, the good news of Jesus had circulated amongst the beggar crowd. Perhaps Bartimaeus was fortunate to be blind or he wouldn't have called out to Jesus. It is only when we recognize our spiritual blindness that we call out to Him. If you recognize your blindness, *Be of good cheer!* Jesus is calling you! Jesus is always calling out to us, seeking, loving, yearning to give us spiritual sight. In Matthew 11:28, He urges us to come to Him for rest from physical and emotional strain.

Others had tried to shut Bartimaeus up (Mark 10:48). Satan's minions are always at work trying to derail the work of God. How many times can you remember that someone has tried to quiet your relationship with Jesus? People will say you are a fanatic, or crazy, or a Bible thumper. Satan's followers have all kinds of derogatory things to say. But this man, realizing that this might be his only chance, threw away his house blanket, his only possession - his only defense against the world – that he might receive his sight!

He rose and came to Jesus!

The story of Bartimaeus is one of those historical parables that provide a lesson as well as a miracle. This one outlines the salvation experience of many Christians who have realized their spiritual blindness and have come to Jesus for spiritual sight. How does it compare to yours?

Prayer - Dear Father, thank You for calling me. I *throw away* all that I have for You.

July 20   Judgment

1 Peter 4:17 *For the time has come for judgment TO begin at the house of God; and if it begins with us first, what will be the end of those who do not obey the gospel of God?*

TO means make happen.

Q Where does God's judgment begin?

It begins in the church, the Body of Christ.

Who - believers and *those who do not obey.*

What - *judgment.*

Why - *the time has come for judgment.*

How - in God's call for righteousness through grace.

When - now.

Where - in the *house of God* and outside.

Whatever *time* Peter was referring to, now is the right time; now is the best time for us to consider God's judgment. After we die, it is too late. There will be judgment - we reap what we sow. Fortunately for us, be it known – God made Christ to be our sin so that we might be made His righteousness (2 Corinthians 5:21). O what grace, that God should reach out to us and take us into relationship with Himself!

What will be the end for the disobedient? They choose to die as they chose to live - without God. Part of God's will is that man should have the wonderful horrible power of choice. Wonderful if we chose Him, horrible if we reject Him. God doesn't need puppets; he wants humble, thankful, obedient servants who choose to receive and give love to Him and to each other.

If you haven't chosen, realize that a choice must be made. Not to decide is to decide. Choose, this day - now, whom you will serve. If you choose Satan, at least admit to it.

Prayer - Dear Father, thank You that You have led me to choose to be obedient to You.

July 21   True and Righteous

Revelation 19:1b-2 ... *Alleluia! Salvation and glory and honor and power belong TO the Lord our God! For true and righteous are His judgments ...*

> TO – means in His character.

Q Why don't we have to worry about letting those who have abused us "off the hook"?

> Because they are on God's hook. ... *true and righteous are His judgments ...*

> *His* judgments – because mine may be neither true nor just. I have read the Bible through every two years since I was 16 years old and about the twelfth time through, this verse exploded in my mind. His judgments are as true as His redemptive work. I don't have to hold grudges or resentments any more. (Actually, they held me.)

> When I was doing linguistic work at the University of Oklahoma, Native Americans helped us in working to translate the Bible into languages with no written word. When I asked my helper about the atrocities of some settlers, she said, in proper English, "They will get theirs."

> Holding a grudge doesn't hurt offenders. They don't worry about the offense or they would do something about it. Holding a grudge does hurt me though, it uses up emotional energy and saps my joy and peace. Part of the word forgive is give - give it to God, His judgments are *true and righteous.* "*Vengeance is Mine and recompense; their foot shall slip in due time*" ... Deuteronomy 32:35. And this verse is quoted by Paul in Romans 12:19. Both Moses and Paul felt vengeance was best left to God.

> A lot of people don't want to forgive because they feel their abuser should suffer as they did. The problem with that is every time they re-member, it gives new life to the offense. They are practicing being an abused person and the abuser does it to them again, and again, and again. Don't give them the satisfaction. Instead, give it to God, in *due time,* trust Him - He will judge righteously.

Prayer - Dear Father, I gratefully yield to You all the pain, abuse, and neglect I have experienced and felt from interactions with Satan's followers. Release me to love, joy, and peace in Your continual presence.

July 22   Slaves

Romans 6:16 *Do you not know that TO whom you present yourselves slaves TO obey, you are that one's slaves whom you obey, whether of sin leading TO death, or of obedience leading TO righteousness?*

TO – means given to that person or being.

Q How do we gain righteousness? We present ourselves obedient to God.

Q What do you call people who obey Satan?

Isn't it obvious? They are slaves to him.

You don't want to admit that? Then you are right in Satan's palm. Satan's slaves have a mindset against God. They say, "There is no God" or "God is bad," therefore, any event is interpreted against God. Any positive evidence is discounted. It is like the vote counters. They found a vote they didn't like so they laid it aside. When they found another like it, they assumed someone had voted twice. So they threw them both out.

There is no middle ground (Matthew 12:30). When we are with Him, we are committed slaves to Him. KISS – Keep It Simple Slave. We cannot present ourselves to Jesus as a present marked "Do not open."

There are people who knowingly worship and obey Satan. If they insist on following their wicked ways God gives them what they want, their despicable desires (Romans 1:26a). What a horrible thought - to present yourself as a present to Satan. Let's face it. We are a slave to Satan or to Christ. To deny that is to have one's head buried in the sin. (Intended).

The path of obedience to Satan leads to death, wages earned.

The path of obedience to Christ leads to life and righteousness, gift given.

Romans 6:23 makes it very clear – sin brings death, Christ gives life.

Which do you choose? Again, not to decide is to decide.

Prayer - Dear Father, I continue to choose You as my Savior, Lord, and Master.

July 23   "I"

Mark 14:19 *And they began TO be sorrowful, and TO say TO Him one by one, "Is it I?" And another said, "Is it I"?*

> TO – means being sorrowful, TO say, TO Him.

Q Why were they sorrowful?

> Eleven of them were worried that somehow they would betray Jesus (v18).

> They didn't go on the defensive. They didn't start a denial process. They didn't start blaming someone. They each, individually, opened himself to examination. All except Judas. What did Judas do? He got up, left, and betrayed Jesus. How did that work out for him? When we are betraying Jesus, we get up and leave too.

> Our relationship with God is the most precious thing we have. Our desire to live in Him and present Him to the world as a wonderful Savior should be our utmost passion.

> To betray the gift of grace and forsake trust in Him is the last thing we want. We can't just pay lip service to our faith. We should look at ourselves and give God a search warrant to have permission to inspect our entire person and premises to find anything nasty that we, or others, have put there (Psalm 139:23-24). If the Holy Spirit convicts us of any sin, we should not argue, or try to justify our action, blame the weather, or parents, or someone else, or society. We should own it, repent, and ask forgiveness. *"Is it I"?*

> We need to be sensitive to the word and have an accountable friend from whom we receive guidance (Proverbs 27:6a).

Prayer - Dear Father, may I never have to be sorrowful and ask, *"Is it I."*

July 24   Determined

1 Corinthians 2:2 *For I determined not TO know anything among you except Jesus Christ and Him crucified.*

TO is rigidly install.

Q What is one of the most important segments of knowledge about Christianity?

It is *Jesus Christ and Him crucified.*

In this passage Paul is talking about salvation. At another time he might say, "I am determined to know nothing among you except Jesus risen from the dead."

These are to be our mindsets. We will take hold of every bit of evidence of these truths and we will reject any accusation against them. Thankfully there is a mountain of evidence supporting the reason for, and effectiveness of, the crucifixion and resurrection of our Savior.

Today's verse is emphatic! *I determined* ... The letters to the Corinthians were written because the church there was in turmoil. Careful readers will see a series of problems handled with Spirit led teaching. One of the continual problems was an argument for salvation by works. Paul cut right to the heart of the matter with his foundation premise - *Jesus Christ and Him crucified.*

If you can imagine a group of overlapping circles around a point, the point in the center is the central truth about Christianity built around belief in Christ (John 3:16), new creations (2 Corinthians 5:17), and grace through faith (Ephesians 2:8-9).

Unfortunately, there are many denominations and denominations within denominations. If the crucifixion and resurrection of Jesus is not at the center of their theology, they are not of God. What is of singular importance is still best defined by variations on the foundation verse which is John 3:16. There are many spinoffs from this verse: (See John 1:12, Romans 10:9-10, 1 John 1:9).

Prayer - Dear Father, thank You for the totality and simplicity of knowing Christ Jesus.

July 25   Discerned

1 Corinthians 2:14 *But the natural man does not receive the things of the Spirit of God, for they are foolishness TO him, nor can he know them because they are spiritually discerned.*

TO – entrenched in his mindset.

Q What are *the things of the Spirit of God* to *the natural man?*

Foolishness. So don't look for guidance from him, his way leads to death.

Paul had played on this theme before: People who are languishing outside of Christ find information about the cross to be foolish (1 Corinthians 1:18). Why are things of the Spirit foolishness to the natural man? Because the wisdom of the natural man is foolishness when compared with the wisdom of God.

The *natural man* is the person who is not in relationship with God. He does not have the Spirit of God so he cannot discern *the things of the Spirit.* The natural man has had a physical birth but has not had the born again experience of spiritual birth. Simply put - no second birth, no see the kingdom (John 3:3).

The natural man does not receive - doesn't know - *the things of the Spirit of God* because a person needs the Spirit of God in order to see and understand the things of God. Does anyone want the Spirit of God? All they have to do is ask Him and He will immediately give the Holy Spirit to all who ask (Luke 11:13). Does anyone want spiritual discernment? All they have to do is ask Him and he will receive abundant wisdom with no qualifications (James 1:5).

So let us lay foolishness aside, take on wisdom, and proceed in faith with spiritual discernment.

Prayer - Dear Father, thank You for the Spiritual discernment to receive *the things of the Spirit.*

July 26   Given   (Revisited, see January 28)   <u>1 Corinthians 12:2</u>
But the manifestation of the Spirit is given TO each one for the profit of all: for TO one is given, ... a word of wisdom ... a word of knowledge ... faith ... gifts of healings ... working of miracles ... prophesy ... discerning of spirits ... different kinds of tongues ... interpretations of tongues. But one and the same Spirit works all these things, distributing to each one individually as He wills (vs8-11) (Shortened version).

TO - is given. Manifestation means demonstration or expression.

Q What is the origin of Spiritual gifts?   They are GIFTS *of the Spirit*! We need to review this truth from time to time.

Spiritual gifts had become one of the problems Paul addressed in his letter to the Corinthians. His teaching is very clear here and needs to be studied and heeded by the Body of Christ today because some people are told they are not part of the Body if they don't have a particular gift. Some people try to make work out of a gift.

We are to want to have spiritual gifts (1 Corinthians 14:1) but we need to remember they are gifts, not something we demand to have, or that others demand we have. No gift or any amount of gifts are a requirement for salvation. Nowhere in Scripture does it say we have to demonstrate a certain gift to gain or prove our salvation. That smacks of works. For instance, the gift of tongues, God speaks English, and all other languages.

The manifestation of the Spirit is given for the profit of the Body. God distributes gifts as He wills. A person does not necessarily have a certain gift. A gift may be a onetime thing or it may last for a period of time depending on the *Spirit's distribution as He wills*. INSTANT REPLAY - depending on the *Spirit's distribution as He wills*.

Gifts are not for bragging rights nor given so people can be excluded. Neither should one be envious of, or covet, another's gift. Gifts are to complete the Body, not separate it into sects. The gifts are equally distributed so that the sum of gifts equals the whole. If there is one person, that person may have several gifts. If there are several people the gifts may be distributed. Remember – gifts are for edification, not qualification. People may ask, "What is your gift?" Correct answer, "Whatever God wants me to have." Bottom line, be open for whatever gift the Spirit may give you at any given time.

Prayer - Dear Father, please gift me as You will that I might be used to build up the Body.

July 27 Receive

Romans 14:1 *Receive one who is weak in the faith, but not TO disputes over doubtful things.*

TO – to be involved in.

Q Should we argue about laws and rules not clearly defined in the Bible? No.

What should we do? We are to receive the weak and welcome them as siblings in Christ. As Paul goes on in the chapter, he explains our attitude should be one of reconciliation, making sure our actions do not encourage others to violate their consciences. He does say that our choice of conduct, as long as it doesn't violate clear teaching, is acceptable as long as we don't wear a sign on our chest (v22). He also essentially says, "If in doubt, don't" (v23).

Romans 14 is a great chapter to help in understanding Christian conduct and common activities in our daily lives. It also gives that powerful summation of the essence of Christianity: *… for the kingdom of God is not eating and drinking, but righteousness and peace and joy in the Holy Spirit* v17. Don't get caught up in rules. Paul dismisses food and religious days as being insignificant theological factors. He calls the Colossians to task, reminding them that they had died to legalism and wondering why on earth they were burdening themselves with another set of rules (Colossians 2:20-23).

We are saved through the gift of faith (Ephesians 2:8-9). The faith given by God is a faith with sufficient strength.

Those who are *weak in the faith* think they need rules in order to please God. That means they try to bolster their weak faith with works. They don't have faith in their faith.

Those who are strong in the faith ask for, and receive, the Holy Spirit to direct their lives in freedom. Now, one thing should be crystal clear, when we are led by the Spirit, we don't go looking for sin. We keep the commandments, etc. But, bottom line - *The kingdom of God is righteousness and peace and joy in the Holy Spirit.*

Enjoy your freedom while being conscious of your siblings' needs.

Prayer - Dear Father, help me be firm in my faith and not be involved in petty arguments.

July 28   Cling

Romans 12:9b *Abhor what is evil, cling TO what is good.*

TO – is to install.

Q How are we to react to *what is evil*?

Abhor it.

Q How are we to react to *what is good*?

Cling to it.

More than Velcro, more than static cling, more than a piece of cellophane stuck on your finger. We need Jesus glue.

We need to use the KISS (Keep IT Simple Slave) method. The message here is clear, evil is not a disputable matter. If you find yourself trying to justify something the Holy Spirit is warning you about, *abhor* it. Abhor evil means to detest, loathe, despise, be repulsed by, hate with a passion, what is evil. Don't do anything you think you are going to have to lie about, to God, to others, or to yourself. Run, don't walk, the other way. Trust the Holy Spirit; ask Him to guide you. He will not lead you do what He abhors.

Sin is detestable to God; sin is not part of His desire for us. God does not even allow evil and sinfulness to exist in His presence (Habakkuk 1:13). That is why sin pays off with death (Romans 6:23).

And we are asked in 2 Corinthians 6:14-15, should law abiding citizens make friends with crooks? Can light and darkness coexist? Should Jesus agree with Satan? More rhetorical questions.

Resist the devil - his end is death.

Listen to Jesus - His beginning is life everlasting.

When I was a boy, on a farm, we used a separator to extract cream from milk. It wouldn't have made sense to stir the cream back in. Christ separates us from sin. Can it been made any clearer? Evil and good do not mix.

Prayer - Dear Father, may I never try to mix sin in with Your goodness.

July 29   Knew

John 2:24 *But Jesus did not commit Himself TO them, because He knew all men.*

To commit is when you willingly entrust or choose to obligate yourself.

TO – is in their power.

Q Why didn't Jesus *commit Himself?*   *Because He knew all men.*

There were many who desperately wanted to be rid of Jesus. They didn't succeed through trickery so they finally crucified Him. The unredeemed heart is deviously clever and dreadfully depraved (Jeremiah 17:9). Jesus, of all people, knew that about mankind. After all, He created them and observed all the disobedience before He came in human form. Jesus certainly knew Satan and how he deceived people. Jesus knew Judas and He knew Peter; He knows us.

Let's not kid ourselves; there are precious few that can be trusted these days. Certain vocations have come by their reputations dishonestly, yes, dishonestly. The hackers seem to be one step ahead of the antivirus geeks. Video telephones and cameras spy on people. Credit card information is stolen. Nations are strutting nuclear arms, deranged individuals are murdering singly and in mass. There truly is no safe place - church, school, office, etc.

But, *Do not be afraid, for behold, I bring you good tidings of great joy which will be to all people. For there is born to you this day in the city of David, a Savior who is Christ the Lord.* Luke 2:10-11.

THE *GOOD TIDINGS* IS TO YOU!

This day is the day that Christ is born in a person's heart. Have you had your "birth" day?

Jesus knows us; He knows our hearts and our earnest desire to commit ourselves to Him. So you won't find us in a resale shop. We are new in the store. If people check our tags they will find, "Made in Love", "Permanently laundered". Our price tag will read "Paid in Full" (Revelation 3:12b-13).

Prayer - Dear Father, search me and know my heart. Thank You for committing Yourself to me. I gratefully commit myself to You.

July 30   Gather

<u>Matthew 23:37b</u> *O Jerusalem ... how often I wanted TO gather your children together, as a hen gathers her chicks under her wing, but you were not willing!*

TO – desire to make it happen.

Q What did Jesus want to do for Jerusalem?

He wanted to care for and protect them.

Jesus made a plaintive cry, *"O Jerusalem ..."* His compassion for them, and for us, is unparalleled in human history. He knew that Jerusalem would eventually become the arena of His crucifixion which probably added to His sorrow. To be lost and not know we are lost is unfortunate. To be lost and refuse to be found is tragic. You may have been in a situation where someone refused your offer to help and failed in their own efforts. The responses to such a refusal range from anger and disgust to sorrow and compassion.

As today's verse tells us, *"How often I wanted TO gather your children together ...".* The predator <u>scatters</u> the flock and chooses the weak, lost, and confused as prey. Jesus comes to <u>gather</u> the flock as a hen gathers her chicks under her wings for warmth and protection.

But you were not willing - Why? Why? Why unwilling? Why would anyone refuse God's incredible offer. If you have any reservations about the care and keeping of God through Christ and the Holy Spirit, decide now to accept His invitation and take refuge in Him. He is alive and is completely able to intercede for any person who comes to Him for forgiveness (Hebrews 7:25).

And for you.   And for me.

Prayer - Dear Father, thank You for the protection You desire to give to me. I joyfully accept.

July 31   Came

Luke 15:11-32

But when he came TO himself, he said, "How many of my father's hired servants have bread enough and TO spare, and I perish with hunger."

TO – means recognition of his situation; means abundance.

Q What brought the "prodigal son" to repentance?   Hunger.

God can use the adversities of life to give people the option of coming home to Him. The prodigal son must have had some idea that his father would accept him. After all, it was not the father's will that the son would leave in the first place. Eventually he came to himself when he only had pig food to eat. Give a person enough pig food and they may come to their senses

What a fortunate chain of events. We wouldn't have heard of him otherwise. This is another living parable that has many lessons. The key lesson is that when we come to ourselves we can turn to God and He will joyously accept us. *I say to you that likewise there will be more joy in heaven over one sinner who repents than over ninety-nine persons who need no repentance* Luke 15:7. (Who feel no need for repentance.)

The wayward son was seen when he was still a great way off. The father was watching for him. The son got hugs and kisses, a robe, a ring - a sign of royalty, and sandals. Sandals even - an indication of wealth and social position. And the fatted calf which was saved for special occasions was served! And they all had a merry party. Can you believe it? The Father is watching for us!

And then there was the other brother, the righteous church member. "Humph, here I am working my butt off and this disreputable person gets a party. Well, I'm not going." Have you met any righteous church members?

Even with that, the compassionate father assured the other brother of his position in the family. Two lessons: (1) we can come to God whatever our bad choices have been and get a joyful reception, and (2) we should join the party and celebrate whenever anyone joins the family.

Prayer - Dear Father, thank You for giving me a place at Your table.

AUGUST

IT   AS   AM

Meditation Aids

IT - a personal pronoun of the third person, it means "this" and refers to objects.

WE and US are first person and apply to people.

HE and SHE apply to living beings.

AS - adverb - modifies a verb - defines something - in like manner - same or similar.

AM - verb - an identifier of existence, present, indicates being, similar to IS.

Examples:

Consider IT pure joy when you face various trials James 1:2.

IT refers to various trials.

But AS for you, you meant evil against me, but God meant it for good, in order to bring it about AS it is this day... Genesis 50:20.

AS, in these two adverbial phrases, helps clarify *meaning* and *time*.

I know whom I have believed and AM persuaded that He is able to keep what I have committed to Him until that Day 2 Timothy 1:12.

AM indicates persuasion.

August 1   Strange

1 Peter 4:12-13 *Beloved, do not think IT strange concerning the fiery trial which is to try you, as though some strange thing happened to you; but rejoice to the extent that you partake of Christ's sufferings …*

> IT refers to a fiery trial.

Q Should we think that fiery trials are strange?   No.

> To have joy in suffering sounds like an oxymoron. This might be a tough one to take, but we are told to rejoice. Jesus said we <u>will</u> have tribulation. We wouldn't know what joy is if we didn't have sorrow in suffering. We can be cheerful despite our troubles because Jesus has overpowered the things of the world (John 16:33b).
>
> We are addressed as *beloved,* in this case, a word of compassionate endearment. It is helpful to know that we have someone who understands the struggle that goes with resisting Satan in a trial.
>
> The attacks of Satan are not to be confused with God's chastening. God's corrective measures, though they sometimes sting, enhance life in Christ (Hebrews 12:11). We get what we need in order to grow spiritually (Matthew 6:34b). After Satan attacks us, we feel weak and defeated, but when God chastens us we feel strengthened and at peace. God allows Satan's attacks so we can rejoice in victory over him. Check out Joseph's story in Genesis 50.
>
> Peter was no stranger to strange things; he knew we are involved in spiritual warfare. Our enemy, Satan, prowls around looking for people he can consume (1 Peter 5:8-9). Fight him off, rejoice in, and reap the benefits of tribulation.
>
> Get used to it. Even look forward to trials. Paul looked at trials as good times because they increased his dependence on Christ (2 Corinthians 12:10).
>
> We are not alone in what the Bible calls tribulations (Hebrews 13:5, Joshua 1:5). Jesus helps in all tribulations. His grace is wonderful, is within us, and is sufficient!

Prayer - Dear Father, help me to know the difference between Satan's meddling and Your instruction, to grow in grace with either, and to rejoice in the victories you give.

August 2   Testify

John 7:7 *The world hates Me because I testify of IT that its works are evil.*

IT means the world.

Q What word describes the works of the world?

Evil.   Evil is selfish, it does not care for others. Evil creates hate.

You don't think the world will hate you? Try telling someone their works are evil. What does Jesus mean by *the world*? He is speaking of Satan's realm (John 12:31). Satan is the ruler of this world. If we are not in God's camp, we are in Satan's. There is no middle ground. But, praise be to God, as we read yesterday, Jesus has overpowered the world.

We can recognize and accept the devil as an enemy or we can deny and ignore him and, knowingly or unknowingly, play into his schemes - which lead to death.

Consider the following court scene. We are the jury. God is the judge. The matter being judged is whether or not the world, the realm of Satan, is an evil place. Jesus testifies about the world. While he created the world, the world did not recognize Him. Even when He came to the "chosen people", they didn't accept Him (John 1:10). The good that we see is brought about by the Spirit of God. The evil we see is brought about by Satan.

Once we have considered Jesus' testimony, and are shown some TV clips, we are to give our verdict. Are the works of the world good or evil? Is the world guilty or innocent? Our decision affects our eternal destiny. What is your decision?

Once we have made a decision we often will be called upon to defend it. If our decision is in favor of Jesus, it won't be cheerfully received by the juries of the world but we rejoice that we share in the sufferings of our Lord and Savior, Jesus Christ! Eventually, because of the condition of the people of the world, those who follow Satan, they and their ruler will be removed (John 12:31), and we are vindicated.

Prayer - Dear Father, help me make an informed choice about Jesus' words and to choose Him.

August 3   Joy

<u>James 1:2</u> *Consider IT pure joy when you face various trials.*

 IT refers to facing various trials.

Q What is to be our reaction to *trials*? Our reaction should be *pure joy.*

Consider is con-side – with sides. One side is resentment, thinking God is uncaring or mean. James opted for joy, pure joy. Not fake joy, or forced joy. *When* - This is not an i<u>f</u>, it is a *when.* We are to *face* the trials, not deny or run from them. There will be *various trials* - a variety of trials. Each day will give an adequate growth experience (Matthew 6:34b). We won't be bored. The Scripture states, *pure joy* - Holy Spirit joy. There is a four-step process that helps us joyfully deal with trials. This process helps in resolving any difficult situation.

<u>Name it</u> - Examine the evidence. Clearly define the trial.

<u>Claim it</u> - It <u>is</u>. To deny or resent it is to give it power over you. Rejoice and face it.

<u>Blame it</u> - Is it my bad, or from God or from Satan. Will it bring peace or sorrow?

<u>Tame it</u> - Ask for and receive the Helper's assistance for the process and its use. Then don't return to the scene of the crime.

We are to *consider it pure joy.* This isn't mere happiness. If you feel you are being tested, don't be resentful, look for a positive result. If the test seems too severe, trust that God will provide *the way* to get out of the situation (1 Corinthians 10:13b). Many people quote the first part of this verse and then in despair say, "God has a higher opinion of me than I do." They don't finish the all-important end of the verse – He will provide the way out. Notice it says <u>the way</u>. There will be a specific way. We need to pass the test or, if it is too much at the moment, look for <u>the</u> escape route. If you don't find it, go back to seeking what is good about it (Romans 8:28).

We have been given victorious faith so that we can handle any problem (1 John 5:4). So the next time you experience a trial, and you will, rejoice, face it, and pass the test. If necessary, look for, and find the escape route that God has given. There is a warm feeling when we overcome a trial.

Prayer - Dear Father, thank You for escape routes and the faith to find and use them.

August 4   Good Work

Philippians 1:6 ... *He who has begun a good work in you will complete IT until the day of Jesus Christ.*

IT refers to good work.

Q Is God's work in us finished?

No.

I like the T shirt that has these words written on it —

Don't criticize,

God isn't finished with me yet.

Once we are born in Christ, we continue to increase in our entire relationship with Christ Who is our Spiritual Leader (Ephesians 4:15). This process, often called sanctification (being set apart), is accomplished by God through the work of our Helper, the Holy Spirit - from beginning to completion.

WHO? He - God.

WHAT? Has begun a good work - sanctification.

HOW? Through the work of the Holy Spirit.

WHY? To glorify Jesus.

WHEN? to completion - until the day of Christ's return.

WHERE? In us, His body.

We are like the reverse of a burning candle. It continues to give off light until its life is completed and it is consumed. Unlike the candle whose life is diminished, our lives increase in Christ-likeness until we go to Him or He comes to us. In the meantime, we give off Light.

Prayer - Dear Father, may I not hinder, but encourage, Your *good work* in me.

August 5   Heard

John 21:1-8 *Now when Peter heard that IT was the Lord, he put on his outer garment ... and plunged into the sea.*

IT means the Lord.

Q What would we do if we heard that Jesus was nearby?

I hope we would jump at the chance to see Him.

Peter had totally accepted forgiveness, the past was behind him, and he was able to exuberantly go meet with Jesus. Unlike those who would run from Him because they haven't accepted His grace.

Apparently, Peter had given up and he, and others, had returned to their former occupation. They hadn't netted anything until, under Jesus' direction, they cast their nets on the *right side* of the boat. (Jesus helps us know what the right side of life is.) John recognized Jesus, told Peter, and Peter couldn't wait to get to Jesus. The others came in the boat dragging a huge load of fish.

Being his impetertuous self, Peter put on his outer garment, which could have impeded him, and *plunged*, a joyful jump, into the sea. There was no thought of walking on the water.

Then came the question - *Do you love Me?* John 21:15-17 - three times. Peter wasn't thrilled with this but Jesus wanted to emphasize the three times Peter had denied Him and the three times he had slept during Jesus' need. Jesus then said, " *Feed My sheep."*

What would we do if we heard that Jesus was near? Do all the negative issues of the past flash before our eyes or do we so completely understand grace that we can run to Him unimpeded? What would be His message for us?

Ask Him.

Prayer - Dear Father, I eagerly come to you, realizing that You have removed all barriers. What would You have me to do?

August 6   Better

<u>1 Peter 3:17</u> *For IT is better, if IT is the will of God, to suffer for doing good than for doing evil.*

IT refers to suffering for doing good.

Q Is it the will of God that we suffer?   Yes, if it is for doing good.

We suffer as Christ suffered and we rejoice that we share in His sufferings. The evil world causes suffering but God gives us strength to forgive and endure. I find joy, even while suffering, because I join with Christ in being afflicted for you. His suffering was not inadequate, it is just that we have His mind and continue His work in the church. (Colossians 1:24). Forgiveness sometimes requires suffering as we suffer, and forgive the indignities that are foisted upon us. We, as His body, now suffer in forgiveness for others. His primary affliction was death which speaks to the high price that is paid in the act of forgiveness. As we forgive others, we fill up in our bodies the affliction, the sometimes excruciating demands of forgiveness.

The church, His body, has been, is, and will be the object of attack by Satan and his followers. Part of the Good News is that Christ has overcome the world and has provided faith, armor, safe guards of comfort, escape routes, and Scripture to give us victory. But the question sometimes remains: Why suffer? - Why? Because we share with Christ the necessary act of forgiveness so that relationships may prosper.

> The world hates us because our lives and testimony expose them to the light. They will try to defeat us and make us suffer so we will go away. There was a day that evil was roundly condemned. That condemnation has gradually decreased until evil has become the norm and Christianity is now frowned upon. Society is reaping the sorry crop of what it has sown.

Why me? Because, you have a unique mission field. No one else is you or where you are. Whether in words or actions, you are God's ambassador in your situation. You are the Bible those around you read. You are often the one from whom forgiveness is required. It is the will of God that the church should thrive. Therefore, we will survive suffering.

Prayer - Dear Father, thank You for allowing me to share in Your suffering so that all those who see how I handle suffering would see You and come to repentance.

August 7   Heart

Jeremiah 17:9 *The heart is deceitful above all things, and desperately wicked; who can know IT?*

> IT refers to the heart.

Q Who can understand the *deceitful* heart?

> Jeremiah didn't seem to know; *who can know it?*

> We can know it because Jesus told us. Some people are so much under the influence of Satan that they think his ways of robbery, murder, and destruction are the thing to do (John 10:10). We know the struggles we have avoiding and rejecting sin. Paul knew it and wrote about it in Romans 7:14-25. Paul knew that the ability to sin was always present and that a spiritual war was going on in his heart and mind. He also knew that God gave him strength and that he was not condemned (Romans 8:1).

> What is the condition of the heart if Satan rules it? The heart is the source of many nasty things. *See* Matthew 15:19 for a short list.

> The unredeemed heart is *desperately wicked*. But, GOOD NEWS! Because of your faith, Christ has evicted Satan, has moved into your heart, and has cleaned house. We now have a continual house warming party (Ephesians 3:16-17).

> The heart is deceitful until God's love dwells in it. Hence, the need for Christ to die for our sins; our deceitful hearts need to be changed to be made His dwelling place.

> We don't get a heart transplant - we do get a heart transformed. Our heart is cleaned out and occupied by Him Who helped create us in the first place. Truly, this is Christ in us. When He is in our hearts, we not only have the mind of Christ, we have the emotions of Christ.

Prayer - Dear Father, thank you for transforming my heart into a suitable dwelling place for Jesus Christ and Your Holy Spirit.

August 8   Testimony

Luke 21:12b-15 *You will be brought before kings and rulers for My name's sake. But IT will turn out for you as an occasion for testimony. Therefore settle IT in your hearts not to meditate beforehand on what you will answer; for I will give you a mouth and wisdom ...*

IT refers to being brought before an audience.

Q Will it be a bad thing to be brought before people for the sake of Jesus' name?   No. *IT* gives us a chance to witness of what Jesus has done for us.

We may not be brought before kings and rulers but we are certainly in the audience of many people of high and low authority. In Acts 1:8 we find that we are to be witnesses at home and abroad. Whenever we are in public we are *before* someone. We do need to *settle in our hearts* that each aspect of our lives will always be in service to God. Every word and activity is an occasion for testimony.

In Exodus, Chapter 4, we find Moses being prepared to talk to Pharaoh.

Peter wrote a companion verse: Be constantly prepared to defend your hope in Christ, if anyone asks, but do it with gentleness and respect for their needs (1 Peter 3:15b). We don't want to insult them or scare them off. The readiness may be constantly allowing the Holy Spirit to speak to the general public or it may be preparation for a specific kind of audience – anyone who asks.

The Holy Spirit can use our lives to generate a question. Like, "How can you be so calm in this turmoil?," or "How can you take abuse like that without striking back?"

Life is full of chances for verbal testimony. Be alert for them. Remember however that much of communication in social gatherings is non-verbal. Our social language testifies loudly and clearly about Who dwells in our hearts and minds.

The nature of the world and the nature of mankind will give us ample opportunity to testify about the nature of Jesus. Let us always be ready, whomever God presents to us, to enthusiastically show them or tell them the Good News, with boldness.

Prayer - Dear Father, thank You for endless opportunities to testify for You. I want to be alert for them.

August 9   Prepared

1 Corinthians 2:9-10 *As IT is written: Eye has not seen nor ear heard, nor have entered into the heart of man the things which God has prepared for those who love Him.* (Quote from Isaiah 64:4). *But God has revealed them to us through His Spirit.*

IT refers to what God has prepared.

Q What was there, up to that point, that man didn't know?

Things for which God has prepared us.

We love Him. So what has He prepared for us and how are we to see, hear, or receive in our hearts about His preparation? We need to look at the following passages to determine some answers to this mystery.

We now have the mind of Christ (1 Corinthians 2:16). This is part of what God has prepared for us. Another part is that He has prepared in us a dwelling place for His Spirit. The Holy Spirit now dwells in us (1 Corinthians 3:16). We are now called God's temple. All of this is what was beyond the capabilities of humans to think of or to accept. But now it is true. We are His temple; the Holy Spirit is alive in us; and we have the mind of Christ. Mystery solved, WOW!

As we learned yesterday, Christ now dwells in our hearts because of the faith given to us by God. Jesus and the Holy Spirit now live in our hearts. God is no longer some exterior being. He is alive in us and brings us to life in Him. He has now gone through our eyes, ears, and the internal information of the Holy Spirit, and ended up in our hearts. He has prepared this for us because He loves us and we love Him. We love Him because He first loved us. John, in his gospel and shorter letters taught us a lot about God's love. It is interesting that John paraphrased his own statement of John 3:16 in 1 John 4:10. Jesus' love gives us eternal life.

Now, our eyes see, and our ears hear. Christ has entered our hearts because God has prepared us to love Him. The Holy Spirit dwells in us and we have Christ's mind, so we can think as He thinks. He has prepared eternal life for us. Thanks be to God!

Prayer - Dear Father, I love You and thank You that I can trust the things You have prepared for me.

August 10   Not My Will

Mark 14:35-36 *Jesus went a little farther, and fell on the ground and prayed that if IT were possible, the hour might pass from Him ..."Take this cup away from Me; nevertheless, not My will but what You will."*

IT means the hope that crucifixion would not be necessary.

Q What is the possibility of another means of relationship with God?
None.

No person or religion outside of Christ can save us; nor should there be. It is only in His name and nature that we must find salvation (Acts 4:12).

Why look for another way when God offers the *way* of forgiveness and relationship with Him? Such a futile senseless and unproductive waste of time leads to a dead end.

Some people resent Christians because we testify to God's promise of everlasting life (John 6:68). They shouldn't blame us, it wasn't our idea. Ask them, "Do you have a better way – a sure way - or any way at all?"

Today's Scripture tells us that *Jesus went a little farther, and fell* – He didn't casually lie down, He *fell*. This was an excruciating time. He was in Gethsemane, the oil press, and the pressure on Him was intense. He was considering the awesome, ugly task of taking all the sins of all time in His Person through the act of crucifixion. Was it possible that the *hour might pass*? No, sin is so indescribably horrible that something indescribably terrible had to happen to pay the price for your and my redemption.

When receiving the *cup* of communion we testify that communion is serious business. We are not to take of the *cup* in an unworthy manner or we share the blame of re-crucifying Christ (1 Corinthians 11:27).

Nevertheless -- In this incredible night in history, a most important question was asked and answered - Is it possible? No. And His death, and our life, were sealed.

Not My will. The humanity of Jesus was speaking here. *But what You will.* The divinity of Jesus overcame the humanity. These phrases became the bottom line of all prayer for followers of Christ, "*Not my will, but what You will.*"

Prayer - Dear Father, in my Gethsemanes, *not my will*, but Yours be done.

August 11   Intercession

<u>Isaiah 53:10-12</u> *Yet IT pleased the Lord to bruise Him, He has put Him to grief. When You make His soul an offering for sin … My righteous Servant shall justify many … He shall bear their iniquities … and* (He) *made intercession for the transgressors.*

> IT refers to the bruising (crucifixion) of Christ.

Q How could it please God to sacrifice His Son?

> God wanted relationship with us. But we were infected with sin. He had to remove our sin to establish relationship. There was only one way to do this. God had to separate Himself from Jesus and place our sin on Him. This met the need and fulfilled God's desire.
>
> The awfulness of sin required a tremendous sacrifice. <u>He gave His only Son.</u> The prophecy in Isaiah was fulfilled in God's gift in Christ (John 3:16). Jesus died that we might live in love, joy, and peace, now and forever.
>
> In today's verse, *Him, His, He,* all refer to God or Christ. Jesus was the focal point of creation and He is the focal point of re - creation – redemption.
>
> Further, *He has put Him to grief.* Yesterday we considered the grief that Jesus endured in the second garden. Jesus remarked that he was so grief stricken that it felt like the sentence of death (Matthew 26:38).
>
> What love! What fantastic, wonderful love, that God has shown for us - that we are His children! (1 John 3:1). Only a fully dedicated life can express what our words are not sufficient to say.

Prayer - Dear Father, words cannot express our gratitude for Your inexpressible love. I thank You with my life.

August 12   Blessed

<u>Luke 11:28</u> Jesus said, *"More than that, blessed are those who hear the word of God and keep IT"*

Blessed - given extreme favor.

IT refers to *the word.*

Q How can we be blessed?

Hear and *keep the word of God.*

What is the word of God? The Word of God is the instruction that we have in the Bible.

We are blessed, first of all, when we hear of the Word. Of all the billions of words that are spoken and printed, the most precious are those that tell us of our Redeemer and our redemption.

We are to read the word: think of the Bible as a nourishing beverage (1 Peter 2:2b), and

we are to listen to the word. We can trust what Jesus tells us (Ephesians 1:13a).

Another blessing comes when we remember and keep the Word (James 1:22-25).

There is no way of estimating the trouble we avoid by living according to the teachings of God. When one thinks of the financial burden placed on the United States tax payers as the result of law breakers, self-abuse, fornication, and breaking other of God's rules, the amount is staggering. That total is compounded by individual hardships and tragedies. Thankfully, we have the mind of Christ and the guidance of the Holy Spirit to think things through to the likely end of positive personal and godly social choices.

To receive the blessing of God is so much better than anything else we can imagine.

Prayer - Dear Father, thank You for Your Word, Jesus, and Your word, the Bible.

August 13   Returned

Luke 22:31-32 *And the Lord said, "Simon, Simon! Indeed, Satan has asked for you, that he may sift you AS wheat, but I have prayed for you, that your faith should not fail; and when you have returned to Me, strengthen your brethren."*

AS means like sifted wheat.

Q What if we get sifted? Satan keeps the chaff and throws away the wheat.

God sifts us and keeps the *wheat.*

Not to work the parable too hard, but we are a combination of *wheat* and chaff. Chaff is the husk that encloses the kernel of wheat. The threshing process, in those days, was to put the heads of the wheat stems on the threshing floor, tread on them to separate the wheat from the chaff, and then throw the mix into the air to let the wind blow away the lighter chaff. Hopefully, through the process of sanctification, we get rid of more and more chaff. Sometimes oxen were used to walk on the heads. God uses different methods to separate us from our chaff.

"Simon, Simon" was equivalent to an exclamation point "!". What was Peter's chaff? He didn't want Jesus to be killed (Matthew 16:23). It is interesting to consider the life of Peter between this pronouncement and the events following the resurrection - Peter's desertion at the arrest site, his denial by the fire, his despair when Jesus looked at him, his discovery at the empty tomb, and his dive into the Sea of Tiberias, - all led to his dedication and he said, "*Lord, You know all things; You know that I love You*" John 21:17b. What is your journey?

In an Old Testament parallel Satan also asked for Job (Job 1:12). Satan is still asking. He asks for you and me. As we consider our desertions, denials, and despair, followed by discovery, dives, and dedication, we are thankful that Jesus prays for us then as now and doesn't allow Satan to have us. As for Peter, so for us - that our faith should not fail. We rejoice because *we have an inheritance incorruptible and undefiled and that does not fade away, reserved in heaven for you, who are kept by the power of God through faith* … 1 Peter 1:4.

The *brethren* are strengthened by our discovery of Christ, our dive into Christ, and our dedication to Christ.

Prayer - Dear Father, thank You for your prayers and for allowing me to return again and again.

August 14   Faith

Romans 4:16 *Therefore IT is of faith that IT might be according to grace.*

IT refers to the promise that Abraham was declared righteous.

Q Why must it be of faith?

So that grace may abound (Romans 5:15).

Faith and grace are two very important words in our relationship with God. They are far more important to relationship than they are to religions. Remember, religion is a set of behaviors. Relationship is a state of being.

Faith, in religions, is something the believer has to conjure up. But faith, in relationship with God is a gift. Grace is not a big word in religions because religious people depend on works. Ephesians 2:8 wraps them together in a powerful statement that does not depend on our efforts. There is nothing we need to do except to accept.

Once we know and accept, believe and receive, that faith is a gift from God, we don't have to worry if we have enough faith or if our faith is good enough. He has given us the necessary and sufficient faith so it is perfect. The promises of God are faithful as they are received by perfect faith that is given to us.

Grace, also is a gift – Paul was always thankful for Jesus' gift of grace (1 Corinthians 1:4). Grace, as we have studied, is total forgiveness and acceptance that we don't deserve. Grace, for the world, is one of the most difficult attributes of God to understand. When something, often sinful, isn't working, Satan's answer is, "Do it harder". Grace, for Christians, is one of the simplest things to understand. Once we come to the understanding that we can't do IT ourselves, and that God has done IT for us, we confess our sins and our needs and come before Him in humble gratitude. Then grace can abound and bounce and reverberate and fill our lives with the fullness of God. I wouldn't have seen grace if I hadn't received God's gift of faith to believe it.

God's gifts of faith and grace combine to make us righteous before Him.

Prayer - Dear Father, thank you for the gifts of faith and grace. I accept them in their simplicity and power.

August 15   Right

<u>John 1:12</u> *But AS many AS received Him, to them He gave the right to become children of God, to those who believed in His name who were born, not of blood, nor of the will of the flesh, nor of the will of man, but of God.*

AS refers to receivers.

Q What is the importance of receiving Christ?   We become children of God.

This is another powerful salvation verse. It was, and is, my salvation verse.

WHO? *As many.*

WHAT? Were born of God.

WHY? *He gave the right to become children of God.*

This right is a gift, not something we deserve or earn. It follows that we were not His children before.

HOW? *... as received Him - to those who believed in His name (nature).*

Not of blood – Not of earthly parents; God doesn't have grandchildren,

Nor the will of the flesh – not by our devices or the strength of our personal will,

Nor of the will of man – no one else's will, no matter how good their intentions.

WHERE and WHEN? Right here, right now. When we believe and receive Him.

The transaction is immediate because it is affected by God's grace, not our efforts.

There are those who believe but don't receive. Let us do both.

Have you done it? If not, do it, and pass from eternal death to eternal life.

Prayer - Dear Father, "I receive Jesus into my mind and heart and I believe He is my Savior. I'll trust Him to show me the details later."

August 16   Grieve Not

1 Thessalonians 4:13 *I do not want you to be ignorant about those who have fallen asleep lest you grieve AS others do who have no hope.*

Hope - anticipation about something we want to have happen.

AS refers to grievers.

Q Why don't we grieve as others do?

Because we have hope. We do grieve at the physical death of a loved one but there is comfort if that person is in Christ because we will be reunited. Our hope is in Jesus Who gives us victory over death!

Make a special place in your hearts for God; be quick to defend to anyone who wants to know why you hope in Him (1 Peter 3:15). USE THE FOLLOWING THREE VERSES for the defense of your hope. Look them up.

Confession leads to cleanliness   (1 John 1:9).

Hope leads to purification   (1 John 3:3).

God's greatness leads to assurance   (1John 3:19-20).

I used these three verses consistently with clients and the verses were a powerful aid in improving mental and spiritual health. Study them, accept them for yourself, and ask the Spirit to give you clarity in presenting them to those whom He has prepared.

1. *I do not want you to be ignorant* - that is, I want you to know the truth -
2. *About those who have fallen* asleep - that have experienced physical death -
3. *So you don't grieve as others do who have no hope* - we grieve, but not without hope.

We can thank God that He has given us victory over sin and the law through the redeeming work of Christ (1Corinthians 15:56-57).

This is our hope.

Prayer - Dear Father, thank You for the truth about loved ones having left this life in Christ.

August 17   Walk

Ephesians 4:17 ... *you should no longer walk AS the rest of the Gentiles walk, in the futility of their mind ...*

AS refers to the way the world walks.

Q How should we walk? We should walk in the purpose and power of God.

Futile is defined as meaning incapable of producing any useful result. To be futile of mind makes a person's life seem rather pointless – a sad commentary.

Speaking of the futility of the mind – Man's best thinking leads to death (Proverbs 14:12). The teaching is clear - the world walks in sin. Read God's spiritual lips. The wages of man's futile best thinking is death (Romans 6:23).

The worldly things of extramarital sexual desire, lascivious looks, and pride in personal achievements is not of God (1 John 2:16). Living in lust sounds like another oxymoron. Lust is not living; it is the futility of a pointless life.

So, what is the answer? How can we avoid the consequences of sin? In order to have a meaningful walk, we need to walk in the Spirit (Galatians 5:24). Jesus gave His life for us that we might reach a transition point. We can leave the way of death and enter the way of life everlasting. It goes like this:

Our way = death. Jesus, Holy Spirit way = life.

As Christians we no longer walk as the "Gentiles" walk. Gentiles are anyone who is spiritually blind, leading or following a spiritually blind person. Don't let Satan's lies prevent you from knowing the truth about the Holy Spirit. Are you going to trust the father of lies?

When we are in Christ we are capable of thinking as He did (1Corinthians 2:16b). Let us follow His thoughts and teachings and ask for and receive God's gift of the Devine Director. If we would just ask, God will cheerfully gift us with His Spirit (Luke 11:13). Then, and only then, does our walk shift from futility to productivity.

Prayer - Dear Father, may I consciously let every step be guided by Your Spirit.

August 18   Led

<u>Romans 8:14</u> *For AS many AS are led by the Spirit of God are the sons of God.*

AS refers to the sons of God. This is another look at being led by God's Spirit. Here, the emphasis is on the fact of being led.

Q Why should we seek, receive, and be *led* by the Spirit? That we might become children of God and be *led* by Him.

We will be guided in all truth when the Holy Spirit comes to us (John 16:13). The truth that sets us free! On the other hand, we could follow Satan – he will guide into all error. Is that what you want? Be warned: The only reason Satan enters our lives is to rob, murder and destroy any semblance of God's goodness and grace (John 10:10). A classic example of this in Scripture is the story of Judas. Satan entered into Judas (Luke 22:3). After Judas betrayed Jesus, feeling remorse, he tried to give back the bribe money but was scornfully rejected (Matthew 27:3-5). What a payment for following Satan! Satan entered into Judas, Judas followed Satan's lead, and the whole process ended in Judas' death. Once you have done Satan's bidding, you get nothing from him but a scornful laugh. The *thirty pieces of silver* take on many disguises to tempt us.

Spending time with evil people will rot your good intentions so don't try to join in with their activities (1Corinthians15:33, 2 Corinthians 6:14). Don't bow to negative peer pressure; choose companions wisely.

Choice is an interesting thing. We make thousands of choices every day, every act - every step, and a choice is made in what we do with every thought. After enough practice a choice becomes a habit. Wisdom has it that 15 - 20 repetitions make a choice a habit. Choice is a wonderful thing when we choose to be *led by the Spirit* and make the right choice. Choice is a terrible thing when we choose wrongly. We get good at what we practice. If we want to change a habit, we need to make the choice to do the new behavior - again and again. Don't despair. God is patient and He isn't through with you yet. Whew! – a lot here. We should be sick and tired of being sick and sinful. We should resent the results of following Satan. Choose, this day, whom you will serve – follow the Holy Spirit.

Prayer - Dear Father, I choose You, knowing that You know everything about me and love me anyway. Turn my rebellion to renewal and my resentment to rejoicing.

August 19   Heart

<u>1 Samuel 16:7b</u> *For the Lord does not see AS man sees, for man looks at the outward appearance, but the Lord looks at the heart.*

AS refers to the outward appearance.

Q How does God look at us?

He looks at our hearts.

... man looks at the outward appearance ...

<u>Is this ever true</u>! The whole cosmetics industry, and so many other industries, capitalize on this. Women are often introduced as - "The beautiful -," or "The lovely -." Flatter a woman, give her candy, flowers or a piece of jewelry and she is supposed to melt in your arms. Really? Why not - "The intelligent -?" or "The competent -?"

Physical beauty, enhanced by fancy hairdos, jewelry, and clothes, is only surface deep. Real beauty comes from the heart that shows itself in God's precious attributes of gentleness and a calm spirit (1 Peter 3:3). <u>This applies to both genders</u>.

Clothes make the man. Really? Only if there is a man inside them. Now Peter does say, " *not ... merely outward ...".* But the outward appearance doesn't change a wolf into a sheep. How people look and what they do are often two different things.

We need to look at what is on the inside - the heart. A pure spring yields clear, fresh water, a clean heart is the source of positive action (Matthew 12:35).

If our hearts are clogged with the arteriosclerosis of sin, God, Who created us, has a pill for that, the Gospill (Intended). Therefore, our prayer should be that God would make our hearts pure and sanitary (Psalm 51:10). Notice that we need to ask. We have the wonderful gift of choice of what we do with the answer.

Prayer - Dear Father, I give You my heart, and my whole body. Please make me all You want me to be for Your purposes.

August 20   Good

Genesis 50:20 *But AS for you, you meant evil against me, but God meant it for good, in order to bring it about AS it is this day ...*

AS refers to a situation of intended evil.

Q What is to be our attitude about evils?

If you love God and believe it to be true, God can bring good out of any circumstance (Romans 8:28). If there is a lot of manure around, look for the pony.

See Genesis Chapter 37, and following, for the entire story of Joseph. The words convenient and prevenient apply to this historical narrative. They are based on avenue - a pathway of opportunity. The prefix con- means with and pre- means before. God's convenient grace is with us in the now and His prevenient grace is there before we are.

So, in God's prevenient grace - all the events in the saga had to occur. With a little thought, you can recall many things that may have seemed inconvenient, painful, or even tragic at the time that have resulted in bringing meaning and glory to God's love and purpose. Inconvenient (not with avenue) means they seem out of place in our journey.

Tribulation brings comfort. Receive His comfort. Share His comfort. If we trust God, seek and receive His comfort, even in the worst of our troubles, we'll get comfort for ourselves and be prepared to be a true comfort for anyone whatever their problem (2 Corinthians 1:3-4).

Don't worry about anything. Anything and everything can be used by God to bring incomprehensible peace (Philippians 4:6-7). Ask Him how He can use the event. Share in the sufferings of Christ. When you are able, ask, "Why is this the best thing that could happen?"

Discipline brings righteousness. An experience that isn't fun at the time will often result in a new mindset that brings us peace (Hebrews 12:11), and prepare us to be a comfort for others.

Joseph's experience brought about the saving of his family from starvation.

Prayer - Dear Father, if evil befalls me, I know that You have allowed it and You will work in it for good.

August 21   Remind

2 Peter 1:12-13 ... *be even more diligent to make your call and election sure, for if you do these things you will never stumble ... For this reason I will not be negligent to remind you always of these things, though you know and are established in the present truth. Yes, I think it is right, AS long AS I am in this tent, to stir you up by reminding you...*

AS refers to being alive in His body.

Q Should we be reminded and told again and again?

Yes!

Reminders are so important. There is a standard app on cell phones for reminders. We make lists so we don't end up a day with unfinished business. Our spiritual life, of great importance, deserves due diligence of reminders. A set time, each day, for Scripture and prayer, icons around the house, encouragement from friends – there are many ways to keep the pot stirred.

Peter was aware that even servants of God can become complacent. Peter was going to continue reminding them as long as there was breath in his body. So, to stir them up, Peter felt it was his duty and privilege to remind them of the sum and substance of life in Christ.

I have followed Peter's example, as you have noticed, in examining the same passages in different ways, often using a different LITTLE WORD to emphasize the same truth. I want you to become close friends with these passages so they are stored in your heart and mind.

As far as I am concerned, I want, and appreciate, frequent reminders of what is required to be a faithful servant, and what it is like to obtain the manifold gifts of God.

Prayer - Dear Father, I thank You for those who remind us of the truth about Jesus and how the Holy Spirit helps us live in Him.

August 22   I AM

Exodus 3:14 *And God said to Moses, "I AM Who I AM."*

AM refers to the name of God.

Q What is God's name?

I AM Who I AM.

This is not only God's name, it describes His eternal being.

This is kind of a Pete and Repeat thing. Pete and Repeat were sitting on a fence and Pete fell off. Who was left? Repeat. Etc.   Who is I AM that I AM? I AM. Who is I AM? ... God always was, is, and always will be. Nothing else makes sense.

Those who say, "There is no God," have a lot of explaining to do. The Big Bang Theory just doesn't cut it. Something doesn't come from nothing. Intelligent Design is inadequate. That doesn't explain emotionality. Evolution of man from apes isn't a good explanation because it isn't still happening. To find one skull and base a whole theory on it is curious thinking. The idea that man developed from some organism that started in an oil puddle is preposterous.

God sent Jesus into the world to show His existence and His purpose. Jesus said, "If you see Me, really see ME, you have seen God!" (John 14:9b). The disciples saw God in the earthly form of Jesus. Jesus may have been referring more to God's character than His Person. We who know Jesus today know His character.

Jesus prayed. *"O righteous Father! The world has not known You, but I have known You; and these have known that You sent Me. And I have declared to them Your name, and will declare it, that the love with which You loved Me may be in them, and I in them"* John 17:25-26. As stated earlier in this passage, *them* refers to all who believe in Jesus. The *name* of God is His nature.

As examined in January 18's devotion, Jesus used the I AM identifier many times, most often to describe a work or an attribute. As far as our eternal destiny is concerned,   we are because He AM (is).

Prayer - Dear Father, I accept You as God and I enjoy our loving personal relationship.

August 23   Denied

John 18:25b ... *they said to him* (Peter), *"You are not also one of His disciples are you?" He denied it and said, "I AM not!"*

Here, AM refers to a negative use of I am. A denial of identification.

Q ... *You are not* ... are you? What? "Yes, I mean No", What? Many of us share this confusion today.

Note how the question was worded. This is one of those "Do you still beat your grandmother?" questions. Whether you answer, "Yes", or "No", you are a bad person. If Peter had said, "Yes." then he would have denied Christ because he would be saying, "Yes, I am not." They meant, "Are you a disciple of Christ?" Peter, out of fear, fell in line and said, "I am not."

People don't always ask; they may just look at us with an evil eye and we fold. Quite often by being in a given place at a given time, we deny being a disciple. When we can avoid those circumstances, it is best to do so. If we are unfortunate enough to get blind-sided, and can't take a verbal stand, we need to leave. Look for one of God's means of escape. It is easier to stay out of trouble than to get out of trouble. INSTANT REPLAY - It is easier to stay out of trouble than to get out of trouble.

The main reason we may deny Christ is that the place or people who are around us are more important to us than our relationship with God. INSTANT REPLAY - the place or people who are around us are more important to us than our relationship with God. Give that due thought. Jesus, on the other hand is not ashamed to be called our Savior. Jesus is the positive I AM.

In Mark 9:38, we find the sobering thought that, when He returns, He will be ashamed of us if we are ashamed of Him. What is necessary is that the power that comes to us in Christ is greater than the power that Satan wields over us.

We can join with Paul in saying, "I'm proud of the good news of Jesus because it powers believers into salvation" (Romans 1:16).

Are you one of His disciples?

Prayer - Dear Father, may the world be so dead to me that I never hold any part of it more precious than confessing You as my Lord and Savior.

August 24   Deliver

Romans 7:14-25 *I AM carnal, for what I will to do, that I do not practice; what I hate, I do. It is no longer I who do it, but sin that dwells in me. … O wretched man that I AM, Who will deliver me from this body of death? I thank God through Jesus Christ our Lord!*

AM - Paul identifies himself as carnal and wretched.

Q What is Paul's struggle? He finds himself doing what he hates. (Carnal - worldly desires and appetites.)

There are those who say this is Paul's pre-Christian condition but he uses present tense words. Perhaps he is in process, thinking of during and after. This passage does not name his struggle; maybe it was his *thorn in the flesh* (2 Corinthians 12:7). Perhaps the lack of identification is best because it may apply to any struggle we have. The good news is that Jesus delivered him, and us.

Meanwhile: The question - *"Wretched man that I am, Who will deliver me from this body of death?"* The answer, Christ Jesus; because those who reside in Him are not condemned by anyone, self, or others (Romans 8:1).

No condemnation! (What a shout of victory! We not only have victory over death, we have victory over life. Paul did not feel he was given permission to sin. He had covered that in Romans 6.

I have joined Paul so many times in his lament. It is a continual war. Perhaps you have also had this experience. But, take heart. The fact that we hate what we do is evidence of our position in Christ. If we ever get to the point that we are comfortable in sin, we have a real problem.

We strive to go forward in the process of sanctification. Don't return to a wallow.

God would rather have us rejoice in His grace than to spend our days agonizing over our weaknesses. *There is no condemnation …* And, we are not to retain our sins against ourselves. That can be a sin in itself. Why sin against ourselves? How have you been spending your days, lamenting or rejoicing? Focus on grace, rejoice!

Prayer - Dear Father, thank you that I can rejoice and find strength in Your sufficient grace!

August 25   Ambassador

Ephesians 6:19-20 ... *the mystery of the gospel for which I AM an ambassador in chains ...*

AM refers to being an ambassador - a representative.

Q What was Paul's primary identity? An ambassador.

For which? Which is the *mystery of the gospel.* The gospel was a *mystery* because it was difficult for people in that time to see Jews and Gentiles in relationship with each other, let alone the two groups in relationship with God.

Paul was in prison because of his work in and for the Gospel of Christ. That had resulted in his being chained between two guards.

What are our *chains?* An illness? A handicap? A mental condition? Our station in life? Whatever the chains, we are ambassadors for Christ.

What is our responsibility in the *mystery of the gospel?* It is, like Paul's, bringing people together in Christ. There are many people today who do not see the possibility of different denominations in relationship with each other. But, what about heaven? Do we all tiptoe around?

Anyway, In our times in "chains", others see our real selves come out. In those times when we are where nobody knows who we are, who are we? We can be positive or negative. We are either the fragrance of Christ or the stench of a sneak. People will notice. We are witnesses of something to someone all of the time.

It should be obvious that griping about our God given circumstances is not attractive to observers or to Him Who loves us.

He has given Himself to us as a present. We are to re-present Him, sharing our present with others (2 Corinthians 5:18). It is our desire to represent Christ, to show others Who He is. We re-present Him one way or another. Let it be joy in His presents (intended) and His presence.

Prayer - Dear Father, help me at all times and in all circumstances to show others that Jesus loves and transforms us into His image.

August 26   Midst

<u>Matthew 18:20</u> *For where two or three are gathered together in My name, I AM there in the midst of them.*

AM means existing with them.

Q Why meet with siblings in Christ's nature? So Christ is in our gathering.

This is another example of the "I AM" nature of Christ going back to God's declaration to Moses,

"I AM WHO I AM" <u>Exodus 3:14</u>.

Jesus is the most significant Log in the fire when two or three are gathered together. This occurs when we are gathered in His name, that is, His nature. The nature of Christ is to be our Savior, that is, He Who justifies us so that we have relationship with God. When we gather, His attributes of love and forgiveness are shared and we can rid ourselves of self-accusations and be assured of forgiveness. When we look into eyes of love and forgiveness, we see ourselves as God sees us. Therefore, we don't go out and kill ourselves in sinful activities.

As we have learned, He not only is in our midst, He is IN each of us in the Person of His Spirit Who is IN us, assuring our spiritual selves that we are God's children (Romans 8:16). In turn, His Spirit in each of us testifies to His Spirit in each other of us so that love and forgiveness are shared. The fruit of the Spirit, love, joy, peace, etc., is strongly active in these gatherings. What a party!

We are to gather In His name so that we don't become complacent in our relationship with Him (Revelation 2:4). We have His word that He will be there. If and whenever we feel our flame is dying out, we need to gather with Christian siblings in His nature. The less we feel like doing that, the more imperative it is that we gather together.

Prayer - Dear Father, thank You for Your presence in our gatherings.

August 27   Believe

John 11:25-27 *Jesus said to her, "I AM the resurrection and the life. He who believes in Me though he may die, he shall live. And whoever lives and believes in Me shall never die. Do you believe this?" "Yes, Lord, I believe that You are the Christ, the Son of God ..."*

AM refers to Jesus as the means of resurrection and life.

Q What is our assurance that we have eternal life?   Jesus said so.

Martha affirmed her belief and stated why Jesus had the authority to make His claim. Jesus echoes the words God used as He told Moses His name, "I AM Who I AM." Jesus is God and He is the I AM of God. With this authority, He plainly tells Martha the result of His work in human form.

Before we can have life after death, we need to have life in life, our own resurrection to newness of life. This occurs when we make the decision to accept Christ as our Savior and Lord. Jesus used the physical death of Lazarus to give evidence of His authority to grant eternal spiritual life.

Today's scripture essentially says, "Whoever believes in Me Lives in Me". We live in Christ because He lives in us and we are in Him through the work of God.

And when Jesus says, "*shall never die*," He is speaking of eternal, spiritual life. In order to enter eternal life we must give our life to Him. This is not a loss we regret but a gain in which we rejoice.

It is through belief in Jesus that we gain everlasting life. Those who reject Jesus have an eternal existence but it is a miserable everlasting death (Matthew 8:12). This thought is so terrible that many people want to deny it. But, Jesus said it, so if you have a problem, talk to Him. Simple answer - don't worry about everlasting death, believe in Christ and have everlasting life! And tell your friends and family and anyone else.

The same promise is ours today. *And whoever lives and believes in Me shall never die.*

Prayer - Dear Father, thank you for Your life in me that gives me life in You, now and forever.

August 28   Receive

<u>John 14:3</u> *I will come again and receive you to Myself, that where I AM there you may be also.*

AM refers to where Jesus is.

Q Will we be with Jesus?

Yes, *where I AM there you may be also.*

John 14:1-4 is one of the most comforting passages in the Bible. It is often used at funerals and gives solace to believers. If you need a boost to your faith in a challenging time, don't be in distress, turn to, read, and meditate on these words of comfort and strength.

Jesus will come and get us so we can be with Him. It is as if we fall asleep on the couch and our Heavenly Father carries us so that we wake up in bed. In Christ, death is just a shadow. We enter the valley of the shadow of death and come out in the Sonshine (intended).

After the promise of the resurrection, we have the promise that He will come for us – He will receive us unto Himself. In John 1:12 we are told, "Believe and receive Christ. That gives you the privilege of becoming a child of God". We have received Him and He promises that He will receive us.

Jesus has prepared a place for us and He will be there also. Don't be confused because, as the world turns, what was up is down. Wherever heaven is, it is with Jesus.

We won't have to stumble around in the darkness of death to find where Jesus is. He will come and get us. We are His precious children, purchased at the highest price ever paid. What a homecoming!

Prayer - Dear Father, thank You for being with us in life and giving us hope in death. We rest in Your care.

August 29   Teach

Exodus 4:10-12 *Then Moses said to the Lord, "O my Lord, I AM not eloquent ... but I AM slow of speech and slow of tongue."... so the Lord said to him, "... go, and I will be with your mouth and teach you what you shall say."*

AM refers to Moses' feeling of inadequacy.

Q What does God do with our excuses?

He promises to be with us and supply strength for any weakness. We should not seek a way out of what God wants us to do. We should seek His way of enabling us to do it. INSTANT REPLAY - We should seek His way of enabling us to do it.

Here is a negative use of I am. In this case, not the awesome power of God, but the weakness of humanity. Whatever our reasons for not following the urging of the Holy Spirit, God will gift us for the task to which He appoints us. There have been many times in my psychological practice that I have prayed for direction in a circumstance and have been led to work in a way that had never occurred to me before. In the preparation of this collection of devotions, I have continually prayed for and received direction to verses and thoughts that fit together like a neat puzzle. Sometimes, the devotions seem to write themselves.

Moses may have had a legitimate excuse or he may have been remembering the fear he had for Pharaoh that caused him to run from the Egyptians in the first place. He thought he was going to be killed because he had killed an Egyptian (Exodus 2:11-15).

God assured Moses, *... I will be with your mouth and teach you what you shall say.* Jesus gave a similar promise to His disciples,"*... for I will give you a mouth and wisdom which all your adversaries will not be able to contradict or resist"* Luke 21:15.

This reminds us again of the wonderful passage in 1 Peter 3:15 – always be armed and ready to share the good news with anyone who wants to know why we have hope, especially during rough times.

Don't worry about it, ask Him.

Prayer - Dear Father, thank You for the words to say when the opportunity arises.

August 30   Persuaded

2 Timothy 1:12 *I know whom I have believed and AM persuaded that He is able to keep what I have committed to Him until that Day.*

> AM indicates confidence.

Q Why did Paul believe?   He was persuaded.

How was Paul persuaded? His conversion experience, many miracles, his conversations with the Apostles, and the sufferings that Jesus predicted he would experience all convinced Paul of the truth about Jesus (Acts 1:3).

Paul's original mindset was that Christians were the enemy and that they should be exterminated. However, Paul was well versed in the Scriptures and knew all the prophesies about Jesus as well as what happened during Jesus life, death, and resurrection. These were the "goads" against which he was kicking (Acts 9:5). He had to know the church leaders were wrong. Jesus confronted Paul and Paul made a U-turn, committed his life to Christ and gave up all else for a life of service to God. He was made blind so he could see.

When my wife and I were on a vision mission to Honduras with our optometrist son, we saw a two wheeled cart, piled high with branches, pulled by two oxen. The driver had the reins in one hand and a long pointed stick (a goad) in the other. When he wanted the oxen to move, he would poke them. They could either move or kick. This scene brought Paul's experience to life.

Because of all that had happened in his past, Paul was certain of his future in Christ. Life or death, which? Hard to choose, the advantages of life now in Christ or the benefit of life eternal (Philippians 1:21).

God doesn't want blind faith; *come now and let us reason together, though your sins are like scarlet, they shall be as white as snow ...* Isaiah 1:18. As we have examined, and will continue to examine many scriptural passages that speak so eloquently to our personal experience, we too, are persuaded that Jesus is able to keep our lives that we have committed to Him.

Prayer - Dear Father, thank You for His story, the his-story of our faith, and the witness of Your Spirit persuading us of the validity of Your commitment to us and our commitment to You.

August 31   Righteousness

Proverbs 16:31 *The silver-haired head is a crown of glory, if IT is found in the way of righteousness.*

IT refers to a silver-haired head.

Q When is a silver–haired head to be honored?

When it is found righteous.

Many "silver-hairs" know a lot about inadequate things, see the list in Colossians 2:21-23. Christianity is not a religion based on actions. We are not just a group of actors (act or). We are the Body of Christ. Understanding the mystery of the Gospel is knowing that we are saved by grace - through faith - for works. Christianity is a relationship.

What does give a silver-hair a *crown of glory* is expressed in Colossians 2:2b-3.

Obviously a *silver-haired head* belongs to an older person. With age is supposed to be accumulated wisdom. True wisdom is to find the way of righteousness - Jesus Christ.

Today's Scripture, *... if IT is found ...* implies that the bearer of silver hair may not find the way of righteousness. Many are not even looking for it. Thankfully, God is ever seeking to convict us of thoughts that cause us to consider Him (John 16:8b).

When, and if, we attain that age where we have a *silver-haired head,* may it be found in the *way of righteousness*! Jesus said, "I am the way ..."

Prayer - Dear Father, thank You for leading me in the way of *righteousness.*

SEPTEMBER

DO

Meditation aids

DO is a verb, usually used as an auxiliary word making up a verb phrase. The phrase combines the verb with its auxiliary partner and modifies another word in the verse. Many of the verses use the phrase, *Do not* which helps us know that we should DO the opposite.

Uses of DO: Achieve or complete an action

Example:

I can DO all things through Christ Who strengthens me <u>Philippians 4:13</u>.

Do all things is a verb phrase with *all* as a modifier.

Things are the object of the verb DO.

September 1   Name

Colossians 3:17 *Whatever you DO in word or deed, DO all in the name of the Lord Jesus, giving thanks to God the Father through Him.*

DO means to act.

Q What should be our goal in life's activities?

Whatever we do, do all in the name of the Lord Jesus. All:

In word - everything we say.

In deed - everything we do.

EVERYTHING

There should not be a difference between what we say and what we do because what we do may drown out what we say. In Philippians 4:9, we find a powerful motto:

Whatever I do

You do

And God's peace will be with you

This is one of the guiding principles for my life. We need to remember that the *name* of Jesus refers to His nature, that is, His being. What we want to do is to reflect His Person in us.

To say that, "Jesus is Lord," brings all that we do in subjection to Him. Since I was a freshman in college, I never worked for anyone else. Other people and corporations signed my paychecks but I have worked as unto the Lord.

Our life is to be lived as an offering of thanksgiving to God the Father. Doing all that we do in the nature of Jesus makes our thanksgiving *through* Him. *Through* the Lord Jesus is an important and powerful aspect of our behaviors. He is our conduit to God.

Prayer – Dear Father, guide me so that whatever I do will be in the nature of Christ. Let the words of my mouth, the emotions of my heart, the actions of my body, and the thoughts of my mind be delightful in Your sight.

September 2   Wrestle

Ephesians 6:12 *For we DO not wrestle against flesh and blood, but against principalities ... powers ... rulers of the darkness of this age ... spiritual hosts of wickedness in the heavenly places.*

DO means strenuous action.

Q What is spiritual wrestling?   Spiritual wrestling is spiritual warfare.

There is a common statement sometimes called Murphy's Law. It goes something like this, "Nothing is as easy as it looks; everything takes longer than it should; and, if anything can go wrong, it will." This is really Satan's law going way back to John 10:10a and 1 Peter 5:8. If you are trying to do something good, you will often run into unreasonable circumstances. Even *in the heavenly places!*

We have reasonable expectations in life or else life becomes unpredictable and scary. We have to be reasonable. However, one of our reasonable expectations should be that Satan will buffet us at every turn, especially if we are on track for God. If we expect everything to go right, we'll live a life of confusion and resentment.

Quite often, people ask, "Why is this happening to me?" Well, let's look for clues. Is there theft? Murder? Destruction? If any of these, or any other ungodly thing is going on, we know why (John 10:10a). Satan is why.

Peter tells us not to be worried about some weird circumstance that is occurring in our life (1 Peter 4:12). We know it is just Satan messing around and that we are safe in God's care. Jesus told us we will, not may, but will have tribulation. But we can be happy because He has conquered the world (John 16:33b).

Jesus has overcome all the noxious things mentioned in today's verse. Do you have a problem? Jesus has conquered it. Look for His fingerprints on the carcass.

Sin can exist anywhere. Be wary but claim victory! *And this is the victory that has overcome the world – our faith* 1 John 5:4b.

Prayer – Dear Father, thank You that the victory over Satan is won, and I can claim victory because of Jesus' presence in me.

September 3   Things

1 John 2:15 DO *not love the world or the things in the world. If anyone loves the world, the love of the Father is not in him.*

DO means we should love the Father.

Q What does love for the world do?   Love for the world excludes God.

Loving the world means to fall into Satan's trap. Love is a strong word, not like the watered down "making love" version we hear today. If we love the world, as indicated in this verse, we are devoted to the world and spend our time and resources seeking what it offers and satisfying its requirements. We become what we worship. The things of the world, Satan's tools and temptations, become our god.

One way to catch a monkey is to put a banana in an old fashioned glass milk bottle and tie it to a tree. The monkey can reach in with an open paw but once it grabs the banana he can't pull it out. The hungrier he gets, the more he hangs on to the banana. Meanwhile, captors throw a net over him. We have to check and make sure we aren't grasping any bananas that trap us. Any time we become angry, bitter, resentful, or disappointed about something or somebody in the world, we have made IT/THEM our banana god and the love of the Father is not in us. Let go of the "banana". Let the love for God overcome any worldly love.

Serving two different bosses is difficult unless they agree on everything. God and world wealth are mutually exclusive, don't try to worship both (Matthew 6:24). If you try to live in two different minds, you will be unsteady in everything you do (James 1:8). We can't love God AND the world at the same time.

Two men were considering the rubble that was left of their homes after a cat 5 hurricane. One had invested his life in his possessions and cried out that he has lost everything of value to him. The other had invested his life in God and observed he had lost nothing of lasting value. When the love of the Father is in us, the things of the world are of no account. If we lose "everything", we have lost nothing (Philippians 3:8-9a). The main thing is to make the main thing the main thing. Do not love the world. Do not love the things in the world. The main thing is to love God and the things of God.

Prayer – Dear Father, help my love for You extinguish any worldly affection.

September 4   Temple

1 Corinthians 6:19 *Or DO you not know that your body is the temple of the Holy Spirit Who is in you … For you were bought at a price; therefore glorify God in your body, and in your spirit, which are God's.* (See also 1 Corinthians 3:16).

A temple is a holy place of worship. The Holy Spirit worships in and through us!

DO implies understanding that we are temples of the Spirit of God.

Q Do we know whether or not we are temples of the Holy Spirit?

We do now.

How could we, in good conscience, act in a way that defames a temple of the Holy Spirit? We should not mistreat or abuse our bodies or use them to use or abuse others. It is important to realize that we become what we worship and worship accordingly.

Again, *do you not know that you are a temple of God?* The Spirit of God lives in us. How should we respond to being a temple of the Holy Spirit? By glorifying God in body and spirit. Not only do we want to keep our temple clean, He helps us keep it clean. When the Holy Spirit is in us, we have all His attributes at our disposal. (See November 11.)

We are to copy the holiness of God (1 Peter 1:16, Leviticus 11:44). Practice the presence of Jesus. When a question or challenge arises, think or say, "Jesus is Lord." Thank Him in all circumstances.

You were bought at a price. Do you realize the price? God sacrificed His Son for you!! That makes you of extreme value to God!! You didn't know? You do now!! The Holy Spirit is in us! INSTANT REPLAY- The Holy Spirit is in us! We are His temple.

How should we treat a building that is a temple? We need to keep it in good repair, neat and organized. What we wouldn't do in a temple, we shouldn't do in or to our bodies. Don't have any rooms marked, DO NOT ENTER.

Prayer – Dear Father, Thank You - what an awesome truth – that You consider my body to be a dwelling place for Your Holy Spirit.

September 5   Press

Philippians 3:12-13 *Not that I have already attained, or am already perfected; but I press on, that I may lay hold of that for which Christ Jesus has also laid hold of me. Brethren, I DO not count myself to have apprehended; but one thing I DO, forgetting those things that are behind ... I press toward the goal for the prize of the upward call of God.*

DO means the intent to forget and go on.

Q How do we get past the past?

We spell FoRGeT backwards. We Talk to God and others, we Grieve and Get rid of Garbage, we Recycle any good stuff, and we Forgive ourselves and anyone who has offended us. Talk - Grieve - Recycle - Forgive. Memorize these steps and print them on your mental windshield. Windshields are bigger than rear view mirrors.

What a joy to know that forgiveness is possible and real. We don't have to go through life with a hampering weight of balls and chains dragging along behind us. Satan, as the accuser, would have us re-member or retain all the sins of commission and omission, which would ruin our peace and joy, and make us feel too ashamed to tell others about God's marvelous love. But, good news! Christ has taken hold of us! We need to know that the past does not have to be a continual present.

We long for forgiveness for ourselves but we need to know that, what we can't forget, we can't forgive. REVERSE INSTANT REPLAY - WHAT WE CAN'T FORGIVE, WE CAN'T FORGET. If I am busy licking the wounds of the past, I won't have healthy energy to go on towards the goal. Also, what we don't forgive, we won't forget. Wallows and vomit.

Know this: Satan's call is a downward call. He and his minions are real downers. God's call is an upward call. The upward call of God is called a prize to be awarded when we reach the goal. Paul is saying he hadn't reached the goal of perfection yet but he was not quitting. He knew that he was perfected in Christ. He longed for Christ to be perfected in him. Perhaps he was thinking of his lament in Romans 7:14-25.

Jesus has laid hold of us! He wants us to live in grace with love, joy, and peace! Press on!

Prayer – Dear Father, thank You for laying hold of me, help me keep my eyes on the goal.

September 6   Keep

John 17:15 *I DO not pray that You should take them out of the world, but that You should keep them from the evil one.*

DO shows intent to protect His disciples from Satan.

Q How can we be in, but not of, the world?

God has given us a suit of Spiritual armor so we can be protected from the attacks of Satan (Ephesians 6:14-18). Therefore we don't need to escape from the world. We are in the world but not under Satan's control. God has given us His Spirit with all of His guidance and help (See November 11 devotion).

John 17 contains wonderful information about Jesus' relationship with God and with His disciples. He not only prayed for them, He extended His prayers to us. Everything He granted to His disciples is ours to enjoy (John 17:20). WOW!

It is so wonderful that Jesus is always praying for us. We have an everlasting prayer warrior Who is able to totally save those who enter God's Kingdom through His door (Hebrews 7:25).

Knowing that Jesus is praying that we would not follow the lures of Satan, we can agree with Him in prayer and feel safe in living the life He gives us on earth. Part of our life in Christ is showing and telling a clear message about Him. A surgeon has to have confidence in surgery or the patient will feel insecure. If we aren't feeling safe and confident in God's care, those with whom we interact will be unsure of our message.

When our children know that we hold them in high esteem, evidenced by the investment of our time, energy, and prayers, they are far less likely to become involved in the world.

No one can hurt me because I have a forever helper. I am bold in Christ Who takes away all my fears (Hebrews 13:5b-6). Satan is in the world, but Christ is in us. Don't sublet an apartment in the basement.

Neither man nor Satan can inflict eternal harm on us so long as we are in Christ. Anything else that God allows can, and will, be used to glorify Him and comfort others.

Prayer – Dear Father, thank You for protecting me from Satan.

September 7   Through

Philippians 4:13 *I can DO all things through Christ Who strengthens me.*

DO means act.

Q How can I do all things?   Through Christ's strengthening.

Jesus said to him, "If you can believe, all things are possible to him who believes" Mark 9:23. No thing is excluded. However, the things must be in the realm of God's wisdom and desires for us. It becomes our part to ask and then accept God's answer: Go - do it, Slow - don't get ahead of Me, Grow - this will be helpful, or No - not My will for you. We have to be careful to know, and to teach children, that God always answers prayer but that He does it with His plan and our best interests in mind.

There is no such thing as unanswered prayer. INSTANT REPLAY - There is no such thing as unanswered prayer. One of the great things we can do is to rest in Him when our prayer doesn't go the way we hoped it would. We definitely need to remember for ourselves, and to teach children, young in age or young in Christ, that God answers according to His will, not our whim.

When we are facing a problem, no matter how great, we need to remember that we have Christ's strength. We, as limited mortals, have God, Who is capable of doing anything. This makes our relationship with Him invaluable (Matthew 19:26). We know (1.) All things are possible, and (2.) God loves us. Therefore, the answer He gives is that of an all wise, all powerful, loving Father. God created everything and He has power over everything.

All things are possible. Don't fail to ask. One way to find out God's will in a situation is to present the matter to Him in prayer. Again, He will give us the appropriate answer – Go, or Slow, or Grow, or No. Only believe that the answer you get is the way of grace, mercy, love, joy, and peace as we submit ourselves to Him. God won't give us a *stone* when we ask for *bread* (Luke 11:11).

It is through Christ that we receive strength. He is our pathway. Don't wait to pray when all else fails. Go to Him first and the way will be smoother.

Prayer – Dear Father, help me not to fall into the trap of relying on my own strength but to have power in the strength of Christ.

September 8   Freedom

Galatians 5:1 *For freedom Christ has set you free, DO not be entangled again with a yoke of bondage.*

DO means to live free in Christ.

Q What is a yoke of bondage?

The yoke is being harnessed to laws and works instead of grace.

In order to be saved by following every law, we must be perfect. We aren't. One problem is that we don't have to break a lot of laws to forfeit our relationship with God. One transgression is the same as a hundred (James 2:10). God's grace sets us free from our inability to keep the whole law.

Bondage can be shown in habits of what we say or what we do. Christ can set us free from bad habits if we utilize the gifts given to us in the Holy Spirit.

Christ has set us free from laws and works so we know our freedom is a true and effective condition. He did NOT set us free for lawlessness. He did NOT set us free so we have freedom to make dumb choices or say dumb things. Again - Never do anything you think you are going to have to lie about. That will go a long way towards keeping you untangled.

God didn't leave us in a life full of fear because of our sin, He gave us the joyful inclusion in His family so we can shout, *"Abba, Father"* (Romans 8:15). We aren't caught in fear, we are released in freedom.

The yoke of bondage is like being caught in a mesh of fish line, a person can't tell an end from a beginning. Do not be entangled – if we are trying to be saved by law there is always the fear of not doing it right, or to be good enough. When we are free in Christ, our life becomes unsnarled.

Satan is always trying to get us to take our eyes off Christ and worry about some law. Thankfully, we need not be concerned with rafts of lies or tangles of fish line. We are to live as people who are free in Christ; let us stay that way.

Prayer – Dear Father, help me live responsibly in the freedom that grace provides.

September 9   Training

Ephesians 6:4 ... *fathers, DO not provoke your children to wrath, but bring them up in the training and admonition of the Lord.*

> Training - guidance, instruction. Admonition - counsel or advice, gentle reproof, caution.
>
> DO means the intent to raise children in a Godly environment.

Q What is the way to raise a child? With firm but gentle instructions about the teachings of Jesus. If we don't train them, we provoke them.

> These instructions are given by, through, in, about, and of, the Lord. Think each prepositional phrase through for instance: the guidance *of the Lord* -- but not in a way that would cause anger. What parents do, and what they don't do, can provoke wrath. If we don't raise them according to Godly training and admonition, we encourage wrath. So many of the harmful and criminal actions of children, that we see and read about, are a result of poor parenting.

If we raise a child right, he may deviate for a few years but he will return when he gains the wisdom of age (Proverbs 22:6). TV is filled with encouragement to have some kind of training program. Each one has a discipline we can follow in raising children. The main thing is to be consistent with an appropriate combination of love and discipline.

How do we know what is the correct way to go? We look to God's word. *All Scripture is given by inspiration of God, and is profitable for doctrine, for reproof, for correction, for instruction in righteousness ...* 2 Timothy 3:16. Be sure your children have a steady diet of the Bible. Teach them the five spiritual food groups - Bible study, prayer, fellowship, meditation, and service.

Children are provoked to wrath when they see trivial, and or sinful, things in their parent's lives – when parents don't practice what they teach (intended). Child - "Hey dad, let's play catch." Dad - "Not now, I'm watching a football game." Child thinks, "What am I? Chopped liver?" If the children sense some unnecessary thing or act is more important to their parent than they are, they will be resentful. More of life's lessons are caught than taught.

Prayer – Dear Father, thank you for Your words of instruction and the gentle admonition of the Holy Spirit. May I teach as You have taught me.

September 10   Quench

1 Thessalonians 5:19 *DO not quench the Spirit.*

Quench – extinguish, smother, stifle.

DO is the intent for us to allow and encourage the Holy Spirit in our lives.

Q How can we increase the Spirit's activity in our lives?

By not extinguishing or ignoring the Holy Spirit's directives.

We need to know there is a Holy Spirit and that the Holy Spirit is a good and desirable Person. Jesus wants us to have, and He has prayed that God would give us, His Spirit (John 14:16). Then, we need to want the Spirit, ask for Him, and know that God has given Him to us (Luke 11:13).

It is so incredibly important that we practice the existence and importance of the Holy Spirit. Remember, anything you think is negative about the Holy Spirit is blasphemy promoted by Satan, the destroyer.

One of the ways we can quench the Spirit is to cause Him grief (Ephesians 4:30, see September 29). It is important to know that our actions result in pleasure or grief on the Holy Spirit's part. As an instructor is troubled when a student knowingly or unknowingly violates a clear message, the Holy Spirit is sad for us when we ignore His teachings.

When we follow the Spirit's instruction, our position with the Father is confirmed. We have a wonderful warm feeling of agreement with the Spirit within us that we are behaving as God's children (Romans 8:16).

The Holy Spirit is Christ's presence and action in our lives. We should rejoice in the Spirit in every aspect of our lives. Then He will not be grieved nor quenched.

Prayer – Dear Father, thank You for not leaving us as orphans but giving us Your Holy Spirit to affirm us, empower us, gift us, and lead us in a life pleasing to You.

September 11   Know

Mark 14:70-71 *Then Peter began to curse and swear, "I DO not know the man of whom you speak."*

DO means denial.

Q How should we react when confronted about our relationship with God?

Hopefully, we confess Him and speak with boldness about what God means in our lives.

We do not know what curse words Peter used but he swore that he didn't know Jesus. We can testify that we know that Jesus has forgiven our sins and has given us a loving relationship with God.

After Peter was accused for the third time of being a follower of Christ, he denied it vehemently. It is interesting that it was his accent that gave him away. There are people who can name the county in which we were born by our accent.

Our verbal accent is not our choice. However, our choices in life give it a chosen accent. Our actions can have the "accent" of a life in Satan's corner, OR, a life in Christ.

What counts is the way we act and speak now that we are born again - what we choose to do and say. What does our speech say to others about our citizenship? If we were accused of being with Christ, would there be enough evidence to convict us?

I once told an English woman that she had an interesting accent. She drew herself up haughtily and crisply said, "You, young man, have the accent!" The world has its "Accent," which is different from ours. May others recognize Christ's accent in us.

Having Me (Jesus) confess people before God has a requirement; they must confess Me before people (Matthew 10:32). This is true for words and actions, We confess with both. Jesus will confess us. It is nice to know that He will say, "Yes! I know who you are talking about. I love him".

Prayer – Dear Father, may the words of my mouth gladly and thankfully confess that I know Christ and that I am with Him.

September 12   Approve

Romans 1:28-32 ... *God gave them over to a debased mind, to DO those things which are not fitting (*see list of evil*) ... they ... not only DO the same but also approve of those who practice them.*

DO means doing evil.

Q Does God allow people to choose Satan and Satan's ways?

Yes, if people allow it and insist on it.

You can be sure this is not God's plan or desire. He doesn't give up on us until we flat out refuse His grace up to the time our last breath is exhaled. He desires remorse and confession, not that we should perish (2 Peter 3:9).

It is uncomfortable to watch people promote evil and approve of those who perform evil. TV sitcoms treat drunkenness, drug abuse, fornication, and adultery, as if they are funny. Some TV adds promote lying and misbehavior. We live in a world where a lot of social media is dedicated to violence of every description. Video games are marketed where people can inflict all kinds of mayhem on persons and property. One can go to school on the evil shown by some TV shows. News media, when reporting news, often show how to perform criminal acts. Even some sporting events are marked by violence to the delight of screaming fans. (I went to a boxing match and a hockey game broke out.) It is possible that people lose their distaste for evil because they see so much of it.

In the book of Luke, a discussion is held with a man who had been buried and was in torment in Hades. He appealed to Abraham to send a message to his living brothers, but as the story goes, If people do not listen to live testimony, they won't be convinced even if the word comes from someone who has been resurrected (Luke 16:26-31). Even though Jesus rose from the dead, people choose not to believe and adhere to God's commandments.

If you are not *persuaded*, you should try disproving the resurrection of Christ. Your decision will dictate your quality of life and where you spend eternity.

Prayer – Dear Father, thank you for rescuing me before I became so hardened that I chose against You.

September 13   Good

2 Thessalonians 3:13 ... *DO not grow weary in doing good.*

DO means to continue in good deeds.

Q What do we do when practicing our faith seems tedious? We keep on keepin' on.

We need to nourish our spirits by feeding on the word, practicing His presence, and by being active in fellowship and prayer. Then, we will not *grow weary*, get tired, or be bored. Our second wind comes from the breath of the Spirit

Burn out, in the people business, comes from trying to do someone else's work for them. Burn out, in Christianity, comes from trying to do God's work for Him. Sometimes we need to step back, lean on the everlasting arms, and give the Holy Spirit a chance to do His work. Slow - don't get ahead of Him.

If, or when, you feel weak,

call on Jesus for strength.

He will give you the power to do anything within His will (Philippians 4:13).

God's goodness is refreshed in us at the beginning of each day. He faithfully restocks our shelves so we have a continual supply of whatever we need for that day (Lamentations 3:22-23).

We need to know that God will not ask us to do the impossible (1 Corinthians 10:13). He will never give a challenge that is beyond our ability to handle. He will give us an out.

We need to keep our eyes on the goal of doing good. How do we keep enthusiasm? We constantly plug ourselves into the Holy Spirit. Just like we plug in our cell phones so we can communicate. We use power and we receive power whenever we ask for His refreshing presence in our lives.

We will finish our race, we will keep the faith (2 Timothy 4:7).

Prayer – Dear Father, may Your Spirit of life continue to fill me with grace, mercy, and peace that comes only from You.

September 14   Gift

1 Corinthians 12:30 *DO all have the gift of healing? DO all speak with tongues? DO all interpret?*

DO means have possession of a spiritual gift.

Q Do we have to demonstrate a certain gift in order to be a Christian?

The implied answer to this rhetorical question is, "No."

These are rhetorical questions the answers to which are obvious. No, no, and no. Some people DO, but not all. God gifts people or groups according to His purpose for the need at the moment. The Spirit controls the distribution of gifts, giving each individual the appropriate gift, according to His plan, for the best interest of the person and the Body of Christ (1 Corinthians 12:11). Note – As He wills, not the notion of another person or group.

God may give the gift of healing to a diseased person, or He may give a gift of faith, which may be a greater, more compelling testimony to His grace. God may gift a person with a different language to help someone of a different nationality. He may give a different tongue for edification but He will always give another person a gift of interpretation for the tongue.

Being ill doesn't mean we are horrible or sinful; even the apostle Paul had his problems. If someone troubles your faith by saying you need a certain act or a certain gift, be aware they are violating Scripture. Refer them to 1 Corinthians 12:30, our verse for the day. There are times a problem is meant to show the glory of God (John 9:3).

Recognize they are weak in the faith and treat them with kindness. If they are open to instruction, help them to accept the answers Paul gave to the Corinthians who had the same lack of understanding. If we have to have a certain gift, it becomes a work instead of a grace gift.

Do all have whatever gift is in question? No, claiming otherwise is to exclude people whom God has accepted. Gifts are for edification, not qualification. Be open at any time for any gift.

Prayer – Dear Father, help me not to exclude anyone based on gifts.

September 15 Say

Mark 8:29 *Jesus said to them, "But who DO you say that I am?"*

DO means to realize.

Q Did the disciples realize Jesus' true identity?

Yes!

The disciples had witnessed many signs and wonders. They had observed many Old Testament prophecies fulfilled in the person and works of Jesus. They knew the Messiah had come and *immediately* they left their nets and followed Him (Mark 1:18). God had given them eyes to see and ears to hear.

Others did not recognize or want to admit that Jesus was the Christ of God. There are many people today of the same mind.

It is interesting how often the "I AM" declaration shows up in Jesus' discourses. This is a short description but an important link between Him and God. (See the I AMs of Jesus in the January 18 devotion).

When Moses asked God how to identify Him, God said, "*I AM WHO I AM*" Exodus 3:14. We say, "You are Christ, the fulfillment of the prophesy and plan of eternal God " (Matthew 16:16). We take God at His Word.

When we recognize and accept Jesus as God's Son, the Savior of the world, we open up the treasures of heaven. Once we see it, we will have all kinds of evidence to believe it. I wouldn't have seen it if I hadn't believed it.

Who do YOU say Jesus is? This is the most important question you will ever be asked to answer.

Prayer – Dear Father, it is clear to me and I say, "Jesus is the Christ, Your Son and my Savior."

September 16   Peace

<u>John 14:27</u> *Peace I leave with you. My peace I give to you; not as the world gives DO I give to you. Let not your heart be troubled, neither let it be afraid.*

DO means giving peace.

Q Does the world give peace?

No.

Jesus told us that the world gives tribulation. However, we are to rest in the promise that He is more powerful than any worldly problem (John 16:33b). God knows our tribulation. He has allowed the tribulation. He has a solution or the escape so we, or someone else, will benefit from our tribulation.

We should follow Paul's instructions in Philippians 4:6-9: Don't worry, be thankful whatever the circumstance, and state what you feel you need. God will answer in a way that will give you perfect peace to settle your thoughts and emotions.

The peace of Jesus - this isn't just any old peace. There is no greater peace than that which Jesus gives. Jesus doesn't always give us peace without problems but He always gives us peace within problems. INSTANT REPLAY – Jesus doesn't always give us peace without problems but He always gives us peace within problems.

Don't let your emotion depend on the ebb and flow of circumstance. Our boat floats above the turbulent sea.

Don't be upset. Take anything you are worried about to Him and talk to Him about it. Always be aware that He is concerned for your welfare (1 Peter 5:7).

If you are troubled or afraid, ask for the Holy Spirit's fruit, part of which is peace (Galatians 5:22). Whenever we ask for something from God, He will give us the answer immediately, couched in peace.

Prayer – Dear Father, thank You for *the peace that surpasses all understanding.*

September 17   Third

John 21:15-18 *He said to him the third time, "Simon, son of Jonah, DO you love Me?" Peter was grieved ...*

DO means complete devotion.

Q Why did Jesus ask Peter three times?

Peter had denied Jesus three times. Also, Peter slept three times while Jesus agonized in prayer Mark 14:41, so Jesus asked Peter three times if Peter loved Him. Possibly a bit of humor. Maybe there was emphasis:

Do YOU love Me? Do you LOVE Me? Do you love ME?

Previously, Jesus had predicted that Peter would deny Him three times (Mark 14:30). Jesus knew Peter would deny Him but He didn't deny, give up on, Peter. There is hope for us.

In the third denial, Peter's accent gave him away (Mark 14:70). Then the "accent" of his personality took over and he used foul language and swore that he didn't even know Jesus (v71). When pushed to the limit, Peter used his bluster and bravado to shut the accusers up. It is interesting that Jesus then reverted to Peter's original name – *Simon.* Peter realized Jesus knew he had reverted to his old self. This added to his remorse. We should feel grief if Jesus has to ask several times about our devotion. Peter knew he hadn't lived up to his bragging.

Why did Jesus ask three times? Asking the same question several times is a good technique to get at the core of a situation. Interrogators use it on criminals because liars will eventually change their stories to try to make them more credible. "Truthers" will keep on telling the truth. Jesus pursues us until we get to the truth. Peter kept on saying, "Yes ..."

When we are at crisis points we need to ask ourselves, "Do I really love Him?" When tempted to lie, cheat, or steal, "Do I *really* love Him?" If necessary ask several times. "Do I really love Him?" At these points Jesus gives us extra chances to choose for or against Him. If we insist on being against Him, He gives us our chosen consequences. If we have remorse, confess and accept His forgiveness, we proceed in newness of life.

Prayer – Dear Father, yes, I love You and I will follow You.

September 18   Present

Romans 6:13 *And DO not present your members as instruments of unrighteousness to sin ...*

DO not means to avoid.

Q Do we have choices to what or to whom we present our members? Yes - and choices have consequences (con - with a sequence of events).

> The members of our bodies are any part that has an exterior function – hands, feet, eyes, ears, tongue, etc. We are to take care not to speak out of both sides of our mouth as the saying goes – or foot, etc. The tongue, for example, can state a blessing for God in one minute and turn right around and blaspheme a person the next (James 3:9). Each member has the ability to do good or to do evil. Any one member of the body, or any one act, can cause a great deal of trouble.

Think of the members of a symphony orchestra. Each member, from the string bass to the piccolo, plays a part, sometimes solo, sometimes in harmony. One person, out of tune, places a blight on the whole symphony. Think of the members of a sports team. The weakness of any one person, or one error, will often bring about a loss for the whole team. Likewise, one member of our body can besmirch the rest. As your pilot goes through a checklist before takeoff, check each part of your body to see if it is ready for flight. God has given specific armor for common Satanic attack points (Ephesians 6:14-18).

> We are to present our members as presents to God as a response for His Gift to us. God does not force us to do His will or extract favors from us. If we don't give cheerfully, the gift is tainted. It is in the giving of ourselves that we gain the joys of servanthood.

> The parts of our bodies are not to be tools of Satan. Any evil we don't think of, Satan will provide through his minions or circumstance. But, the Holy Spirit is faithful and He will convict us of sin if we have not hardened our hearts against Him. Place each decision before the Holy Spirit, especially if there is a time you are trying to justify something the Holy Spirit says is wrong. Ask Him what you should do, or ask for a "Yes" or "No" answer, and He will guide you.

Prayer – Dear Father, may every member of my body be an instrument of righteousness.

September 19   Happy

Romans 14:22   *DO you have faith? Have it to yourself before God. Happy is he who does not condemn himself in what he approves.*

DO means to take ownership of faith.

Q How do we rest in our faith? Don't condemn yourself for what you feel is approved.

Here, Paul is writing about things that may seem right to one person but wrong to another. If you have a practice that is not forbidden in the Bible, but may be a problem for another person, don't wear it on your shirt. There are two definitions of sin that help a lot in directing our choices. They bear repeating over and over.

If you don't do what you know you should do, this is sin (James 4:17) - a sin of omission. If you do what you know is wrong to do, this is sin (Romans 14:23b) - a sin of commission.

These statements about sin give guidance for what we should do and what we should not do. If we know it is good, do it. If we believe it is wrong, don't do it. KISS, Keep It Simple Slave.

If you find yourself in some big debate about an activity, it's probably wrong.

If you are saying, "I guess it wouldn't hurt," it probably will hurt.

If we ask, "Why not?" - then there is usually a reason, so, "Not." Don't do it.

The Holy Spirit will guide us as we lay debatable things before Him. Don't be afraid that He will ruin your fun. Actually, He will lead you into all truth and help you avoid the consequences of sin. Guilty pleasure is no substitute for joy.

Do you believe what you are doing is acceptable to God? Don't brag to the world about it. Keep it to yourself before God. Don't second guess yourself. Live in the freedom that grace gives, with concern for members of the Body, and constant referral to the Holy Spirit for guidance.

Prayer – Dear Father thank You for the freedom in grace that sets us free. Help me not to flaunt my freedom or to abuse it.

September 20   Yoked

2 Corinthians 6:14   DO not be unequally yoked together with unbelievers. For what fellowship has righteousness with lawlessness?

DO means have fellowship with believers.

Q Why choose good friends?

Being yoked with an unbeliever is a yoke of bondage. Being yoked with believers strengthens good habits. When our log is in the fire, we not only receive encouragement from others, we give encouragement to them. God does not intend that we be spiritual hermits. (Or hismits)

Don't be taken in and misled by Satan or his disciples. If you run with the wrong crowd, they can, and will, wear you down and lead you into sin. Don't kid yourself or let anyone else fool you. If you try to fit in with bad people, you'll become like them. They'll drag you down to their level (1 Corinthians 15:33). Sorry, it doesn't very often seem to work the other way. One person usually can't lift a group. It takes a church.

In the Middle School where I taught, each new student was paired with a member of the Honor Roll for the first few weeks of school. Hopefully, this helped the newbies get off on the right foot.

In my doctoral internship, I worked with many people who struggled with dependencies on drugs, alcohol, or various deviant habits. They would come for treatment, get clean and dry, and go out with confidence. After a while, overconfidence led them back to their previous "wet faces" and "wet places" - people and hangouts. Soon, they were back, going through the revolving door of treatment.

There is a lot of folk wisdom about companions. "Birds of a feather flock together." "One rotten apple spoils the bushel." "Guilt by association." Like "oil and water," good and evil don't mix.

So, yoke yourself with believers. Make them your birds.

Prayer – Dear Father, help me choose associates with good habits.

September 21   Whatever

1 Corinthians 10:31 *Therefore, whether you eat or drink, or whatever you DO, DO all to the glory of God.*

DO means DO it.

Q What should our actions do?

Bring glory to God.

Watch for the "therefores". In this case the discussion was about a practice that may offend or cause a sibling to stumble. The solution offered was not to satisfy personal bias but to do what would glorify God – deny the self.

There is that word ALL again. What does *all* mean in our lives? Everything we do should bring glory to God. Every thought, every act - nothing is omitted. Christianity is not a part-time endeavor. Whatever you do with food, beverage, whatever - extend the concept to the universe of behavior, do it *all* with the purpose of pointing others to His glory.

We need to realize that whatever we do with earthly endeavors is a response to grace, not a payment for justification by good works. Any person or group who claims status by what they practice has not gotten the message. In reality, human habits are not the essence of life in Christ. Rules about eating and drinking are not what God's kingdom is all about (Romans 14:17). However, we definitely should not misuse food or beverage. The best "food" we find in His kingdom is the fruit of the Spirit.

We have to be careful that meaningless arguments do not take glory FROM God. We cause people to shy away when we disagree and form denominations to show we have a toe-hold on God. Is there anything we do that doesn't bring glory to God? Ditch it!

Everything we do or say should reflect and fulfill the nature and expression of our Lord and be an offering of thanksgiving to God (Colossians 3:17).

Prayer – Dear Father, may all that I do

bring glory to You

September 22   Love

Matthew 5:44 *But I say to you, love your enemies, bless those who curse you, DO good to those who hate you, and pray for those who spitefully use you …*

DO means play nice.

Q How should we treat people who hate us because of our faith?

Love them, *bless* them, *do good to* them, *and pray* for them.

When people despitefully use us, we know we're winning the battle. When we are being kicked in the rear, it means we are out ahead. Our Light exposes their darkness. Satan increases the attacks on us when we move out of the twilight into the full light of Christ.

Make sure they hate you because you are doing good. Social suffering is proof that we are on the right track. Spiteful use goes with the territory.

Pray for those who misuse you

1. The way of the world is to hate their enemies, return a curse for a curse, and to condemn those who treat them with disrespect. This is not so in Christ.
2. It should be reasonable to suffer for doing bad but in today's world people are likely to suffer for doing good and be rewarded for bad behavior. No good deed will go unpunished.
3. The idea of an abundant life is the opposite of the intent of Satan (John 1:10).

HOWEVER

4. 1 Peter 4:14 informs us that we are blessed when we are verbally chastised for doing things in the nature of Christ.
5. We are totally secure in Christ and we can cheerfully take up any cross that people force on us. To respond evil for evil is to sink to their level. To do that is to lose our spiritual fruit (Galatians 5:22-23).
6. We can deny our "self" (our earthly self) and take on the nature of Christ.

Prayer – Dear Father, help me show You to those who abuse me.

September 23   Sufficient

Matthew 6:34b *DO not worry about tomorrow for tomorrow will worry about its own things. Sufficient for the day is its own trouble.*

What a great promise for the process of sanctification!

DO means mental intent to be content.

Q Should we be anxious about the future?

As our grandson used to say, "Don't wuddy about it."

Could trouble be a good thing? Jesus, Paul, James, and Peter all speak of how our reaction to tribulations can develop positive things (see November 9). Verses we have looked at before point to God's good use of *trouble*. Not only is God's grace sufficient for our bodily ailments (2 Corinthians 12:9), His grace is sufficient for spiritual growth.

His grace is *sufficient for the day* because His grace is sufficient.

Each day's *trouble* is adequate for personal growth. A good trainer knows the client's potential and sets appropriate goals. A good trainer knows the client's limits and doesn't ask the client to overdo. God is the ultimate trainer.

Don't worry about being overwhelmed when God gives you a growth experience, He knows our strengths and weaknesses and will give us the escape route if necessary so we can handle it (1 Corinthians 10:13). Don't get bogged down in the struggle, keep an eye on the escape hatch.

When I was rehabbing my torn rotator cuff, there was a big sign in the Physical Therapy room: NO PAIN – NO GAIN. (Easy for them to say.) But then, they put sand traps on golf courses. Why should we, in our faith, expect anything less than challenges that give us a chance to grow in faith.

I trust you, Lord, to be my master Trainer.

Prayer – Dear Father, help me use *troubles* as an opportunity for growth.

September 24   Do

Matthew 7:12 *Therefore, whatever you want men to DO to you, DO also to them, for this is the Law and the Prophets* (Quoted from Leviticus 19:18).

DO means doing to gain a return.

Q What is the Law and the Prophets?

The law of the Kingdom (the Royal Law) is to extend the same care and comfort to your neighbor that would make you feel nourished and cherished (James 2:8). Reminder, the Royal Law is more commonly called The Golden Rule. There are jokes about The Golden Rule: "Do unto others, first" - "Do unto others and then split" - "Do unto others before they do unto you" - "Those who have the gold rule." I don't know any jokes about grace.

Now we know that rules and laws are to be followed but rules and laws are not grace. When people say they abide by The Golden Rule they are expecting a return. Following the Golden Rule doesn't bring salvation. People need to be sure they know they LIVE by grace. Grace doesn't expect a return.

You are to love your neighbor as yourself. What is also true, and often happens, people hate others as they hate themselves - HATE YOUR NEIGHBOR AS YOURSELF is also true. Many people show their disgust for themselves by the way they treat others. When we are at peace with our self, we have peace with our neighbor.

Paul extends the rule to marriage. Each member of the couple should operate under the same set of Kingdom rules. Love your spouse as yourself (Ephesians 5:28). Show me a man who mistreats his wife and children and I'll show you a man who hates himself. Likewise with women and their husbands.

In order to love our neighbor/spouse as ourselves we must first get right with God; then we need to accept His love for ourselves. When we love ourselves as He loves us, we can love our neighbor as ourselves.

It's okay to love whom God loves. You can love yourself because God loves you. You can love others with agape love.

Prayer – Dear Father, help me to know Your love for me and may I extend it to others.

September 25   Living

<u>Luke 24:5</u> *Why DO you seek the living among the dead?*

DO means futile intent.

Q To whom were the two men (angels) referring?

Jesus.

The two men knew that Jesus had fulfilled His prophecy that He would rise from the dead.

<u>Who was seeking?</u> Women who had supported Jesus during His ministry had come to embalm Him (Luke 24:1). They didn't know He was already wrapped in 100 pounds of spices (John 19:39-40). They thought Jesus was dead. (Another proof of the resurrection.) Anyway, it was women who were first to find that Jesus had risen from the dead.

<u>Who were they seeking?</u> They were seeking the corpse of Jesus so they could anoint it. They were asked why they were looking for a dead person when He was alive.

<u>Who is dead?</u> Those who are really dead are those people who are outside of Christ (Ephesians 2:1b).

<u>Who is living?</u> Jesus, (1Corinthians 15:2), AND, those of us who are in Christ. He has given life to those of us who are in Him (Ephesians 2:1a).

Don't look for life in those who don't believe - they are spiritually dead. Seek and find the living among those who are spiritually alive. Doves of a feather flock together.

Prayer – Dear Father, thank You that Jesus is alive and living in the living. May we have fellowship with Him and them.

September 26   Woe

1 Corinthians 9:16 ... *yes, necessity is laid upon me; yes, woe is me if I DO not preach the gospel!*

DO means act.

Q What is the Gospel we are to preach?

We are to spread the Good News Gospel that God has brought us into relationship with Himself through the redeeming sacrifice of Jesus Christ.

Paul had a dramatic conversion experience, changing from being a person who persecuted Christians to being a devoted preacher. Paul went from sinful blindness to spiritual sight. His conversion came about through a communication from God – "What is this persecution of Me all about?" (Acts 9:4b). This was followed by a session with Ananias and baptism. Then, in behavior befitting an audience with the Creator of the universe, Paul was transformed into the world's greatest exponent of the message of Christ (v20).

His conversion was not the only thing dramatic about his life. He became God's spokesperson to the non-Jewish population and wrote some of the most beloved and productive letters of all time. Even so, he referred to himself as a second rate apostle. He was honestly humble, never forgetting that he had worked against the very people he now called siblings in Christ (1 Corinthians 15:9).

For all of this, Paul felt a tremendous sense of gratitude to God, such that he felt compelled, such that he should suffer woe, if he did not respond by proclaiming the gospel. He not only preached the gospel, he practiced it to a fine degree. Paul presented a positive role model which we would do well to emulate to the best of the abilities that God gives us.

Bringing it home to us - your conversion is/was/will be a dramatic and monumental thing. God's angels respond with joy over every single person who follows the directives of Christ and enter His kingdom (Luke 15:1). Isn't that great? Have you given them a party yet?

Prayer – Dear Father, thank You for the amazing fact that heaven rejoices about my coming into relationship with you.

September 27   Meditate

Joshua 1:8 *This Book of the Law shall not depart from your mouth, but you shall meditate in it day and night, that you may observe to DO according to all that is written in it. For then you will make your way prosperous, and then you will have good success.*

DO means intent.

Q What are we to do with the Bible?

We are to think about it and talk about it.

The Lord spoke to Joshua and said to heed all that Moses had written, that is the Pentateuch, the first five books of the Bible. That was what they had then but it is not a stretch to extend this mandate to all scripture

Be very clear on this - We are justified by faith through grace. We are not saved by the law but it is still in effect. *Do not think that I came to destroy the Law or the Prophets; I did not come to destroy but to fulfill. For assuredly, I say to you, till heaven and earth pass away, one jot or one tittle will by no means pass from the law till all is fulfilled* Matthew 5:17-18. There are some laws that just make good social and business sense.

In today's verse, we see the phrase, *shall not depart from your mouth.* Don't let any negative person or negative emotion cause you to be quiet. INSTANT REPLAY - Don't let any negative person or negative emotion cause you to be quiet. This may not mean that we always talk about the Bible but it does mean that we talk about it at appropriate times. We should talk with knowledge and conviction based upon our meditation which should be a constant thing, directing all our thoughts and steps.

The verse also says, *"Observe to do according to all that is written."* - We are to look upon the Bible in its entirety to give instruction in life. By following the precepts of God's word, we will find success in our business endeavors and social pursuits. The 10 Commandments are a case in point (Exodus 20). God is primary and basic rules for social success are clear.

Prayer - Dear Father, thank You for Your word that I can think about it and share it with others, and by using it, prosper and have good success.

September 28   Test

1 John 4:1-2 *Beloved, DO not believe every spirit, but test the spirits, whether they are of God ... by this you know the Spirit of God: Every spirit that confesses that Jesus Christ has come in the flesh is of God ...*

DO means have mental toughness.

Q Are we to believe every spirit?

No

The spirits are prevailing thoughts that may affect our mental processes. These thoughts come to us from many sources. There are spirits that say that Jesus was never human. Whatever moves them, there are people who say we can do anything we want to because we are saved by grace. These are just two of Satan's lies. We are not to believe the lies or the people who tell them. They are children of Satan – like father, like son, Satan is a liar and his children are liars (John 8:44).

We know from Jesus' teachings, and from other Bible passages, that there is an evil force in the world and that he wants to harm us any way he can (John 10:10). He attacks us with things about ourselves, things in the world, and things that we know very little about (Ephesians 6:12). To deny the existence of Satan, or to deny that he is actively trying to destroy the word of God, is to be wide open to attack.

We need to know about the enemy and how he works. Satan is the ruler of this world and has many people in high and low places who knowingly or unknowingly work for him. We need to know how to fight against Satan. *Be sober; be vigilant; because your adversary the devil walks about like a roaring lion, seeking whom he may devour ... Resist him, steadfast in the faith* 1 Peter 5:8.

For you science students, the Litmus Test for activities is – Is this something that Jesus would do? WWJD?

Prayer - Dear Father, thank you for alerting me about the enemy and teaching me how to defeat him.

September 29   Grieve

Ephesians 4:30 _And DO not grieve the Holy Spirit of God, by whom you were sealed for the day of redemption._

DO please the Holy Spirit

Q What does the Holy Spirit do for us?

He seals us.

How do we grieve the Holy Spirit?

1. We blaspheme Him: to blaspheme the Holy Spirit is to accuse Him of being evil.
2. We refuse Him: we don't accept the gift given to us by Jesus. There are groups today who deny that the Holy Spirit and/or Jesus are part of the Godhead.
3. We refuse His gifts - Love, joy, peace, abiding presence, etc. There are those who accept Satan's lies and don't allow the Spirit to become active in their lives.

The contents of a personal letter are sealed to keep the message safe from being lost or getting dirty. In like fashion the Spirit seals us with protection that ensures our safe delivery (2 Corinthians 1:2). In olden days hot wax was poured on the edges of a document and imprinted with a signet ring. We have the blood of Christ poured out for the remission of our sins. We have the mark of the Holy Spirit signifying our life in Him. We glorify God by being, and bringing, His message to the world.

A girl was searching through her Animal Crackers. When asked by her mother what she was doing, she replied, "Well, outside the box it said, ' Do not eat if seal is broken'. I'm looking for the seal." We live to show that the seal of the Spirit is not broken in us.

What is the day of redemption? We are redeemed by the sacrifice of Christ. Our redemption is validated when we accept His sacrifice. The _day of redemption_ in our physical life is when we accept Christ as Savior and in our eternal life when we pass from this life to the next.

Prayer - Dear Father, may the words of my mouth, the emotions of my heart, the actions of my body, and the thoughts of my mind delight the Holy Spirit.

September 30   Complete

Hebrews 13:20-21 *Now may the God of peace ... make you complete in every good work to DO His will, working in you what is well pleasing in His sight, through Jesus Christ, to whom be glory forever and ever.*

The benediction at the end of Hebrews begins with the word *Now* which puts an exclamation point on everything that was presented previously from Chapter 12:1. Chapter 12:1 begins with the word *Therefore* which is based on the information given in Chapters 1 through 11. As you reflect on the *Now's* and *Therefore's* of the Bible, realize that previous information is important to know in understanding what follows.

> DO is to enact His will

Q How are we completed?

> We are completed through Jesus Christ, God's instrument for completion.

> Who completes us? *The God of peace.* The writer of Hebrews took a cue from the writings of Paul.

> Why are we completed? To be sanctified and to *DO His will.*

> How are we completed? God works in us.

> What completes us? God's work in us. ... *work out your own salvation with fear and trembling; for it is God who works in you both to will and to DO for His good pleasure Philippians 2:12-13.* We are to work OUT what God has worked IN. By saying that we need to be completed, it becomes known that we are not complete without God's handiwork. He makes us complete so we can do what He intends for us to do.

> In our verse for today, the writer of Hebrews says, "... *what is well pleasing in His sight* ..." Paul writes, "... *for His good pleasure.*" Both indicate that when we do God's will, we are fulfilling His desires for us as we live in Christ Jesus and bring Him eternal glory.

Prayer - Dear Father, forever complete and sanctify me so I am pleasing to You.

OCTOBER

OF

Meditation Aids

OF – Preposition. A preposition (pre-position) usually is a word used before a noun or pronoun to form a phrase that modifies (qualifies, describes, or limits) some aspect of the sentence. The object of the preposition could be a noun, a verb, or an adjective. Check the objects of the preposition OF to understand its impact.

Uses: as a result – because of – from – part of – concerning.

Example:

> ... that which is born OF the Spirit is Spirit _John 3:6_.

Spirit is the object of the preposition.

Of the Spirit is a prepositional phrase that describes that which is born.

October 1   Thoughts

Jeremiah 29:11 *For I know the thoughts that I think toward you, says the Lord, thoughts OF peace and not OF evil, to give you a future and a hope.*

Q What does God think towards us?

God thinks thoughts of *peace, a future,* and *a hope* that are fulfilled in Christ.

PEACE -The Scriptures tell us we can have the same peace that Jesus had – "My peace is a peace I want you to have and I'm giving it to anyone who will accept it" (John 14:27b).

FUTURE - We need to know that we have *a future* – Do not despair of tomorrow because of today's sorrow. Windshields are bigger than rear view mirrors for a reason. God's grace is not only convenient (With our avenues), it is prevenient (At the destination of our avenues). He not only is with us along the way, He is there before us when we arrive. God knows all the different paths we may take to reach each destination. In John 14: 1-4 we are told that we can look forward with peace to a *place* that Jesus prepares for us.

HOPE - And we have *a hope* – Our hope is that we will live forever with Jesus (Thessalonians 4:13). In 1Corinthians 13:13 we are advised that *hope* endures.

We are not to dwell on evil but we should be aware that Satan does not want us to have *peace, a future, and a hope*. He will do anything we allow him to do to take those gifts from us (John 10:10).

I have chosen a chapter and verse of Scripture to match each of our children's and grandchildren's birth dates. I couldn't find a suitable verse for one granddaughter's birth date of 11:29 so I chose Jeremiah 29:11 for her.

It is such a comfort to know that we are in God's thoughts. God's thoughts are toward us. His thoughts are true and effective if we choose for them to happen for us.

Prayer – Dear Father, may I accept and grasp the *peace* and *hope* that make today full in itself and a foundation for the *future.*

October 2   Lamb

<u>John 1:29</u> *Behold! The Lamb OF God Who takes away the sin OF the world.*

Q What is God's purpose in Christ?

> God's purpose in Christ is to take away *the sin of the world.*
>
> Once and forever, for all time, with my acceptance and consent, my sin is gone. Jesus does not have to climb back up on the cross every time I sin. However, the transaction is only completed if I confess and accept Him as Savior and Lord. This is also true for *the world.*
>
> Please note – sin is a condition and sins are actions as a result of our condition. My sin and sins are forgiven but it does me no good if I don't accept forgiveness. Then Christ's death on the cross is for nothing. His sacrifice is effective only if it is accepted.

Behold! He is the One *Who takes away* our sin(s). WOW!   Do you really behold Him? Do you recognize Him for Who He is? Jesus is the lamb, the Son of God, given as the sacrifice to pay for our sin(s). He has taken away all sin for all time - past, present, and future. Sin is still on us only if we choose for it to be so.

Some people hold on to their sins because they want their sinful life instead of a relationship with God. They do not want to deny themselves. They are selfish.

Others don't want to forget what is behind - they live in the past. They lick their wounds; they think, "How dare they abuse or neglect me this way." They want to take vengeance away from God and wreak their own punishment. They trade joy and peace for retribution - my way or the highway and if not you are roadkill.

Some hold on to their sins because they doubt the truth of salvation; grace seems so preposterous they can't believe it. Some feel they are too awful or too damaged to be purified. That is really a reverse form of pride. "Look at me, I'm so sinful". The truth is, forgiveness and purification are ours for the believing and receiving. Give it to God, He will take away all your doubts and fears and give you faith and joy.

Prayer – Dear Father, I accept Your sacrifice and thankfully give up my sins.

Tomorrow, we look at what replaces our sin.

October 3   Fruit

Galatians 5:22 *The fruit OF the Spirit is love, joy, peace, patience, kindness, goodness, faithfulness, gentleness, and self-control.*

Q Fruit or fruits?

Note that the word fruit is singular. The fruit of the Spirit isn't separate graces, it is like a team. We have the whole team when we are filled with the Spirit.

The fruit is *of the Spirit*. I have heard sermons on how to get joy, or patience or self-control through some effort or activity on my part. While the fruit comes in different ways, all the fruit of the Spirit is *OF THE SPIRIT.*

I heard another sermon on how we "leak" the fruit. I think a better explanation is that we use the fruit as fuel in His service and can be refilled each time we ask. He restocks the shelves of my *soul* (Psalm 23).

Looking back at yesterday's verse, we find that the Lamb of God takes away our sin. Today we see that the Spirit of God gives us His fruit. What a fantastic trade off. If I need *love, joy, peace* or any other member of the team, I pray to be filled with the Spirit and I have God's love, joy, peace and all the rest. Let's examine the first three more closely:

Love -   beyond our ability to comprehend -   Ephesians 3:19.

Joy -   beyond our ability to put into words -   1 Peter 1:8b.

Peace - beyond our ability to understand -   Philippians 4:7.

What great assurance that the graces of the fruit pass *knowledge*, are *inexpressible*, and surpass all *understanding* – WOW!!! The *fruit of the Spirit* is beyond the ability of human understanding but within the ability to have and use through His power of installation.

All of the parts of the fruit are beyond our comprehension, therefore beyond our ability to bring to be, yet through His grace, are ours for the asking to have and use.

Prayer – Dear Father, Help me avoid the effort of striving for what I can't do and to accept what is mine as Your gift.

October 4   Love

<u>Colossians 3:14</u> *But above all these things put on love, which is the bond OF perfection.*

Q – What forms a perfect relationship bond?

Love.

This type of love is "Agape" in the Greek - An emotion that expresses the preciousness of the one who is loved and the desire that they receive all that is best. Agape is unique to Christian relationships.

Imagine this scenario: You are shopping and see that there is a store offering a free suit, available for you. It fits perfectly, looks great: all you need to do is pick it up. Some people don't know it is there and drive past; some know but are too busy and drive past; some go in and look but reject it for whatever reason; some try it on but decide against it; while others put it on, appreciate it, and walk out in newness of life looking and feeling like a million dollars! We need to, and can, *put on* Christ and His attributes.

See the list of *these things* in Colossians 3:12b-13.

God loved us so much He experienced the death of His Son for us (John 3:16). He loved us enough to give His Son as a sacrifice for our sins so we could have relationship with Him. WOW! Several verses extol the importance of love: John 15:13 tells us that Jesus' love for us is the utmost demonstration of this emotional verb. Paul mentions many excellent virtues and concludes that love is the greatest virtue of all (1 Corinthians 13:13).

We can *put on the bond of love* and extend it to others. (Agape love.) Think of why the Dead Sea is dead. It has no outlet. Water, containing minerals, flows into the Dead Sea. The water evaporates leaving an ever increasing percentage of salt, until life cannot be maintained. In like manner, the effects of sin can accumulate in our lives without the life changing work of Jesus.

Again, in like manner, if we horde the bond of perfection and do not let love flow on to others, the spark of relationship within us dies.

Prayer – Dear Father, Thanks for loving me so much. I *put on love* so I can bond with You, myself, and others.

October 5   Joy

Nehemiah 8:10b *The joy OF the Lord is my strength.*

Note: *The Joy of the Lord* is not the same as happiness. Happiness depends on circumstance. Joy is part of the fruit of the Spirit (Galatians 5:22). I am happy if my team wins; I am sad if they lose, but despite all the storms of life I have the bedrock *Joy of the Lord* as my anchor.

Q What is one result of joy?   One result is strength!

We are reminded that Joy cannot be expressed in words (1Peter 1:8) and we are to be filled with joy regardless of any tribulation (James 1:2). We can do this with the *joy of the Lord.*

Jesus' words should become part of your being the same way food is distributed to each cell of your body, so that it will become part of you and give you energy (John 15:11). We are to meditate about His joy, receive His joy, thank Him for His joy, and live in His joy.

Isaiah writes of joy _and_ strength: God is vibrant energy and an expression in and of my body and voice (Isaiah 12:2b). He wrote is – not was or will be – but is now, in each moment, and, my – personally mine, not someone else's. Each person has a full measure of joy and spiritual strength.

Whether you need strength for a task, in an illness, or to refuse a temptation, God's joy will enable you to succeed.

If someone says, "I wish I had your outlook on life," you can share with them how they can get joy that makes them strong. Our demonstration of joy in all circumstances is a powerful witness of God's abundant gifts for the asking.

As a final introduction, prior to his wonderful treatise on the installation of spiritual armor, Paul enjoins us to find our strength in the Lord's mighty power (Ephesians 6:10). Joy generates adrenalin which can be as focused as a laser and enables His strength to be released and used in us. Focusing on sadness weakens our abilities to deal with life's tribulations. Joy and strength are better. You think?

Prayer – Dear Father, Thank You for Your gift of joy and the strength and energy it provides.

October 6   Peace

Philippians 4:7-9 ... *the peace OF God ... the God OF peace will be with you.*

Q What is the difference between these two phrases? The *peace of God* is a gift to us while the *God of peace* is the Giver of the gift.

WOW! We have the *peace of God* because it is given by *the God of peace.* Today we consider several passages regarding peace.

What is peace? Peace is the opposite of anxiety. Philippians 4:6-7 begins with anxiety and ends with peace. In between are the ingredients of a peace sandwich: whatever your circumstances, be thankful, and ask for God's will in all things.

In Philippians 4:7 we see that God's peace is beyond human understanding. *Therefore, d*on't try to understand it, just know the *peace of God* is possible and receive it.

In Philippians 4:8-9 We are given a model of behavior that promotes God's peace.

In John 14:27 Jesus said, "Don't try to compare the peace I give you with what the world calls peace. This is the peace I have, secure and settled in My Father's arms. World peace is just absence from war. My peace is the presence and power in the purpose of God ". Not just peace, but My *peace*, Jesus' peace.

How do we receive His peace? Besides being part of the fruit of the Spirit, we are told in Isaiah 26:3 to fix our minds on God so that we will have perfect peace. Whenever you feel anxious, turn your mind to Jesus and claim His peace. In Christ *we* have perfect peace, not just a piece of peace.

Paul writes in Ephesians 2:14 that Jesus is the personification of *peace.*

And in Colossians 3:15, Paul tells us that peace should control our *hearts* ... God gives us peace to rule in our hearts because the heart is the seat of emotions and can promote negative thoughts and actions. If peace rules, the negative thoughts and actions are controlled and positive actions result.

Prayer – Dear Father, thank you for these wonderful promises; help me to believe in, accept, and live in Your peace.

October 7   Godliness

<u>1Timothy 6:11</u> *But you, O man OF God … pursue righteousness, godliness, faith, love, patience, gentleness.*

Q As we think about our goals and the meaning of life, one question is, what is our purpose in life? What's it all about?

> To be people of God.

> Paul warned Timothy not to be like those who desire riches but to make it a goal to obtain *righteousness*, etc. These virtues compare with what Paul described as the fruit of the Spirit (Galatians 5:22-23). We too, as people of God, can have these earmarks of Christianity by pursuing them with the same intense effort as Timothy. This happens when we utilize the power of the Holy Spirit. We are to study the Scriptures so He can bring to our recall everything that is true (John 16:13). The neat thing is that when we pursue them, we find the Holy Spirit is pursuing us and they are ours with no effort on our part.

> Let's examine the meaning of the above stated virtues:

> <u>Righteousness</u> is right living, a right relationship with God and His people.

> <u>Godliness</u> is the sum total of Christian character and actions.

> <u>Faith</u> is unwavering trust in light of all else.

> <u>Love</u> is a desire for, and actions that benefit, the welfare of others.

> <u>Patience</u> is strength under control - long fuse - endurance under trial.

> <u>Gentleness</u> is calm tenderness.

> The opposites of all these virtues can happen when Satan does his <u>worst</u> to make sure that opportunities will arise that could shipwreck our best intentions.

> We should select what we want in our lives. Do we want sin, evil, doubt, hate, impatience, and hardness, or do want these virtues that characterize God's children?

Prayer – Dear Father, I choose to pursue Christian virtues.

October 8   Fervent

<u>James 5:16b</u> *The effective, fervent prayer OF a righteous man avails much.*

Q – What are descriptors of appropriate prayers? Let's examine each descriptive word:

> *Effective* - When we pray, we often end the prayer by saying, "in Jesus' name, amen," but what does that mean? In this case, name means nature or likeness. We pray in the nature of Christ if we pray with His goals in mind.

> *Fervent* – We don't pray in a panic but we need to be strongly sincere. In some societies there are prayer wheels. One hard spin and several "prayers" go up to God. While we often pray for the same thing, we need to be careful not to just say the words and forget what was said.

> *Righteous* – We are not fair weather prayers. There is a saying, "There are no atheists in foxholes." Many people only pray when they are in a dire situation. They pray as a last resort - "The only thing we can do now is pray." Prayer is the FIRST thing we should do.

Some people say, "God knows His will and our needs so why pray?" The answer is, God always answers prayer to help <u>us</u> understand <u>His</u> will.

Be careful not to give children the wrong idea about prayer. They should not just be told to pray about it, expecting God to obediently do what they ask. God is not a slot machine where we put in twenty-five cents worth of prayer and expect a payoff in silver dollars. We need to teach children how to understand God's answers. He will answer by saying:

> "Go - This is My will and it should be accomplished."
> "Slow - Don't get ahead of me; some things need to happen before this will happen."
> "Grow - I am allowing this experience to prune you and help you mature in our relationship." Or
> "No - This is not My will and it isn't going to happen."

But, He always answers. He <u>always</u> answers. In any case, pray and see the answer in one of the above stated possibilities. Then our prayers will always have positive results knowing what God does or does not want.

Prayer – Dear Father, teach me the nature of Christ so that I might truly pray in Jesus name.

October 9   Know

Philippians 3:10 ... *that I may* know *Him and the* power OF His resurrection *and the* fellowship OF His sufferings, *being* conformed to His death, *if by any means, I may attain to the resurrection from the dead.* (Emphasis added.)

Q What are the means by which I attain the resurrection from the dead?

The key words are underlined. Use the emphasis tip. The *means* are: that I *may know Him* – really KNOW Him. A lot of people know a lot about Jesus but they don't *know HIM.*

We *may know Him* and we can *know Him.* How do we know Him? To know Him is to know His power, to have *fellowship* with Him, and be *conformed to His death,* joining in the suffering of forgiveness.

The power of His resurrection is in His sacrificial death when He bore the burden of ALL sin for ALL time and that any number of people can be given eternal life through Him.

The *Fellowship of His suffering* – to have fellowship with Christ is to have His empathy. Sympathy means I feel sorry for you, but to have empathy means I feel your sorrow. Paul spoke of his own daily intense suffering for the churches (2 Corinthians 11: 28). Paul took on his body the *afflictions* of Christ (Colossians 1:24).

As we forgive, we also take on His afflictions.

Conformed to His death – there have been thousands of martyrs in Christ throughout the centuries since Jesus' death and resurrection. There may be many more. The thing to remember is that they are not martyred to death; they are martyred to eternal life. In the experience of every possessing Christian we conform to His death by dying to the world.

By any means – We have the way, truth, and life found only in Christ (John 14:6).

Prayer – Dear Father, I rejoice that I KNOW Him. Instill in me every likeness to the life of Christ.

October 10   Hold

Philippians 3:12 *That I may lay hold OF that for which Christ laid hold OF me ...*

Q Why did Christ lay hold of Paul? So Paul could *lay hold* of what Christ had in store for him.

Think of *that* – what is *that* which is His intent? God chose Paul to suffer many things for His sake and to be a witness to the world of all the things God had done for him and us.

In our case Jesus lays hold on us so that we can return to the pre-apple experience described in Genesis. At that time, God wanted a relationship with His created people such that they would choose to have a relationship with Him. Choice is the operative word. The problem is that we have all chosen sin and have fallen short of God's glory. In order to overcome that gap, God gives us the choice of being a new creation in Christ.

First of all, as seen in Philippians 3:10, God wants a personal relationship with us. Do those of us who have children love them? Yes, and God loves His children.

Secondly, God wants feet on the ground. He wants people, redeemed by Jesus, filled with and guided by the Holy Spirit, to live the Gospel and spread the Good News to all the world.

Go therefore and make disciples of all the nations ... baptize ... and teach ... Matthew 28:19 (See also Acts 1:8).

Undergirding all of this is our heavenly Father's love and care for us as His children. We can rest assured because we have this promise – God is our safe house, based on the foundation of His unending strength (Deuteronomy 33:27).

Prayer – Dear Father, Thank you for laying hold of me. May I not struggle against Your hold but relax and rest in Your *everlasting arms*.

October 11   Fullness

John 1:16-17 *And OF His fullness we have all received and grace for grace ... grace and truth came through Jesus Christ*

Q Does Jesus only give us part of Himself?

No, He has given us *His fullness – grace for grace.*

It is grace that enables us to receive grace. Even the faith that we have to receive grace is a grace gift (Ephesians 2:8-9). We know for sure that Jesus is the truth and that grace is favor that we don't deserve and can't earn.

We have received that which we are unable to achieve for ourselves. In a world of lies, exaggerations, empty promises, and disappointments we have God's grace – grace upon grace. The gift of grace prepares for more grace. Grace is God's available more. It is hard to believe that what I can't do is achievable and receivable through the gift of God's grace. Believe the believable and receive the receivable - God's grace.

In my life in Christ, there have been so many times that I have received a deeper grace, so much that it seemed like the previous grace paled in comparison. I now know it was all I could receive at the time. Meanwhile, God was continually allowing and giving experiences and circumstances so that more grace could be received. He gives sufficient trouble and sufficient grace.

When we give our "vine" to God, He will cut off unproductive branches and trim the rest so the best possible harvest will occur (John 15:2). Here is another parable. Our life is like a barrel of rocks. As rocks are removed, there is room for more grace. Grace is available to fill what grace removes.

His fullness is the utmost of grace and He gives us steps of grace so that we can achieve more and more of His fullness.

Prayer – Dear Father, I open myself to the fullness of your grace.

October 12   Sound

2 Timothy 1:7 *For God has not given us a spirit OF fear, but OF power and OF love and OF a sound mind.*

Q What lifts our spirits?

> Power, love, and sanity cast out fear.

The spirit discussed here is in our inner being and is the foundation of our approach to life. Reasonable concern is one thing but negative fear is dread, anxiety, and apprehension.

In Paul and Timothy's days, the opposite of power, love, and a sound mind were much in evidence. Fear, weakness, hatred and mental disorders were the order of the day. Is it different today? Anxiety and depression run rampant among US citizens. We need the above mentioned antidotes for fear in our lives. He hasn't given us fear. When we have fear, we don't have power, love, or focused thoughts. Instead, we are compromised by weakness with feelings of inadequacy, defensiveness, hate, and resentment, all of which result in fearful confusion.

God has given:

Power for our physical and emotional being – I will praise God even if I have a physical or emotional problem so that His power will make any of my weakness a witness for Him (2 Corinthians 12:9b). We get power when we receive the Holy Spirit (Acts 1:8).

Love for our emotional being – I am positive that God loves me so I don't have to fear anything that happens or might happen (1 John 4:18). We get love when we receive the Holy Spirit (Galatians 5:22).

A sound mind for our intellectual operation - *... and the peace of God, which surpasses all understanding, will guard your hearts and minds through Christ Jesus* Philippians 4:7. To reject Christ is an act of insanity.

Prayer – Dear Father, fill me now with power, love, and sanity.

October 13   Forgetting

Philippians 3:13b – 14 ... *but one thing I do, forgetting those things which are behind and reaching forward to those things which are ahead, I press toward the goal for the prize OF the upward call OF God in Christ Jesus.*

The criminal often returns to the scene of the crime. The crime often returns to the victim in flashbacks and other PTSD symptoms.

REPLAY September 5 - Today, we go into greater depth with this verse.

Q What was Paul's goal? Paul's goal was to press on toward the upward call of God.

In order to gain the prize, we need to forget the things that are behind. Forgetting is nearly impossible if we keep replaying the offense in our minds. The consonants in the acronym FoRGeT provide an interesting method for dealing with past hurts. The process actually needs to be worked backwards T - e - G - R - o - F to undo or get past the past.

T - Talk – to God and to a trusted confidant. A problem shared is cut in half.

G - Grieve – Write a letter to God, cry - tears are God's gifts to wash our brains, especially take a walk and talk with God.

R - Recycle – Read, and make it part of your understanding of life, 1 Corinthians 10:13, and 2 Corinthians 1:3-5. Look for God's use of any situation.

F - Forgive – whatever or whomever has offended you – say it aloud. I forgive ___. What we won't forgive, we can't forget. Give it to God. When we forgive, we are forgiven.

Talk, Grieve, Recycle, Forgive. The upward call of God is a relationship of forgiveness and love with Him and His children. The river of relationship is dammed up by a lack of forgiveness. Windshields are bigger than rearview mirrors for a reason. Lack of forgiveness fogs over our windshield making it hard to see where we are going in life.

Thank You Lord for calling me *upward.*

Prayer – Dear Father, help me to forget the past and follow Your *upward call.*

October 14   Spirit

<u>Romans 8:5-6</u> *For those who live according to the flesh set their minds on the things OF the flesh, but those who live according to the Spirit, the things OF the Spirit. For to be carnally minded is death, but to be spiritually minded is life and peace.*

Q On what are we to set our minds? We are to set our minds on *the things of the Spirit.* The *flesh* is anything that is contrary to God.

Once we have a mindset we choose information that supports it and tend to ignore and deny information that goes against it. <u>We get good at what we practice.</u> Possessing Christians practice *the things of the Spirit* and that is what we need to do.

See Mark 7:21 for a list of what Jesus means by the evil that comes from being *carnally minded.* This verse deals with stinking thinking and gives the heart as the source of evil for those who have a mindset based in the *flesh.* They think about and perform deliberate acts, based on what they <u>think</u> is critical thought that supports their activity.

God did not bring inappropriate sexual thoughts and actions, nor smugness about such things to be (1John 2:16). Even if we once had an evil mindset, we have been transformed by the Spirit to have the mind of Christ.

Don't reduce yourself to what the world wants but let the mind of Christ, that you now have, direct you in God's wonderful plan for your life. Don't sink to the world but rise to Godliness (Romans 12:2). Do not let the world define you.

We are to be transformed, that is, some power outside ourselves must do this. Thanks be unto God, part of His redeeming power is to give us a new mind – Christ's mind (1Corinthians 2:16). We now can think as Jesus thinks.

The *things of the flesh* lead to death while spiritual attributes lead to *life and peace.* INSTANT REPLAY - *the things of the Spirit* lead to *life and peace.*

CHOOSE THE SPIRIT.

Prayer – Dear Father, fill me with Your Spirit and set my mind on spiritual things – life and peace.

October 15   Acceptable

<u>Psalm 19:14</u> *Let the words OF my mouth, and the meditations OF my heart be acceptable in Your sight, O Lord my strength and my Redeemer.*

Q What should guide my words and thoughts?

That they would be pleasing to my loving heavenly Father.

Clearly, parts of acceptance are *the words of my mouth* and *the meditations of my heart.*

What I think about in the storehouse of my inner being leads to what I say (Matthew 12:34b-35). These two things need to be acceptable to God.

In James 3:1-5 the tongue is compared to a bit in a horses' mouth, a small rudder for a large ship, and a blaze of fire. The message is that the tongue, although a small thing in the body, can have a great influence, either positive or negative.

Inspect my life. Weed out anything that would take me away from You and increase what leads me towards You (Psalm 139:23-2). Our prayer must be that He would search and know our hearts and remove any darkness. And we need to ask Him to try us and know our anxieties. Then we ask Him to help us and to lead us away from wickedness and towards everlasting life.

Once our hearts are right,

What comes out of our mouths is bright.

Our strength is in our *Redeemer* and He is in us. We need to remember and accept Christ as our source of strength before we succumb to the weakness of the flesh. A lot of words, a raft of emotions, and much activity come from the kaleidoscope of our thoughts.

In my prayers, morning, throughout the day, and at night, I use the following prayer as a check list, sometimes needing to confess and receive forgiveness.

Prayer – Dear Father, let the words of my mouth, the emotions of my heart, the actions of my body, and the thoughts of my mind be <u>delightful</u> in your sight.

October 16   World

John 17:14 ... the world has hated them because they are not OF the world, just as I am not OF the world.

Q Why does the world hate *them*, His disciples, and those of us who believe?

The world hates *them* because *they* keep the word. The world hates us because their deeds are evil and our deeds aren't. Our good deeds shine a bright spotlight on evil.

The world attempts to shape our thoughts, dictate our actions, and put our lights out. It is usually for financial gain, self-gratification, or anything that takes away peace and joy. They do not want to be transformed into the image of God. They have knowingly, or unknowingly, cast their lot with Satan. People who don't stand for something will fall for anything.

Hatred, in its strongest form, is a passionate dislike; it means to detest or loathe. In a weaker sense, hatred implies an oppositional mindset that becomes stronger when pushed to the limit. There is no peace or joy in any of that. If you haven't experienced this hatred, just wait until you take a definite stand for Christ in a given situation. I remember locking myself in the pantry of the fraternity house where I worked to get away from a person who attacked me because I bowed my head in thanksgiving before eating. There may be those who are no longer your "friends" when you change your life to follow Christ. The spotlight makes them uncomfortable.

Possessing Christians are in the world but *not of the world*. The first part of this phrase is not a Bible verse but it aptly describes our situation. We need to exist in the world but we do not act like the world. The world is a good place to show God's love when all good, or bad, things happen.

If we have not died to the world, it can be very uncomfortable to be hated. INSTANT REPLAY - If we have not died to the world, it can be very uncomfortable to be hated. When we have died to the world, it no longer has power over us unless we give it power. INSTANT REPLAY - When we have died to the world, it no longer has power over us unless we give it power. We have to be strong in the power of His might to withstand the fiery darts of Satan (Ephesians 6:16).

Prayer – Dear Father, help me to know Your love so strongly that I don't care about any feelings the world may have.

October 17   Root

<u>1Timothy 6:10</u> *The love OF money is a root OF all kinds OF evil.*

Q Is money evil?

No.

Notice, it says *"a"* root, often misquoted as "the" root. It is not money that is evil; it is *the love of money* that becomes *a root of all kinds of evil*. While roots aren't evil, they do take from the environment where they are growing. When the soil is good, roots take nourishment that contributes to the vitality of the plant. Place a plant in unfertile soil and it won't flourish. Put poison in the soil and the plant will die. Roots take what is available to them. Where we plant ourselves is where we place our roots.

If we sink our roots in money, money becomes the object of our affection and the goal of our efforts in life. Our love for God and others will diminish and the door is opened for evil. If the roots are fixed in *the love of money*, the plant bears *all kinds of evil* fruit. Greed, envy, abuse of employees and nature, etc. become evil fruit.

The love of money pushes out consideration and love for others and may become an obsession. It could even become an addiction that drives our total existence. It is interesting that people with billions want more billions. Too much is never enough.

Even though the love of money is a root of evil, money is a necessary tool and, with God's guidance, can be used to glorify Him. Love should not be for money but, in its purest form, love should be directed towards God. We respond in love to His initiation of love for us (1John 4:19). Now, with this "soil" made of love, we are able to love, not money, but God, ourselves, and others, and use money for His purposes. Be rooted in God.

Prayer – Dear Father, help me direct my love towards You, the root of all kinds of good.

October 18   Born

John 3:6 *That which is born OF the flesh is flesh and that which is born OF the Spirit is Spirit.*

Q What is the origin of *flesh* and *Spirit*?

Flesh and *Spirit.*

If we are only born once, *of the flesh*, we die twice – physically and spiritually. If we are born twice, first *of the flesh* and then *of the Spirit*, we only die once. Jesus taught His disciples that in order to enter the Kingdom of God, people need what can be called the second birth (John 3:3). Belief in Christ makes the second birth possible and allows eternal life through Him (John 11:26).

See a list of activities of those who only have the first birth in Galatians 5:19-21. There is a difference between an occasional error and intentional, practiced evil. Even if we intentionally or unintentionally visit an evil place, we don't need to live there. We have the love and power of God Who will show us how we have gone down a wrong path and He will rescue us. We need to recognize evil and avoid it, or, if drawn towards evil, to immediately retreat.

It is important to know that we are born through the regenerative power of God (John 1:13). This verse makes it clear that God doesn't have grandchildren. Each generation must make its own decision for Christ.

Our first birth was *of the flesh*; we now need to be *born of the Spirit*. When we are born of the Spirit we have the availability of the fruit of the Spirit (Galatians 5:22-23). An interesting bit of humor is attached here - *Against such there is no law.* Unfortunately, many things that promote the Kingdom of God are now illegal or frowned upon. Practically any deviant doctrine is accepted while it is not politically correct to express Christian principles. Be that as it may, possessing Christians are *born of the Spirit,* and have all of the Spirit's power, gifts, and fruit.

Prayer – Dear Father, Thank You for my second birth, that I am a new creation in Christ.

October 19   Filled

<u>Colossians 1:9</u> ... *that you may be filled with the knowledge OF His will ...*

Q What is the will God?

God's will is that we should have eternal relationship with Him. There are several wonderful verses that tell us what the will of God is:

<u>Everlasting life</u> - And this is the will of Him Who sent Me, that everyone who sees the Son and believes in Him may have everlasting life ... <u>John 6:40</u>. We have to *see* Him, really *see* what He is all about. Seeing is believing but also believing is seeing and seeing should not go in one eye and out the other.

<u>Sanctification</u> - For this is the will of God, your sanctification ... that each of you should know how to possess his own vessel in sanctification and honor ... <u>1Thessalonians 4:3</u>. Our *vessel,* our body (and its members) is the vehicle of our actions in the world. Sanctification means we should be set apart and have control of our physical being.

<u>Always rejoicing, praying, giving thanks</u> - Rejoice always, pray without ceasing, in everything give thanks; for this is the will of God In Christ Jesus for you <u>1Thessalonians 5:16 -18</u>. We want to have Joyful, prayerful, thankful lives in Christ Jesus.

We want to use all of the things He wills that we possess:

Knowledge

Everlasting life   Sanctification

Rejoicing   Prayer

Thanksgiving

God's will is clear. We have the foundation for an excellent direction for our lives. When we are *<u>filled</u> with the knowledge of HIS will*, there is no room for Satan to mess around.

Prayer – Dear Father, May I continually seek, and be filled, with the attributes of the knowledge of Your will.

October 20   Promise

Galatians 3:14 ... *that we might receive the promise OF the Spirit through faith.*

Q How do we receive this promise?   *Through faith* that God gives us.

Ask for the promise to be fulfilled, have faith that the promise has been fulfilled, and then live in the promise of the fullness of the Spirit. God strongly desires us to ask for and receive the Holy Spirit (Luke 11:13). The receiving of the Holy Spirit is sometimes referred to as the second work of grace. Whatever, whenever, wherever, ask! Realize Satan will fight you every step of the way but Christ, Who is in us, is greater than Satan who is restricted to the world. If there is any confusion about the Holy Spirit, it is because Satan has prompted people to either ignore or proof text the Bible for their own purposes.

God wills for us to have His Spirit. Jesus' work on earth was restricted to His physical presence. When He left, He gave us His Spirit Who is universally present. Once we have believed in and received Christ, we are able to receive His Spirit and all that the Spirit gives us.

Jesus promised us His Spirit. The Spirit is in us and around us constantly. Jesus knew the will of His Father and He prayed, according to the Father's will, that we receive the Holy Spirit as an everlasting Helper (John 14:16-17).

When we consider the trinity, we need to know the function of each Part. The Holy Spirit is God's presence in our lives. One of the primary objectives of this book of devotions is to encourage you, the reader, to have a full understanding of the power and presence of the Holy Spirit in your life.

Don't expect nonbelievers to understand. They do not have the mind of Christ. When we later examine all that we have in the Holy Spirit, it boggles our own minds (November 11). For now, just ask, believe, and receive.

God wants us to have His Spirit. Jesus wants us to be filled with His Spirit. This is a good thing. We can receive the Holy Spirit. Have you asked for, and received the Holy Spirit? If not, now is a good time. Now is the best time. Why waste time not having God's Spirit within you?

Prayer – Dear Father, thank You for giving us Your Spirit and for the faith to receive Him.

October 21   Armor

Ephesians 6:10-18 *Finally, my brethren, be strong in the Lord and the power OF His might. Put on the whole armor OF God – gird your waist with truth … the breastplate OF righteousness … feet shod with the gospel OF peace … the shield OF faith … the helmet OF salvation … the sword OF the Spirit which is the word OF God … praying always …* (shortened version).

Q How can we have strength in the Lord?

Put on the whole armor of God! Don't leave out any part. The *whole* suit of armor is given for protection and for the ability to witness.

Our fight is not against people (v14). We are given specific armor for Satan's favorite attack points. He wants to destroy truth, righteousness, peace, faith, salvation, the Bible, and our prayers. Satan can't penetrate any part of the armor that we are given.

Gird your waist with truth – We won't be effective if we are tangled up with lies. Gird with Truth – Jesus is the Truth.

Breastplate of righteousness – The breastplate protects the heart which is the wellspring of our emotions.

Shoes of peace – When we are engaged in spiritual warfare, we need good traction, with cleats, so we aren't anxious about slipping. So we have *peace*, part of the fruit of the Spirit.

Shield of faith – Faith is protective and extinguishes the attacks of Satan.

Helmet of salvation – The helmet protects our thoughts and our mouths so they are useful to God and His people.

Sword of the word – Spirit + word = Sword – An offensive weapon which needs to be clear and sharp.

Praying always – Another offensive weapon, our first line of defense and offense.

Prayer – Dear Father, thank you for each piece of armor and each directive. May I check each day to see that each item is in good repair.

October 22   Hope

1Thessalonians 1:3 ... *remembering without ceasing your work OF faith, labor OF love, and patience OF hope in our Lord Jesus Christ.*

Paul gave a similar message in Colossians 1:3-5.

Q Why would others be thankful and pray for us?

Because they have heard of us, our:

Work of faith - Our faith results in good works. A faith response to God is to keep His commandments and express His care to others. Our works show our faith. We are saved by grace through faith for works (Ephesians 2:8-10).

Labor of love – Be fixed on a solid platform, not subject to sin, so that you can be released to bound into God's work. When we are fixed in Him, we are guaranteed a life of productivity (1 Corinthians 15:58). Our labor show our love.

Patience of hope – patience and hope are included in the characteristics of love listed in 1 Corinthians 13:4-8. Our patience and hope come to life in Christ. Our patience shows that our hope is secure.

All of these activities, physical and mental, are done because of our position in our Lord Jesus Christ.

Whether we are yeast or dynamite, we can live our life *in our Lord Jesus Christ.* God sees our faith in action as we labor in love and maintain hope in Him.

Prayer – Dear Father, help me live a life that others will remember as one of work, love, and patience of hope all in response to, and use of, Your Gifts.

October 23   Convict

John 16:8-11 *When He* (the Holy Spirit) *has come, He will convict the world OF sin, and OF righteousness, and OF judgment. OF sin because they do not believe in Me. OF righteousness because I go to My Father, … OF judgment because the ruler OF this world is judged.*

> There is *sin*; there is *righteousness*; so there will be *judgment* depending on choice.

Q How does the Holy Spirit *convict the world of* evil, goodness, and divine retribution?

> He uses His people, nature, and life's events. Jesus convicts (convinces):
>
> *Of sin* - because there are people who do not believe that what they are doing is sin. As we see the results of sin, we are convinced of the errors of sin.
>
> *Of righteousness* - because Jesus' resurrection proves His message is valid. The resurrection of Jesus is the proof of His righteousness.
>
> *Of judgment* - because the tempter, the deceiver, the ruler of this world, has been proven to be a thief, a killer, and a destroyer (John 10:10). The results of sin pass judgment on him who leads people into sin.
>
> The Holy Spirit will convict the world of judgment. Many people do not believe there will be judgment and punishment for sin. They think, "God is too nice for that." They live in sin until it becomes commonplace, almost ho-hum. They ignore the fact that they have made a choice and must live with the consequences.
>
> One way that people are convicted of righteousness is by seeing the actions of righteous people. Righteousness is imputed (placed upon us) through justification. We are not just pardoned, our sins are taken away. We are justified, giving us relationship with God, and are empowered by the Holy Spirit. When we accept His taking away our sin and taking away our judgment, we can live righteously.

Prayer – Dear Father, thank You for convicting me of sin so that I could accept the conviction of righteousness, and helping me know that, through Jesus, I will not face judgment.

October 24   Guide

<u>John 16:13</u> *When the Spirit OF truth has come, He will guide you into all truth.*

Q How do we find the truth?

The Spirit of truth will guide us *into all truth.*

This is another compelling reason to have the Holy Spirit within us. It is important that we know *all truth* because Satan has brought so many lies into the world and into some churches.

This is a *when*, not an *if*. And the Spirit *has come* and <u>is ours</u> for the asking.

This verse is loaded with meaning. We will be guided into all truth when the Spirit has come to us, and He <u>will</u> come to us when we ask the Father for Him (Luke 11:13). First - believe what Jesus says, then claim Jesus' claim of who He is and what He does in our lives (John 14:6). Then ask for, receive, and rejoice in the guidance of the Spirit.

The most important truth is that relationship with God is available through Christ and that through Him, we have life now and forever. To guide us in that life, we have the Holy Spirit. We have tools; we have power, gifts and fruit; we have the mind of Christ. We are in Him and He is in us.

All of this is possible if we allow the Spirit to guide us. We utilize the mental activities given by the Spirit. We need not be lost in confusion and doubt, we have a GUIDE. We need to ask for Him and follow His leading.

It was *WHEN* at the time of Jesus' teaching, it is NOW for us. <u>Every moment of our lives we can live in all truth</u>.

Prayer – Dear Father help me seek and accept the truth in Jesus and give me the courage to live triumphantly with joy and power!

October 25   Keep

<u>John 17:15</u> *I do not pray that you should take them out OF this world, but that You would keep them from the evil one.*

Q Do we need to leave the world to survive as Christians?

No, God will protect us from the evil one.

Satan is in the world, but Christ is in us. As long as we are filled with the Holy Spirit, Satan cannot enter into us.

We need to recognize and identify Satan as the enemy. To deny his presence or his power is to aid and abet the enemy. We need to get it straight that we are fighting a spiritual battle against an unseen enemy and unseen forces (Ephesians 6:12). Trust God, trust His word. Don't let your guard down.

The good news is, we don't need to consider what would take us out of the world. There are those who start communes or communities or cut interaction with society. We need to be in the world to be God's feet on the ground. We know that we have the protection of the Holy Spirit. He will keep us from the evil one, that is, Satan, who is the ruler of this world (John 12:31).

So, how do we live in a world of sin? We accept Satan's law as frequently occurring - If he can make anything can go wrong, he will. We take away the power of sin by being thankful in every circumstance and by letting God use all events to help us mature in Christ and to be strengthened in our faith. We need to be thankful <u>in</u> everything (Philippians 4:6).

We are <u>in</u> the world but not <u>of</u> the world. This is a true statement. We are not out of the world. We are in fellowship with possessing siblings and God through the ever-present power of the Holy Spirit. God's power keeps us in saving faith, the result of which will endure to the end   (1 Peter 1:5).

Prayer – Dear Father, may I be very careful to take each step in Jesus' and the Holy Spirit's care and keeping.

October 26   Riches

Romans 11:33 *O, the depth OF the riches both OF the wisdom and knowledge OF God! WOW!*

Q What is the difference between knowledge and wisdom?

> Knowledge is what we know; wisdom is what we <u>do</u> with what we know.

> This verse is a praise song to God, to His glory. He has done great things with His wisdom and knowledge.

> What we need to know is this – Wisdom starts with, and is founded upon, the awe, respect and esteem for Creator God (Proverbs 9:10). An intelligent, orderly universe, based on a loving God, is now a basis for all succeeding thought. We should have all the attitudes of awe, and respect, and esteem towards God. If our lives are lived in awe of God, that will help us direct our decisions and steps in ways that please Him and are of most benefit to us. The mindset that God is Who He says He is, and that life in Him is possible and essential, starts us out on the right path. Once in Christ and directed by the Holy Spirit, we can obtain His *riches*.

> We need to realize the magnitude of God's wisdom; it is beyond our understanding. In His wisdom, He has provided the Way and will lead us in living the life that He wants us to live (Psalm 23:3b).

> God's ways are often beyond mankind's ways. If we could totally understand God, then we would be God. Well, we aren't God. There are those who think they are smarter than God, but man's wisdom, when it differs from God's wisdom, is stupidity in His opinion (1 Corinthians 3:19). And this warning – The wisdom of men leads to death (Proverbs 14:12).

> Let God be God, I don't, and can't, understand all of God's workings. What I do know is that in Christ we have a life of power, love, joy, and peace.

Prayer – Dear Father, help me not to be satisfied with shallow thought but to explore and obtain the *depth of your riches of wisdom and knowledge.*

October 27   Grace

<u>1 Peter 5:10</u> *But may the God OF all grace perfect, establish, strengthen, and settle you.*

Q How can we be perfected, established, strengthened, and settled in our faith?

> *The God of all grace* will do all of this for us if we seek Him and follow His guidance into truth. All grace is of God. No other being has grace. Only His grace has the attribute of being *all.*

> It will happen through God's grace, *all grace,* described as favor because we don't deserve this state of being. God is described as *of all grace* because there is precious little grace apart from Him. He will:

> <u>Perfect</u> –   He purifies us   (1 John 3:3).

> <u>Establish</u> –   He edifies us.   (1 Corinthians 3:9b).

> <u>Strengthen</u> –   He empowers us.   (2 Corinthians 12:10).

> <u>Settle</u> –   He convinces us.   (Romans 8:38).

> *For I am persuaded that neither death nor life, nor angels nor principalities nor powers, nor things present nor things to come, nor height nor depth, nor any other created thing, shall be able to separate us from the love of God which is in Christ Jesus our Lord.*

> WOW, WOW, WOW, and WOW!

We need to realize that we <u>were</u> the opposite of this state of being until we accepted grace. We were imperfect, scattered, weak, and at loose ends, chasing every whim or no whim before we received God's grace.

Now, we are empowered to live as *perfected, established, strengthened, and settled* people. We are guided by the Holy Spirit and are given power, gifts, and fruit. We need to ask for, receive, and live in the state of grace that God gives us.

Prayer – Dear Father, I accept your grace, help me to accept my total new identity in You.

October 28   Kindness

Joel 2:13b ... *return to the Lord your God, for He is gracious and merciful, slow to anger, and OF great kindness.*

Joel, an Old Testament author, was writing to a people who had drifted away from God. Joel was attempting to encourage a return to a merciful God.

Joel, centuries before Christ, spoke of grace and mercy.

Q How do we receive grace and mercy?

We turn to God and believe and receive grace and mercy from Him. Grace and mercy were offered in Old Testament times also. Jesus, and the Holy Spirit have made them more alive and active in our lives. Paul, and others, used Joel's words in their greetings to the churches.

Again - Grace is getting what we don't deserve; mercy is not getting what we do deserve. Grace and mercy are among the gifts that are given to us. For those who have never accepted God's grace and mercy, this is great, good news.

To return to the Lord is a message for those who may have drifted away, like the sheep that nibbles into danger. Joel is writing to a generation whose ancestors had, at times, worshipped God and followed His leading.

We can return to Him, if we have nibbled away, because God is *gracious and merciful.* He is not one who will punish us but One Who loves us, wants relationship with us, and has given His Son to purify us from anything that would separate us from Him.

God is patient and compassionate and unwilling that anyone would die without having relationship with Him (2 Peter 3:9).

Instead, with *great kindness* God is considerate, helpful, and thoughtful. God's loving kindness is beyond our comprehension but not beyond our acceptance. All of His bountiful gifts are available to us every day.

Prayer – Dear Father, whatever my condition, I thank you that I can return to, and rest in, Your grace and mercy.

October 29   Use

Hebrews 5:14 Solid food belongs to those who are OF full age, that is, those who by reason OF use have their senses exercised to discern both good and evil.

In this passage, the reference is made to those who are more mature in their relationship and growth in spiritual understanding.

Q How do we get ready for solid food?

We exercise the senses. We use them so we become of full age – maturity in Christ.

There are two ways to gain maturity: to live longer or to live harder.

The senses exercised are SSSTT – Sight, Sound, Smell, Taste, and Touch, and then, a sixth Spiritual Sense activated by the Holy Spirit, in some cases, a gift of discernment to determine good and evil (1 Corinthians 12:10). We are to exercise the senses like any physical exercise program that is recommended. We need many reps a day so that exciting growth can occur.

Solid food is food that is beyond the baby food listed in Hebrews 6:1-2. What is beyond the basic rules of life in Christ? The ability to tell the difference between good and evil. Those who are mature can discern good from evil. This is an important concept in today's world where the lines between good and evil have become blurred. As possessing Christians we need to discern evil and avoid it.

In Genesis 3:6, we see how, with Satan's help, we can rationalize some activity that goes against God's commands. (In that occasion, it wasn't the apple in the tree that was the problem, it was the pair on the ground.) "After all, God wants us to be happy" – and away we go. Hopefully, the failures found in our exercises in doing evil help us to change our program to doing good.

Every spirit, every thought, every teaching, should be held up to the reality of the light of Christ to separate good from evil. This can be done by praying, studying the Bible, and getting wise counsel from those who are mature in Christ.

Prayer – Dear Father, Strengthen my desire to discern good from evil and help me live in the good.

October 30   Salt

Matthew 5:13, 14 *You are the salt OF the earth ... you are the light OF the world.*

Q What are some of the metaphors Jesus used to describe us?

Salt and *light.*

The *You,* plural in this case, are the recipients of the beatitudes (Matthew 5:3-11).

Salt - Salt brings out the flavor of food. When food tastes too bland, we say, "It needs salt." Practically every restaurant table has a salt and pepper shaker on board. We have a natural need for salt. Without getting too technical, NaCl, sodium chloride, is essential for many body functions. Sodium helps control fluid balance and movement and aides cardiovascular function and electrolytic impulses. Chlorine is part of the acid that helps in the digestive action in the stomach. It is amazing how the functions of salt in the human body parallel necessary activities in the Body of Christ.

Light – Light dispels darkness. When having trouble working in darkness, we say, "I need light". Those who do evil want the darkness of anonymity. Those who do good do not fear the light. You who are released and radiant, let your aura light up your area so that your Godly works stand out clearly, so they bring glory to God (Matthew 5:16). Some people are so gloomy their works are shrouded in darkness. Some are released in grace, others are bound by rules. We want light.

Salt is attractive. French Lick, a city in Indiana, is so named because it was a source of salt for animals. We are to be salt so that people come to us to receive God's grace. Light is attractive. The Holy Spirit convicts people of righteousness so they are motivated to find people of the light to find light for themselves.

Our lives are to give flavor and light in order to shed light on the fact and features of God in Christ and the power of the Holy Spirit. What a joy to know that we are *salt* and *light.*

Prayer – Dear Father, May my life show forth the light of Christ and give flavor to others around me.

October 31   Feet

<u>Romans 10:15</u> *How beautiful are the feet OF those who preach the gospel OF peace, who bring glad tidings OF good things* (quoted from Isaiah 52:7).

Peace is the absence of conflict and anxiety.

Q What makes feet beautiful?

> They belong to the group who move into positions where they *preach the gospel of peace – glad tidings of good things.*

> Those who are instruments of peace are blessed and will be called God's children (Matthew 5:9).

> We have the *peace of God* given to us by the *God of peace* (Philippians 4:7-9). How many of us, as children, remember the footsteps of an irate parent or teacher who was coming with tidings of woe. What a difference it is for the opposite - sounds of love and rejoicing.

> Peace is part of the armor described in Ephesians 6:15. Once we have the right footwear, we should not be indulging in sinful activities that will wrench weak joints out of their sockets (Hebrews 12:13). Those who observe us should discover *peace* and hear *glad tidings.* We are in spiritual warfare but our object is peace.

> The message given so long ago is still the message that we need to hear and tell today. Every aspect of our lives brings glory to God. We are endowed with peace in ourselves and graciousness to others (Luke 2:14).

> Our paths should always be smooth, our traction secure, and our footsteps gentle. so that others will rejoice at our approach.

Prayer – Dear Father, Thank you for the peace that You have given me. May my feet always bring peace to those around me.

NOVEMBER

BY

Meditation Aids

BY is a preposition. A preposition (pre-position - before the position) usually is a word used before a noun or pronoun to form a phrase that modifies (qualifies, describes, or limits) some aspect of the sentence. The object of the preposition could be a noun, a verb, or an adjective. Check the object of the preposition BY to understand its impact.

Uses of BY – as a result – by what means – from – concerning – as an agent - through.

Example:

> *... be transformed BY the renewing of your mind ...* Romans 12:2.

> Renewing is the object of the preposition BY.

By the renewing is a prepositional phrase that describes the means by which the transformation occurs. The implication is that this is not a do-it-yourself project. We need the agent of the Holy Spirit to accomplish this wonderful task, giving us the ability to think like Christ (1 Corinthians 2:16).

November 1   Made

<u>Romans 1:20</u> *For since the creation of the world His invisible attributes are clearly seen being understood BY the things that are made, even His eternal power and Godhead …*

Q How are the *things that are made* evidence of God? The whole universe testifies of God's glory (Psalm 19:1).

> Sun, moon, stars, galaxies, people and animals, light and dark colors, blue birds and red birds, trees and flowers, oxygen and hydrogen, etc. were made; Somebody made them. Many of these things could not have evolved because they don't have life. It is hard to determine the rationality of those who try to replace a creator God with mindless evolution.

> Take any simple object, for instance a leaf – place the leaf in front of an atheist and say, "This just happened". Then, listen to him struggle to come up with an explanation. How do they explain that bees pollinate, or birds, butterflies, and animals migrate thousands of miles and then come back to where they started? Some of them pass through generations on the trip. Did the first butterfly go one mile, and the next generation two miles, until they go 2000 miles? I'm confused.

> Many people admit to intelligent design but they choke at the thought of a personal God Who is intimately involved with the lives of mankind. This is because they can't explain, and don't understand, love, choices, sin, etc.

> It takes far more faith to be an atheist than to believe in a creator God. Those who take the position that there is no God have to struggle to explain all the things He has made. In their struggle to come up with a first cause they may suggest an oil puddle struck by lightning. God says, "Get your own oil and lightning."

> Where did God come from? He didn't come from anywhere. He always was. Make that your mindset and the rest follows. When we consider first cause, this is all we have to know about God's origin. That is, He doesn't have one. Take comfort in this in your daily walk. God is alive, eternal, and working with power in our lives.

Prayer – Dear Father, I stand amazed in Your presents (spelling intended). Thank You for this incredible world.

November 2   Offense

Matthew 18:7 *Woe to the world because of offenses! For offenses must come, but woe to that man BY whom the offense comes!*

> The word offend is interesting. To offend is to cause displeasure. To fend off is to ward off emotional or physical damage. A fender on a car prevents damage to the rest of the car. A fence keeps in good and keeps out bad. Trespassing violates the fence and is an offense to the person offended. The opposite of fend off is offend.

Q What happens to offenders?   Woe!

> Woe is a strong word. It means anguish, sadness, despair, and misery. Woe is the opposite of blessing.

Jesus was welcoming little, innocent, trusting children when he made this statement. Jesus emphasized that causing children to sin was an offense to them and to God. He went so far as to say that whoever offends by causing a child to sin deserved drowning (v18:6). Think of the many ways the world, in Satan, is offending children.

Why must offenses come? Satan's law. Offenses are Satan's forte. Offenses must come because Satan is the ruler of this world and he steals, kills, and destroys (John 10:10). There must be dark in order to appreciate light. This is earth not heaven.

… if need be, you have been grieved by various trials, that the genuineness of your faith, being much more precious than gold that perishes … may be found to praise, honor, and glory at the revelation of Jesus Christ … 1 Peter 1:6-7. How else would we know that our faith is genuine?

Offenses are needed so that we can have the power of choice. God does not want robots. He wants people who choose to follow Him. Therefore, we have the ability to offend, to choose to follow Satan. The power of choice is the most wonderful, terrible, ability for humans to have. If we choose to follow God, choice is wonderful. If we choose to follow Satan, choice is terrible.

> It is our strong desire to be winsome, not offensive.

Prayer – Dear Father, may the Holy Spirit alert me to any offensive deed or thought that I might have. May I avoid inflicting woe. Instead may I be a blessing to those around me.

November 3   Mirror

2 Corinthians 3:18 *But we all … beholding as in a mirror, the glory of the Lord, are being transformed into the same image … BY the Spirit of the Lord.*

Q What power transforms us from one image to another?

> *The Spirit of the Lord* is our incredible transformer. All the transformers dreamed up by movie or toy makers pale in comparison to a life transformed into the image of God.

When I was in Air Force ROTC at the University of Michigan, there was a full length mirror with the inscription - SEE YOURSELF AS OTHERS SEE YOU. We need to look into the Holy Spirit so we can reflect the image for which we were created. Then God said, *"Let Us make man in Our image, according to Our likeness. … So God created man in His own image; in the image of God He created him; male and female He created them* Genesis 1:26-27. (Note the US and Our.)

When people look at us, as a mirror, and see love, they see themselves as lovable and are more likely to be transformed into the image of Christ. If they see disgust, they may see themselves in the image of Satan and reflect his nature. We can be mirrors for the world.

It is the Spirit Who transforms us. If we choose to follow Satan, we forsake our divine image and become conformed to Satan. Yuk! Our thinking becomes warped. We don't think and act according to God's image for us. Our minds are on earthly things – we have an ungodly mindset.

> We see ourselves according to our mindsets. When we have a certain mindset, we interpret all thoughts in terms of that guiding principle. We will accept any scrap of information that supports the mindset and disregard a mountain of contrary information. A-theists (no God) have a mindset that must be supported by all kinds of ridiculous fabrications. They disregard all the evidences of God and cling to scrappy theories.

When our mindset is that of a loving God, Who cares for us and has given a way to have relationship with Him through Christ and the Holy Spirit, our thoughts become reasonable, and abundant life on earth and eternal life come into focus.

Prayer – Dear Father, transform me by Your Spirit that I may have the image you imagined for me.

November 4   Pursue

Romans 14:17-19 ... *for the kingdom of God is ... righteousness, and peace, and joy in the Holy Spirit. For he who serves Christ in these things is acceptable to God and approved BY men. Therefore let us pursue the things which make for peace and the things BY which one may edify another.*

To *pursue* is to go after with diligence (thorough carefulness) the things that make for peace and edification.

Q What are these *things* that edify each other?

We are to *pursue*:

Righteousness - Righteousness is simply living right – according to God's direction.

Peace - If we consider Philippians 4:6-7 to be a sandwich with anxiety in verse six and peace in verse seven as slices of bread, in between we find the ingredients of peace – don't worry, pray about everything, be thankful, and ask God about what we want. Then His peace will be with us even though we don't understand how it works.

Joy in the Holy Spirit - Believing brings joy and peace which are parts of the fruit of the Spirit (Galatians 5:22).

We need to desire and receive the nine features of Spiritual fruit. Note: fruit is singular. We get it all as a salad when we are filled with the Spirit. Recognize that you have the fruit and allow it to work in you.

Righteousness, peace, and joy build us up and are the things that enable us to edify others. It is incredible that through the power of the Holy Spirit, we have the ability to edify – to build up and increase the faith of others!

Prayer – Dear Father, Thank You for giving me a source of joy and peace in the Holy Spirit. Help me use these gifts to bring joy and peace for the edification of others.

November 5   Hope

Romans 15:13 *Now may the God of hope fill you with all joy and peace in believing, that you may abound in hope BY the power Of the Holy Spirit.*

Q How may we abound in joy, peace, and hope?

> *BY the power of the Holy Spirit.*
>
> We are filled by knowing that the *God of hope* fills us *with all joy and peace in believing.* Believing comes to the fore again. If we don't believe we won't have joy or peace. However, we need to act out our belief. Let us not be doubters, those who don't believe, but let us be believers, who do, and say, "I wouldn't have seen it if I hadn't believed it".
>
> Other words for believing are faith and hope. Faith and hope promote Joy and peace. Joy and peace promote faith and hope. Each element builds on each other and they are steps up the ladder of life in Christ.
>
> We can have joy and peace by exercising the fruit and gifts given to us by and through the power of the Holy Spirit. These are not items to be placed on a shelf and admired; they are not a pretty tractor in a showroom; they are to be used in God's field.
>
> Hope is not pie in the sky, by and by, but trust and confidence in the living God. The God of hope will _fill_ you – not a partial filling. We are like a barrel of rocks. The rocks represent things of the flesh and of the world that hinder our progress in the faith. God will fill us as full as our rocks will allow. As we, through the guidance and power of the Holy Spirit, get rid of rocks, we can be filled more and more with the Holy Spirit.

Prayer – Dear Father, tell me what my rocks are, help me get rid of them, because your joy and peace are my delightful desire!

November 6   Grace

<u>Ephesians 2:9-10</u> *For BY grace you have been saved through faith, and that not of yourselves, it is the gift of God, not of works, lest anyone should boast.*

Q Why *BY grace* instead of works?

It is by grace that we are saved so there is no shred of doubt about the fact of our salvation. Any effort on our part is suspect. If we rely on any work or anything good we do for salvation, we forfeit grace and constantly have to wonder, "Is this good enough?"

There is no caste system in Christianity. We are all level at the foot of the cross because even our faith is a gift. We need to exchange pride for humility. Self pride and boasting only cause resentment and divisions.

Therefore, having been justified by faith, we have peace with God through our Lord Jesus Christ <u>Romans 5:1</u>. (See also Galatians 2:16). His grace for us is perfect. Don't make it difficult. By His grace, we can have peace so rejoice in the peace that His grace gives.

A large part of our peace comes from the fact that our position in Christ is God's grace gift and we can <u>live</u> in Him instead of spending our efforts trying to be good enough to enter into relationship <u>with</u> Him. Through His grace we have arrived. We are there.

When I ask people why they think they are going to heaven, they often say something about church, or Bible reading, or prayer, or tithing, or being a good person, etc. We must be clear, these things are a response to grace, not payment for grace. INSTANT REPLAY - We must be clear, these things are a response to grace, not payment for grace. Paul counted all his personal accomplishments as filthy rags. (Philippians 3:7-8). We know by now, the correct answer to the question is, "Grace."

God does not judge our work for adequacy. He doesn't even consider our works when it comes to salvation. God is merciful in that confession brings forgiveness and cleansing from everything that separates us from Him (1John 1:9). All that is necessary is confession and acceptance of His grace.

Prayer – Dear Father, thank You for the peace that comes from Your gift of perfect, saving faith.

November 7   Healed

Isaiah 53:5 *... and BY His stripes we are healed ...*

Q How do His stripes heal our wounds?

BY Jesus taking our punishment in the most unusual transaction in history.

Peter quotes the fulfillment of Isaiah's prophecy in his first letter when he states that Jesus' stripes bring healing to us (1 Peter 2:2). The verses refer to spiritual healing.

We need to consider the cross and the events that occurred before the crucifixion of Jesus so that we can realize the enormity of sin and the dreadful act it took to purify us.

Jesus was *scourged* (John 19:1). Scourging, or stripes, was either for punishment or cleansing. It was either a gruesome retribution for lawbreaking or an act to correct those who were living in error.

A scourge is a whip or lash, often equipped with bits of glass or metal tied to several split ends like a cat-o-nine-tails. It often tore skin and sometimes caused death through blood loss or infection. The stripes were 40 lashes less one. To prevent excess whipping, the recipient of the lashes got to hit back if the whipper went over 40.

The scourging we deserved was inflicted on Christ. The punishment placed on Jesus fulfilled God's desire for our reconciliation with Him (Isaiah 53:10). This was not a sadistic pleasure but a necessary act. The crucifixion of Christ is God's statement about the horribleness of sin. It is also a statement of how much He wants relationship with us. As weak examples, a surgeon may amputate a limb to save a life or, those who fight forest fires may set a backfire, burning good trees, to stop a raging blaze.

Words aren't strong enough to describe the depth of love required for God to sacrifice Christ that we might be redeemed. However, we need to realize, appreciate, and accept what Jesus did for us.

Prayer - Dear Father, all I can do is to live my life in thanksgiving for your indescribable Gift.

November 8   Fruit

Matthew 7:16-17   *BY their fruit you will know them. Even so, every good tree bears good fruit, but a bad tree bears bad fruit.*

> Who are *them*? Jesus was talking about prophets. Prophets are spokespersons for God.

Q How do we know if prophets are believable?

> By their fruit.

> Fruit will be delightful or it will be scabby and wormy. Each day, we are to examine our position in Christ as to what our fruit belies the type of prophet we are. We want both our words and our actions to tell the truth about God.

> Sometimes it takes a while for good fruit to ripen. We need to tend the soil, plant the seed, give it appropriate "sun and water", keep the weeds and varmints out, and have patience until the crop is ready. (Those of you who garden can have many pleasant, fellowship talks with God as you go about the gardening process.)

> There are other things that add to our fruit baskets: ... *add to your faith virtue, knowledge, self-control, perseverance, godliness, brotherly kindness, and love. For if these things are yours and abound, you will be neither barren nor unfruitful in the knowledge of our Lord Jesus Christ* 2 Peter 1:5-8.

> We, as possessing Christians, are continually bearing fruit, in ourselves, and in the lives of others. We have the fruit of the Spirit (Galatians 5:22-23) and it is such a joy to know that the Holy Spirit constantly enriches our lives. As others look upon us, and see His Spirit in us, they are attracted to Christ Jesus our Lord. Moths are attracted to flames and seekers are attracted to Jesus by the fire of Christ within us. As we give ourselves more and more to Him, we bear more and more fruit.

Prayer – Dear Father, examine me and prune anything, bad or good, that keeps me from bearing fruit for You.

November 9   Obedience

Hebrews 5:8 ... *though He* (Jesus) *was a son, yet He learned obedience BY the things which He suffered.*

Q How did Jesus learn to be obedient? Through suffering.

Many people want to know, "Why?" or "Why me?" Some reject the idea of a loving God, and may even fall away from the faith, because of some tragedy. Therefore, it is important that we examine and understand the place of suffering in our lives.

If the Son of God was subjected to suffering in order to learn obedience, why shouldn't we have growth experiences? People like challenges to prove their abilities, hence sand traps and water hazards on golf courses. And offenses countered by defenses in so many games.

We see in 1Peter 1:6b-7 that trials are to refine us like gold. In 2 Corinthians 1:4 we find that we will be comforted so we can give comfort. In James 1:2-3 we are to rejoice in trials because they produce patience.

We get an adequate dosage of trouble for each day's growth lesson (Matthew 6:34b). Some people see this verse as a negative statement about troubles. Given all the positive statements in today's study, we can see this verse in a different light. Each day, God gives an appropriate amount of spiritual exercise for our growth. He won't give too much (1 Corinthians 10:13).

Jesus, Peter, Paul, and James didn't complain about suffering; they told about suffering's benefits: growth, obedience, genuineness, contentment, comfort, and patience. We need to know that God is love and that He does not allow anything to enter our lives before it passes His throne. Therefore, we know that whatever happens, happens because it is to be used by Him for His purposes. With that attitude, we can look for His purpose instead of feeling mistreated. He will show it to us. We can then sense the end from the beginning.

Prayer – Dear Father, help me to see adversity as a way to grow and to learn more of Your comfort and compassion.

November 10   Faith

<u>James 2:18</u> ... *I will show you my faith BY my works.*

Q Do works substitute for faith or does faith beget works? We are saved <u>by</u> grace, <u>through</u> faith, <u>for</u> works.

Faith comes first. It is faith that is being emphasized here; *works* is the object of the prepositional phrase, *by my works*, that supports *faith.*

There are many people who simply cannot grasp the concept of salvation by grace alone. Some people try to justify themselves by something(s) that they do - some works. They don't want to give up on the self. They lean heavily on James to lend support to their argument. Now, there may be some confusion in the information in James but Paul made it crystal clear to the Ephesians.

For by grace you have been saved through faith, and that not of yourselves; it is the gift of God, not of works, lest anyone should boast. For we are His workmanship, created in Christ Jesus for good works, which God prepared beforehand that we should walk in them <u>Ephesians 2:8-10</u>. Works don't save us! We were created for works. Works are proof of our faith. Faith begets works. We are not saved by works but works show obedience to God by keeping His commandments. An old saying, "The proof of the pudding is in the eating" probably comes from this passage in James.

Which came first, the chicken or the egg? A strong argument can be made either way. But, with salvation, faith in God's grace comes first. Works are a <u>response</u> to faith through grace, not a purchase price for grace. It is clear, though, that there is truth in James 2:17 – no works means dead faith. We are saved by grace, through faith, for works. Going backwards, no works shows no faith, so grace is not effective. It is possible that faith was never alive in the first place.

Jesus clearly stated that we will keep His commandments if we love Him (John 14:15). We may not do it right at first, or we may never succeed in doing it right, but if a job is worth doing, it is worth doing poorly, yes poorly. So many fail to try because they tried and failed. Keep on keeping on, and trust the Holy Spirit to translate the results of your actions into what the situation calls for.

Prayer – Dear Father, thank You for Your complete work in grace; may Your grace result in works by me.

November 11   Abides

1John 3:24 *And BY this we know that He abides in us, BY the Spirit whom He has given us.*

Q How do we know that He abides in us? We have inside information from the Spirit Who lives comfortably in us.

Compare 2 Corinthians 6:6 with Galatians 5:22-23 to see some evidences of the Spirit's life in believers. In order for there to be evidence, there has to be indwelling and activity. The clues should be evident.

What are some of the activities of the Holy Spirit by which we can learn and commend ourselves? We find that the Gospel of John, chapters 14-16, are a goldmine of characteristics and activities of the Holy Spirit:

He is ever present to help us in every area of life.   (John 14:16).

He lives around and in us.   (14:17).

He will teach and remind us of Jesus' teachings.   (14:26).

He will affirm the truth of Christ.   (15:26b).

He will glorify Christ.   (16:14).

He will convince people of sin, righteousness, and judgment   (16:8b-9).

He will direct us into truth.   (16:13).

And, He will give us power to witness.   (Acts 1:8).

These are not human tendencies. They are evidence of the Holy Spirit abiding and working in possessing Christians.

Satan does not want us to have the Holy Spirit and has generated a lot of confusion about Him. Think of the opposites of the evidence and characteristics of the Holy Spirit and you will see the intentions and activity of Satan. God wants us to have the Holy Spirit because the Spirit is God's representative in the world, and in our lives. So let us ask for and receive this wonderful, heavenly gift (Luke 11:13b).

Prayer – Dear Father, I accept the Holy Spirit as my Helper to help me accept His truth and power.

November 12   Live

Galatians 2:20 *I have been crucified with Christ; it is no longer I who live, but Christ lives in me; and the life which I now live in the flesh I live BY faith in the Son of God, Who loved me and gave Himself for me.*

Q How does faith give life?

The Scripture tells us ... *the just shall live BY his faith* Habakkuk 2:4 (Quoted in Romans 1:17 and Hebrews 10:38).

Paul became deeply personal here and spoke of Jesus' love for him and that Jesus had given His life for him. We need to have that same knowledge and feeling. So often, without realizing it, we think of the Christian experience as being a fuzzy dream or belonging to someone else. Our experience with God through Christ and the power of His Holy Spirit is not a dream. It is an "in me" thing - a powerful reality. Here and now, I know Jesus loves me.

Faith gives us life. It is the use of faith that makes life livable and that gives abundant life. Jesus is our life preserver in an ocean of weights that would drag us down.

Before the Holy Spirit was in our lives we lived under the influence of Satan. Now, the life we live is in, and with, the power of God - often when we don't even realize it. While we still live in an earthly body with all its strengths and frailties, flesh, we are under new management. In Christ, we have the power, gifts, and the fruit of the Holy Spirit.

All this is attained by faith in Jesus. In the same verse in Galatians, Paul wrote that he was no longer alive because Christ had taken over his life. Christ in us allows us to live for Him while still in the flesh. Christ in us makes us one with the eternal God. INSTANT REPLAY - Christ in us makes us one with the eternal God. As He always is, and will be, we will live forever in Him. WOW!

Prayer - Dear Father, Thank You for loving me, giving Yourself for me, and giving me life; live in me.

November 13   Confident

Philippians 1:14 ... *and most of the brethren in the Lord, having become confident BY my chains, are much more bold to speak the word without fear.*

BY – through means of.

Q How do chains help gain confidence? If faith can rise above chains, it is worth sharing. As mentioned in today's verse:

Most of the brethren - siblings in Christ in the family of God. Are we part of the *most* speaking boldly? Or, sad to say, are most of the brethren reluctant to admit their faith, lingering in the shadows, griping about some "chain." Is embarrassment about life in Christ our chain? Should it be?

Having become confident by my chains - Paul did not despair because of his chains but rejoiced that others were made bold by them. Paul was chained to guards on either side 24/7, four shifts of six hours each, for two years. What an opportunity with a captive audience. Who was really in chains? When others think we are in the chains of some supposed adversity we are free in Christ to speak boldly and to accomplish the task God has given us.

We may never know the influence our life has on someone who is watching.

Are much more bold - As others see our faith in trials, they are encouraged and made bold to witness. We, as believers, are not to have shame, we are to have power to tell of the good news of salvation (Romans 1:16).

To speak the word without fear. We only have fear if we love the world more than we love God. The Holy Spirit is in us with all the benefits we considered on November 11. So we can speak out for Christ without being afraid. Now, consider their threats and make us bold to fearlessly proclaim Christ (Acts 4:29).

Whatever "chains" God has allowed us - irritations, illness, hardship, tribulations - let us rejoice so that others can see the fruit of Christ in us and seek Him for themselves.

Prayer – Dear Father, help me see chains as opportunities so I can speak the word with boldness.

November 14   Walk

Philippians 3:16 ... *let us walk BY the same rule.*

Q What is the rule of walk?

The rule is to forget the past and press toward the goal (v12-14).

I now ignore my rear view mirror, get a good look through my windshield, and drive resolutely toward God's prize, which is the increase of my faith (Philippians 3:13b).

There are other rules for walking the Christian life. Remember the acronym General Electric Power Company. It stands for the books of Galatians, Ephesians, Philippians, and Colossians in order. In them we find rules for walking:

We need to live and walk in the Spirit (Galatians 5:25). We are in the Spirit and the Spirit is in us. A walk in the Spirit is a loving, joyful, peaceful walk.

We need to walk with sanctified steps (Ephesians 4:17-24). We need to be filled with the Spirit and to get His help in following God's commandments. Nonbelievers are walking away from God in futile paths that seem reasonable to them.

We need to walk in the manner of possessing Christians (Philippians 3:17) who are successfully walking through the maze of life. They can be a pattern for us to follow.

If we walk worthy of what Christ has done for us, we will please Him and bear fruit (Colossians 1:10).

Meditate on these verses. Meditation is medication for the soul.

Prayer – Dear Father, thank You for my Interior Guide, Your Holy Spirit, Who directs my thoughts and actions.

November 15   Receive

Galatians 3:2   *Did you receive the Spirit BY works of the law or BY the hearing of faith?*

Q Do we EARN the Spirit by works of the law?

NO! The Holy Spirit is a GIFT, received by faith.

There is no law that says we deserve, or can distribute, the Holy Spirit because of some work or merit on our part. There was a person described in the book of Acts as one who wanted to buy the power to be able to grant the Holy Spirit on everybody he touched (Acts 8:18b-19). Peter rebuked him explaining that the Holy Spirit is a gift from God.

Have you received the Spirit? If not, He is readily available. God wants us to have the Holy Spirit and He will give Him to anyone who asks (Luke 11:13). The Holy Spirit is a gift. We don't have any possession or attribute that we can exchange for Him.

Ask for the Holy Spirit. Receive Him. The Spirit is a *much more* good gift. Remember, anything bad that you have heard about the Holy Spirit is a lie of Satan and a misrepresentation of the Spirit's true nature. These lies are brought about by evil people or confused Christians.

Jesus wants us to have the Holy Spirit and prays that we will receive Him (John 14:16-17b).

The Holy Spirit is a grace gift. The Holy Spirit is our Helper. He, and His attributes, are precious gifts that we need for abundant life. Even though the Spirit is equal to God, He is God's presence in the world today, given by Jesus after He had ascended into heaven. And the Spirit is sent to help us. No wonder Satan wants to defile Him. Please, I beg you, receive, and live in the Spirit of God.

Prayer – Dear Father, thank You for my Helper, Your grace gift, freely given and gratefully received.

November 16   Boast

Galatians 6:14   *But God forbid that I should boast except in the cross of our Lord Jesus Christ, BY Whom the world has been crucified to me, and I to the world.*

Q Why does the world need to be crucified in us?

The *world* is Satan's realm.

Things become gods. Harmful rules and acts become accepted practices. So it is a necessary thing for the world to be dead for us and us dead for the world. Why should we want to be alive for something that brings death to us? INSTANT REPLAY Why should we want to be alive for something that brings death to us? The world was dead to Paul and Paul was dead to the world. The same thing needs to be true for us.

We should not be high minded about our faith. As pointed out in Ephesians 2:9, we are totally saved by grace, our sins are totally paid for by Jesus' sacrifice on the cross, so all we have to boast about is the effect of the cross on our lives.

We should speak confidently about Christ's sacrifice and how it unites us with God. The world is not going to die for us. It was necessary for Jesus to die for us. Nothing is necessary for us except to accept.

Jesus was crucified for me to pay the cost of redemption. The world is crucified to me. It became dead for me. As far as I am concerned, the world's attractions, pulls, any tugs on my interests, no longer have power over me. I became dead to the world. Satan wants me to be alive to the world so I will want what he wants to give. No way!

Don't do half a job – CRUCIFY the world. Crucify the power of Satan's lure to total, final, and absolute death. Then don't administer CPR.

Prayer – Dear Father, please try me and know me and crucify any aspect of the world that may be in me.

November 17   Endure

<u>Mark 13:13</u> *But you will be hated BY all for My name's sake, but he who endures to the end shall be saved.*

Q Why will we be hated?   For Jesus name's sake.

I'm a bit troubled by the word endure which might be interpreted to mean we have to tough it out. I agree with the writers in the New Testament that we should rejoice in whatever circumstance. Perhaps the thought should be "lasts" to the end.

My name's sake means the nature of Christ. Look how different Jesus was and how He was treated. Think of how you are treated when you dare to live in His nature. It is so much better to be loved by Jesus even if you are hated by people.

What the world clings to is tolerance, which is expressed in apathy - that is a-path-y, no path - "If it feels good, go with it." If people are pushed to defend their godless position, they usually react negatively. Our faith is read by them to be their condemnation. There may even be those who deliberately try to discredit our witness.

We need to be Teflon, not Velcro. When people say negative things we don't let them stick, we give a Teflon response. He says, "You stink!" I say, "You think I stink? It's your thought, I won't accept or own it". Practice Teflon responses on good comments with agreement.

When the light through us shines on darkness, it reveals terrible things which should make the world ashamed. Sometimes we need to be lasers and sometimes a light bulb. We will be invited to join them in ungodliness but don't give in. Peer pressure shipwrecks many people if they still want the world.

At any rate, we *endure* (enjoy) by knowing that life with, and in, Christ gives us so much more a life of love, joy, and peace. We endure by giving our total self to Christ and by accepting His total self into our lives. We endure by utilizing the Holy Spirit.

The tools of endurance are the five Spiritual food groups: Bible study, prayer, fellowship, meditation, and service. Our endurance insures our salvation. Endure to insure.

Prayer – Dear Father, I resolve, with the help of the Helper, to outlast the haters.

November 18   Win

1Corinthians 9:22b *I have become all things to all men that BY all things I might win some.*

> Q How might we win some?   BY *becoming all things.*
> We become winsome in order to *win some.*

Paul said he had been abased and he had abounded. He lived his life in such a way that others saw Christ living in his humanity. He preached but he also practiced. He had what is called fellowship evangelism. As we mirror a life with Holy Spirit gifts and power, others will see Jesus in us and some will want what we have.

We become *all things,* but not in any way compromising Christ's commandments. We don't lead sinners to salvation by sinning with them. They need to see the fruit of the Spirit, not the trash of Satan. Satan would tempt us to do sinful things in order to be accepted but Paul also wrote, "Should we sin in order to generate grace? Of course not; we can't be dead to sin and live in sin at the same time (Romans 6:1b-2). Christians don't seek sin. We are in grace so we should live in grace.

We are to follow the Holy Spirit Who is continually convicting people of sin, righteousness, and judgment. We always stand ready to testify (1 Peter 3:15).

People ask questions, we need to be prepared to give answers. One of the purposes of this book of instructional devotions is that we not only know our own status in Christ but that we are able to give clear instruction to those whom the Holy Spirit brings to us. We always stand in the word (2 Timothy 2:15).

Paul hoped to *win some.* In the parable of the Sower, only one fourth of the seed was indicated to have yielded a crop but the sower sowed without discrimination (Mark 4:3). What a crop we have if only one person is won to eternal life in Christ.

Eventually we should come to the place in our lives where we have the nature of Christ and live in Him without having constantly to think about acting like a Christian. We never know when or where God has prepared someone for our witness. Just think any time is the right time and only back off if you meet with resistance.

Prayer – Dear Father, thank you for the instruction and encouragement you give in Your word. May I be so much in Christ that He is my new normal.

November 19   Poured

Romans 5:5b ... *because the love of God has been poured out in our hearts BY the Holy Spirit Who was given to us.*

Q How is God's love dispensed to us?

It is *poured out by the Holy Spirit.* It is not a trickle, it is a gusher!

The love of God has been poured out - We have the love of God. Think about that. The Creator of the universe, Who has all knowledge, wisdom, and power, loves us and has directed that love towards us. WOW!

The process of this outpouring is by means of the Holy Spirit Whom God has given us. The fruit of the Spirit not only is given to us, for our own edification, it is given for us to pass on to others. If we don't have the Holy Spirit, we don't have the love of God poured out in us. INSTANT REPLAY - If we don't have the Holy Spirit, we don't have the love of God poured out in us. So stand with uplifted hands, an open heart, and an open mind, ready to receive.

It is important to remember that the Holy Spirit, and all the manifestations of the Holy Spirit, are gifts. There should not be an attempt to fake them nor can they be bought (Acts 8:18-24). God will give the gifts as He wills, when and where, for His purposes. He wills that we have His Spirit AND the appropriate gift(s).

Poured out In our hearts - not sprinkled, not a trickle, but lavishly poured into our hearts, the seat of emotions, into our inner being

When we have the Holy Spirit in us, directing our lives, we have: good thoughts, edification, faithfulness in marriage, thoughtfulness in relationships, generosity, truth, and praise. These are marks of a person in Christ enabled by the love of God through His gift of the Holy Spirit.

Prayer – Dear Father, I open, my hands, my heart , and my head to your generous, unending, outpouring of love. Thank You.

November 20   Kept

1 Peter 1:5 ...*who are kept BY the power of God through faith.*

Q What keeps us through faith?

God's power.

It's as easy as A, B, C.

A. ... *are kept* ... God is our safe place and His arms support us (Deuteronomy 33:27a). He sets a guard for us (Philippians 4:7). He will guard our hearts from the emotion of fear. We have peace when we place ourselves in God's care. When we stray in thoughts or actions, a sense of uneasiness creeps in. Then we need to return to the safety of His keeping (Psalms 61:3). When we pray

B. ... *by the power of God* . He who had the power to create us certainly has the power to sustain us. God is, and has, the greatest power in the universe.

C. ... *c*ared for *through faith.* Even the faith to have faith is a gift from God (Ephesians 2:8). Do not let anyone or anything make it difficult. Do not believe the lie that you don't have enough faith. Just accept God's gifts of faith, salvation, and power for life in Him.

Kept by the power of God. WOW! Because of His great promises, and the power and desire to fulfill those promises in us, we abide in His care and keeping.

Prayer – Dear Father, thank You for keeping me safe in Your care.

Colossians 3:15-17 Let the peace of Christ rule in your hearts ... And be thankful ...

HAPPY THANKSGIVING whenever it falls.

November 21   Refreshed

Philemon 7 ... *the hearts of the saints have been refreshed BY you, brother.*

Q How did Philemon refresh their hearts?

By his love and faith which he had toward the Lord Jesus (v5).

Before we can be re-freshed we have to be "freshed" - be made new - *Repent therefore; and be converted, that your sins may be blotted out, so that times of refreshing may come from the presence of the Lord ...* Acts 3:19.

In my practice as a psychologist, so many people said they could not talk to their spiritual leaders or fellow Christians for fear of being judged and/or shunned. They felt "Defreshed," to coin a word. We should be able to share doubts, fears, temptations, etc., with siblings in Christ and receive encouragement, not judgment. When we look into a mirror, we see ourselves. When we look into the eyes of a Christian, we, and they, should see love and compassion. Remember when Jesus looked at Peter (Luke 22:61). Have you been defreshed by the words or attitude of someone in the church? Maybe you could have courage enough to tell them about Peter.

How important is sibling support? As we see brothers and sisters live for Jesus, we are encouraged and can encourage others (Hebrews 10:25b). Think of a campfire with several sticks burning. Take one stick out and lay it aside. What happens to it? Put it back in with the rest. What happens to it? I'm sure you understand the parable of the stick.

... but be filled with the Spirit, speaking to one another in psalms and hymns and spiritual songs, singing and making melody in your heart to the Lord, giving thanks always for all things ... Ephesians 5:18b-20b.

Think of the word refresh. It is used in room fresheners that take away stink. The best ones don't just cover up the smell, they remove the smell and leave a pleasant fragrance. How great it is that we have the Source of refreshing, are refreshed, and can be refreshment for the saints.

Prayer – Dear Father, thank You for refreshing my life, may I be a refreshment for others.

November 22   Inspiration

2 Timothy 3:16 *All Scripture is given BY inspiration of God, and is profitable for doctrine, for reproof, for correction, for instruction in righteousness, that the man of God may be complete, thoroughly equipped for every good work.*

Q Are there some parts of the Bible that aren't profitable?

No! Every part contributes to completeness.

Scripture is another gift. With it we can be *equipped for every good work.* *All Scripture is inspired and is profitable for:*

Doctrine – principles and teachings of the faith – a set of guidelines,

Reproof – an expression of rebuke – criticism of wrong doing or wrong thinking,

Correction – presenting a positive substitute for something that is wrong,

Instruction in righteousness – what is upright, decent, and virtuous,

Completeness – whole and finished,

Equipped – given whatever is needed for service.

There are some parts that aren't clear in the infancy of our life in Christ. Experience in Him brings them into focus. In my work on this devotional book I have found insights and deeper meanings that I hope are passed on to you.

Some people want to tear the Bible apart to justify their way. There are those, who wish to be God, who question things in the Bible that they don't understand or don't agree with. Let us let God be God and let us live in the light that is clear. Accept the teachings, repent of wrong doing, correct error, live decently, and realize that all of this teaching equips us for good works. If any Scripture seems confusing, always look for a positive spin.

Prayer - Dear Father, thank you for Jesus, the Holy Spirit, and Your inspired word, three wonderful gifts all making me complete in You.

November 23   Faith

2 Corinthians 5:7 *For we walk BY faith, not BY sight.*

Q How do we walk?

> *By faith.*

> Walking by sight presents problems.

Why can't we trust sight? Sight is something we have. Satan is a clever magician who can make that which is evil look desirable. "The devil made me do it" is sometimes given as an attempt at humor to explain deviant behavior. Quite often the results aren't humorous. Sometimes the phrase is used as a weak excuse and often as a statement of remorse.

> Why can we trust *faith*?

Why can we trust faith? We can trust faith because it is a gift from God (Ephesians 2:8). As a gift from God, we know it is perfect. This is not just some personal conviction that we have conjured up.

There was a little girl who did not want to go to school. She said she had a stomach ache. Her mother felt her forehead and said you don't have a fever. Then the girl said, "I have inside information." When the Holy Spirit is in us, we know we have faith to walk.

As well as "Seeing is believing," "Believing is seeing." "I wouldn't have seen it if I hadn't believed it!" Once we believe, all kinds of wonders occur and become clear to us. So many times in Scripture, God's gifts and care are opened up by faith. We are not immobilized by things not seen; we are energized by the indwelling of the Holy Spirit.

Appropriate, effective faith is that which is given by God. We have nothing to do except to accept His faith. Any faith that we might manufacture would generate pride.

> *Walk by faith.*

Prayer – Dear Father, help me to step forth with confidence in my walk with You.

November 24   Shepherd

John 10:14 *I am the good shepherd; and I know My sheep, and am known BY My own.*

Q Does Jesus know us?

Yes.

Jesus has a name for each sheep in His flock. He knows them and they respond to His voice and follow Him (John 10:3b). Once we have accepted the *good shepherd* as our Shepherd, we know His voice; we recognize His voice by the tones of love, joy, and peace. We will not follow a false shepherd.

This verse is one of the I AM's of the Bible that identify Christ with God. In Exodus 14, God gave His name to Moses, *"I AM WHO I AM."* Jesus used this self-definition several times in describing Himself and His ministry.

He is the *good shepherd* described in the Twenty-Third Psalm. We shall not want, we graze in lush pastures, we move by calm waters, our souls are restocked by Him.

Jesus takes responsible ownership of us because we are bought with the price of His own blood. We are the most expensive purchase in the history of the world! Realize your value. Recognize that God paid a high price for your earthly body and your eternal spirit. This is cause for glorious praise to God (1Corinthians 6:20). Let your purchase price define you in all humility and praise.

He knows each of His sheep individually. Each sheep knows His voice and responds only to Him. We know His voice and should respond only to Him. We recognize Him and His voice because He leads us in the right path.

Prayer – Dear Father, help me understand the price My Shepherd paid for me and to follow accordingly in humble servant-hood.

November 25   Sanctify

<u>John 17:17</u> *Sanctify them BY Your truth. Your word is truth.*

Q How are we sanctified, set apart?

> BY God's truth, the *word* is the <u>truth</u>, Who is Jesus Christ. We are sanctified by Christ, in Christ, and through Christ. God's primary communication to us is Jesus, His physical word.
>
> God also speaks to us through His written word, the Bible.
>
> To be sanctified is to be set apart. Many people, and whole cultures, keep some of their old ways and form some mixture of paganism, or their religion, with Christianity. However, white is different from gray. We are to leave all the old ways and become totally new (2 Corinthians 5:17) - <u>all</u> the old ways.
>
> To be Christian is to be obviously different. We just don't fit into the world's mold anymore. We are not to try to fit into the world's mold but to start fresh with a different mindset of what it means to be alive (Romans 12:2).
>
> Jesus taught us a new way of life (John 14:6). This is not only a statement of fact; it is a model for our living. First, we are to accept and believe His declaration, then we are to (1) walk as He walked - *way*, (2) talk as He talked - *truth*, and (3) live as He lived - *life*.
>
> The more we follow this three step program, the more we grow in sanctification. INSTANT REPLAY. The more we follow this three step program, the more we grow in sanctification.
>
> Jesus will lead us into all truth through the guidance of the Holy Spirit (John 16:13b).
>
> As Jesus is the Truth, we know that the Holy Spirit will guide us to Christ and sanctify us in the truth.

Prayer – Dear Father, help me to know, believe, accept, and live in Your Truth that I might be sanctified.

November 26   By

John 14:6 *Jesus said ..., "I am the way, the truth, and the life; no one comes to the Father except BY Me."*

Q What is the way to relationship with God?

By accepting Jesus as Savior and Lord.

Some may ask, "Is Christ the only way?" Why, in heaven's name would they reject the perfect way? Must be they think their way is better. They want their own self. INSTANT REPLAY - They want their own self. Many people want a way that fits their terms. That is like throwing a red life preserver to a drowning man and having him ask, "Don't you have a blue one that matches my eyes?"

This means of salvation is the only means of escape; why would we ignore it? (Hebrews 2:3). This passage was written to encourage people to accept God's truth in Christ. However, there are those who think this means they should try to find a way to escape. What a waste of a Satanic inspired effort. Why seek another way when we know the perfect way that has God's guarantee?

Any way that agrees with human thinking leads to death (Proverbs 14:12). Let that statement sink in; then set about accepting the truth in Christ.

WAY - Don't waste your life by looking for another pathway to God. There just isn't any other person's teaching that leads to life (Acts 4:12).

TRUTH - Examine Jesus' life and teaching. There is nothing false about either of what He said or what He taught (John 17:1).

LIFE - When we experience our second birth, being born in Him, we are able to live, and die, as God intended for us (John 3:16b).

Our physical life begins with conception enacted by our parents. In Christ we have life, enacted by God, beginning at the conception of our belief and acceptance, continuing through sanctification, and going on through eternity.

Prayer – Dear Father, Thank You for Your Way which is the perfect Way to life through Christ Jesus.

November 27   Word

Matthew 4:4 Jesus, quoting Deuteronomy 8:3 said, *"Man shall not live BY bread alone, but BY every word that proceeds from the mouth OF God."*

At that time the word was the Pentateuch, the first five books of the Bible. The bread of heaven was manna. Manna was given a day at a time to sustain physical life.

Q What feeds our spirit?

Our spirit is fed by Spiritual bread.

For the bread of God is He who comes down from heaven and gives life to the world. ... And Jesus said to them, "I am the bread of life. He who comes to Me shall never hunger, and he who believes in Me shall never thirst" John 6:33, 35.

What is the difference between food bread and spiritual bread? Food bread feeds the body and gives strength for temporal things, life on this earth. Spiritual bread is God's Word - all 66 books of the Bible AND the Word by Whom we live (John 1:1). The Word from God feeds the soul giving eternal life. Jesus existed before the Pentateuch and was always intended to be God's communication with mankind. Jesus is the *bread of life* Who satisfies spiritual hunger.

As we partake of Jesus, we have food that empowers us to rise above any tribulation or temptation to a life of grace, mercy, joy, and peace.

Jesus is the Word of God and the Bread of life. The Holy Spirit uses the Bible to guide us into these truths.

Jesus is the bread of heaven, Who is our spiritual food for each day and for eternity.

Prayer – Dear Father, thank You for the gifts of Your Word and Your word;

I choose to live by them.

November 28   Led

Romans 8:14 *For as many as are led BY the Spirit of God, these are the sons of God.*

Q Who are the sons of God? (This emphasis is about Who leads us.)

Those who *are led by the Spirit of God.* Being led by the Spirit is so important we take another look at this grace. Here, the emphasis is on the Leader.

How can we be led by the Spirit of God? Give Him permission. Ask Him to guide you. Jesus promised that the Spirit would lead us into all truth. There is no limit to the number of those who can be led by the Spirit, You and I are included.

In practical terms being led by the Spirit of God means we take everything to God with fervent prayer. We search the Bible for answers. We talk with trusted, mature, possessing Christians.

Who? As many.

What? To be called Sons of God.

Why? To be a member of God's family.

How? Led by the Spirit of God. We are to have faith in His leadership, make sure it is HIS leadership, and follow Him.

When? Now. Why wait? If you have a problem with your decision, decide - and let Him help you. Don't miss out on another day without serving Him (Joshua 24:15).

Where? Two paths need to be considered. One path follows the Spirit and lives in, and continually approaches God; the other path is given by Satan and leads to death.

Whenever we ask for and follow the Spirit into truth, we are, and we will act like, children of God.

Prayer – Dear Father, as Your child, I trust and follow the lead of Your Spirit into life.

November 29   Spirit

<u>Zechariah 4:6b</u> *Not BY might nor BY power, but BY My Spirit says the Lord of hosts.*

Q How do we accomplish God's work?

By and through the Spirit of God.

When it comes to accomplishing any task, as with Zechariah in the rebuilding of the temple of God, we need to enthusiastically enlist and utilize the power of the Holy Spirit in building up our bodies which are His temples.

In order for the Spirit of the Lord to accomplish His will in our lives, we need to recognize that we have to abandon any egotistical idea that we can do His will without Him. Too many times our might and power leave us unproductive and frustrated.

How much of God's work can we accomplish on our own? Very little, if any. However, once we have the Spirit of God in us (Luke 11:13), we no longer waste our time and energy trying to fill our lives with husks. We see trials as growth opportunities instead of occasions for despair. Our life becomes a living letter that tells those who read us that there is life, grace, mercy, and peace in Jesus.

Might refers to personal strength. We cannot force ourselves to be successful workers in God's kingdom.

Power refers to the ways people control their environment - wealth, gender, title, age, social position, etc. We can't use influence to become His people.

But BY My Spirit says the Lord of hosts. – the ultimate authority. We have studied the many ways the Holy Spirit helps us. Let us continue to let Him be built up in us and to guide us in our daily walk.

Prayer – Dear Father, I thank You that Your Spirit is stronger than my might or power.

November 30   Justified

Romans 5:1 *Therefore, having been justified BY faith, we have peace with God through our Lord Jesus Christ.*

To be justified is to be made righteous.

Q What paves the road to *peace with God*?

We are justified by faith.

WE have examined many times the fact that we are saved, or justified, by faith in Jesus (Ephesians 2:9). Saving faith is a *gift of God.* Saving faith can be trusted.

Saving faith leads to peace; works lead to anxiety. The faith that God gives provides peace in this life and overcomes any fear of death. Not only does the darkness of death no longer disturb us, life is now illuminated by the light of Christ.

This is not a faith which we have to conjure up. Many people who depend on their own faith, falter and fail. This is faith given by God so we glow and grow. We glow because Christ is born in us.

We are *justified by faith* - faith that is a gift from God and is complete, lacking nothing. Because we do not have to depend on any works or effort on our part *we have peace with God.*

Do you want *peace with God*? Accept His justifying grace. We can depend on His grace.

Do you have *peace with God*? Rejoice and abide in justifying grace.

Once we have understood and accepted the perfect faith He has given us, we have peace and we can set about our response to His gifts with a life directed and empowered by the Holy Spirit.

Prayer – Dear Father, thank you, that as we have been justified by faith, we have peace through Jesus.

DECEMBER

BE

Meditation Aids

BE is a helping verb - To be some action or to be some thing.

Uses of BE – to exist – to occur – to represent – to become.

Quite often, used in the form DON'T BE, giving the knowledge of what SHOULD BE.

Example:

And do not BE conformed to the world, but

BE transformed by the renewing of your mind Romans 12:2.

Conform is to be with-form. Transform is to be across-form as in transcontinental.

The word BE, in this verse, indicates the change from being what we should not BE to what we should BE. We should not be *conformed to the world* but we should *be transformed* - moved across - to having our minds renewed in godliness.

Sometimes the only thing that causes us to change is that the pain of change is less than the pain of staying the same.

December 1   Perfect

<u>Matthew 5:48</u> *Therefore, BE perfect even as your Father in heaven is perfect.*

BE – to occur. Is this even possible?

Q Can we be perfect?

Yes, by trusting in Christ.

According to 1John 3:3, we are pure in God's eyes through hope and belief in Christ. REALLY? Read it again. Look it up if you don't believe me. Are you pure? Do you hope in Christ? If you hope in Christ, you are pure! We can change the words from a question to a statement! Are you pure? becomes You <u>are</u> pure.

The verse says, "If" but I prefer "When" we confess, God forgives us and washes us clean of all that we have done or not done <u>and</u> all that was done to us, abuse or neglect (1 John 1:9). My wife calls 1John 1:9 God's bar of soap.

Human words cannot fully state the magnitude of the transformation from our condition of sin to purity in Christ. Allow the Spirit of God to impact you with the power of these verses by accepting them without questions or doubt. We are imperfect but we are perfected in and through Jesus Christ by the grace of God. <u>Thank You and Amen!</u> This is the crux of our relationship with God. It is only through His love for us that we have hope in this life and hope for eternal life.

Jesus was sinless but God actually made Him to become <u>our</u> sin so that we would become righteous in God's eyes and have relationship with Him (2 Corinthians 5:21).

By entering into a relationship with Christ, and letting Him dwell in us through the Person of His Holy Spirit, we have His mind and take on His goals as the purpose and fulfillment of our being. We become servants of God and winsome witnesses to the world.

Prayer – Dear Father, thank You for doing for me what I could not do for myself.

December 2   Worthy

Revelation 5:12-13 *Worthy is the Lamb Who was slain to receive power and riches and wisdom, and strength and honor and glory and blessings! Blessing and honor and glory and power BE to Him who sits on the throne, and to the Lamb, forever and ever!*

> BE – to ascribe, to give credit.

Q Who is to receive *blessing, honor, glory, and power?*

> God, because He sits on the throne.

> The book of Revelation has many praise sections for God and Jesus. If we give this high praise to someone or something else, that person or thing is our god. There will never be eternal benefit from that person or those things.

> Jesus was slain to give us relationship with God. The Old Testament background for His death on the cross was the marking on the door posts with lamb's blood to affect the Passover (Exodus 12:13). Through Jesus' sacrifice on the cross, He saves us from spiritual death and eternal separation from God.

> High praise was given to Jesus, the Lamb, and to God, Who occupies the throne.

> Who? Jesus is the sacrificial Lamb for our justification.

> What? *To receive power, riches, wisdom, strength, honor, glory, and* blessings from us.

> Why? He is deserving of every conceivable positive attribute.

> How? By His sacrifice for us.

> When? For all time.

> Where? On the cross.

> Starting now, and forever, we are to remember that God and Jesus, and only God and Jesus, are worthy of supreme adulation.

Prayer – Dear Father, all of my praise is to You for You are my God.

December 3   Transformed

Romans 12:2 *And do not BE conformed to the world, but BE transformed by the renewing of your minds.*

BE – Paul is writing to believers which extends to you and me today.

Q What is part of the newness we have in Christ?

Our minds are renewed. We can now think as Jesus thinks (1 Corinthians 2:16). WOW!

We no longer wish to be conformed to the world. Remember, the prefix "con" means "with." So conform is with-form - with the form of the world. With the mind of Christ we can think of what the world really means and reject it. Do not think about what Satan says you are losing. Think of what God says you are gaining. Trans–form is across form, like trans-atlantic. We cross over from human thinking to godly thinking.

When we purposely allow the mind of Christ be in us, we find that we are to be servants, not lords over others. If others abuse that privilege, that is on them. Jesus, instead of claiming His position as an earthly king, chose to be the Servant of all to the point of washing the disciple's feet.

Now we have the ability to think as Jesus does when it comes to things that are spiritually discerned. That means we are now empowered to think like Him. One of the main things that we need is to reject any feeling of allegiance to the powers of the world which is Satan's realm. Do you really want to take advice from Satan?

There are many advantages to thinking in the way that Jesus thought. For instance, when we think as He did, we see suffering in a different light (1 Peter 4:1b). We are to rejoice if we suffer on Christ's behalf.

Prayer – Dear Father, please give me the mind of Christ in thought, word, and deed.

December 4   Reason

1 Peter 3:15 ... *always BE ready to give a defense to everyone who asks you a reason for the hope that is in you.*

BE – to be enabled.

Q What should we do if someone asks for a reason for our *hope*?

Be ready to defend our reasons for the hope that is within us which is - there is a meaningful purpose to our existence and that we have a relationship with our Creator Who fulfills our hope for eternal life.

As we have seen many times, the Holy Spirit will prepare people to ask if you are prepared to answer. He will also help you formulate an answer. God gives situations, some joyous, some difficult, so people can see our faith. Always be ready in any and all circumstances. We never know when someone is watching and will ask. *Preach the word! Be ready in season and out of season, Convince, rebuke, exhort, with all longsuffering and teaching* 2 Timothy 4:2.

My high school football coach had a motto – The best offense is a good defense. Our offense and our defense is the love, joy, and peace that we have in Christ. In Christ we have the most powerful defense available to people of faith - spiritual armor. We are under spiritual attack and need the full armor of God to protect us (Ephesians 6:13).

To everyone who asks - some will ask, having been prompted by the Holy Spirit, and desire to know how they can get what we got (have). They often first have faith in us, then they copy our faith, then develop a faith of their own. Others will ask to defend their own ungodliness. If they can find a chink in our armor, they will use it to justify their desire to reject God. If we seem to be apologizing for our faith, they will get an uncertain message. However, if they want the peace and hope that we exhibit, we will be ready to share it.

It is good to be well versed in Scripture because the Word of God is guaranteed to achieve positive results (Isaiah 55:11). Added to this is our own experience which, in combination with the word, makes a persuasive case for those who are earnestly seeking.

Prayer – Dear Father, thank you for helping me defend the assurance of the hope of eternal life.

December 5   Faithful

1 Corinthians 4:2 *Moreover it is required in stewards that one BE found faithful.*

> Steward – one who manages the property or affairs of another person.

> BE – to occur.

Q What is required of stewards?   They should be found faithful.

Faithful to what, or to Whom? God's primary purpose is to bring people into fellowship with Him. A faithful steward of the affairs of God is one who faithfully and truthfully presents Christ as Lord and Savior. A good steward takes care of personal property and duties. If we talk about being redeemed through Christ and have a junk littered life, what does that say? Is it a bell with an unclear ring? Or, if we neglect payment of debts, or taxes, or break traffic laws, what does that tell those to whom we witness?

Paul is writing about the work and results of the labors of different church leaders. Some were claiming one leader, some another - much like many denominations today, claiming superiority because of a person or doctrine. All leaders need to be faithful stewards and point people to Christ. This is a super goal.

Faithfulness is a requirement. A requirement needs Someone who requires - God. Those who are stewards of God's purposes among mankind are to be faithful to Him, not some personal agenda. Stewardship extends beyond those in the pastoral ministry. Every Christian is, in some way, an evangelist. We don't have to stand behind a pulpit to be a steward for Jesus.

Always remember, what we do communicates more powerfully than what we say. When we are in Christ we can live without fear of hidden cameras. We can easily tell others that the trash on the internet has no place in our lives.

Whenever and wherever we are found, we are required to be faithful stewards. People should not have to look under rocks to discover our faith. Our faithfulness should be gloriously evident in all that we say and do.

Prayer – Dear Father, wherever You, or any person may find me, may I be faithfully managing my body as your property and my life as an extension of Your dealings with the world.

December 6   Conduct

1 Peter 3:1 *Wives, likewise, BE submissive to your own husbands, that even if some do not obey the word ... they may be won by the conduct of their wives ...*

> BE – to become.

Q What is the goal of a wife's submission? (v1) That the husband be won to Christ. Remember, without a word. Much of our communication is nonverbal. Our actions speak louder than our words! INSTANT REPLAY - Our actions speak louder than our words!

Q What is the goal of a husband's submission? (v7) To give honor to his wife and to free up his prayers. Having trouble with your prayer life? Has it stopped? Check and see if you are honoring your spouse. Many people with a conflict between their faith and their social behavior, back off from Christian behaviors instead of stopping evil activity. How smart is that?

The word *likewise* refers back to 1 Peter 2:21-23 which expresses Christ's attitude toward suffering. Note: *Likewise* is given as a directive to both husbands and wives.

Paul agreed with Peter and used much of the same language when he encouraged mutual submission out of respect for God's gift of marriage (Ephesians 5: 25-33). This is a good passage for spouses to read frequently. Paul gave one directive to wives and four to husbands.

As Jesus loves and cares for us, a husband is to care for the physical and emotional needs of his wife. A wife is encouraged to respect her husband. Even if one member of the marriage doesn't comply with these rules, the other is to be submissive to Christ and to be obedient to Him in the marriage relationship. Act, don't react.

Take note, submission is not license to abuse. Husbands are to love their wives *as Christ loved the church.* They are to *nourish and cherish* their wives as they do for themselves. It is easier for a wife to respect a husband who loves her as Jesus does.

Prayer – Dear Father, I submit myself to You so I can be submissive to my spouse.

For those without a spouse, think of Christ as being the spouse and let conduct be such that it wins others to Him.

December 7   Learned

Philippians 4:11 *Not that I speak in regard to need, for I have learned in whatever state I am to BE content.*

Q What is to be our attitude towards our needs? We are to BE content, no matter what.

This does not mean that we can be content with something that should be changed. It means we accept what can't be changed.

This passage goes beyond our wants to our needs. We trust that God is in control, that nothing enters our lives that doesn't pass His throne first. Don't worry about anything (Philippians 4:7-8). Think about the positive things listed in v8 – things that are true, noble, just, pure, lovely, of good report, things of virtue and that are praiseworthy. (See February 11).

The contents of verse eight imply that we could be thinking the opposite of each item. However, none of the opposite thoughts will promote contentment. Satan would have us dwell on the false, base, unfair, filthy, ugly, etc. If our minds go in those directions, we need to resist and switch back to positive thoughts.

Note – Contentment is not a gift or a talent, it is a learned state. Paul's Ph.D. coursework in contentment is written in 2 Corinthians 11:22-33. He suffered a great deal in many different circumstances but saw suffering as an opportunity to share in the sufferings of Christ and to increase his, and other's faith.

The differences between joy, happiness, and contentment need to be defined. Happiness depends on circumstance; it blows with the wind. Joy is fruit of the Spirit and is a bedrock state, not altered by circumstance. Contentment is a learned state and can exist in joy and/or happiness.

WE have joy and contentment even when we aren't happy. Name it and claim it. Consider what is really important. When we experience adversity, we are to look beyond the discomfort and find God's joy and comfort. With that comfort, we can comfort others (2 Corinthians 1:3-4).

Prayer – Dear Father, when I am confused about my needs, help me depend on You for Your joy, comfort, and sufficient grace.

December 8   Persuaded

Romans 8:38-39 *For I am persuaded that neither death nor life ... nor things present nor things to come ... shall BE able to separate us from the love of God which is in Christ Jesus our Lord.*

1 Peter 1:4-5 *... to an inheritance incorruptible and undefiled and that does not fade away, reserved in heaven for you, who are kept by the power of God through faith ...*

BE refers to an active force.

Q What, outside of ourselves, can separate us from the love and power of God?

Nothing. No thing. We have an *incorruptible and undefiled* inheritance.

We read the messages of two powerful writers. Paul says nothing can separate us from God's love. Peter says our inheritance is reserved and kept for us by the power of God. Paul is convinced of our union with God through Christ. Peter states we are cemented to God through faith. Even this faith is a gift of God so we can trust it (Ephesians 2:8).

God made an investment in us by the loving act of sending His Son to pay the price for our redemption. That investment comes with an ironclad guarantee. His investment comes with interest! You can believe that God is very interested in the return, which is us, His investment through His only Son.

Our inheritance cannot be spoiled. It doesn't disappear in the mists of life. It is reserved with our name on it. Our inheritance is *kept*, that is, closely guarded.

When we are persuaded, it means we have given due consideration to the subject. Paul had been on both sides of this fence and landed on the side of God's love demonstrated by the actions and teachings of Jesus. Nothing can separate us from our position in Christ because we *are kept by the power of God through faith*. WOW!

Prayer – Dear Father, thank You for the assurance of my inheritance given and kept by you.

December 9   Holy

Ephesians 1:4 *He chose us in Him ... that we should BE holy and without blame before Him in love.*

BE – to occur.

Q Why are we chosen?   To *BE holy* which is simply right living.

God is the One who chooses and we are the chosen ones in Christ. In a sense we are made holy - "Holified" through Christ's atoning (at-one) act so that we are without blame because of His love.

Ephesians 1 is the "In Christ" chapter. It expands on Jesus' prayer in John 17. There is much food for meditation in both areas. It begins with a greeting to those in Ephesus who are in Christ. To us, wherever we are, we are in Christ. It is far more important to be in Christ than wherever our geographical location finds us. Look at all the benefits that we have in the 14 "In Christ" statements in Ephesians 1.

As a child on the playground, I was the default kid. I was never chosen; the team with the last choice got stuck with me. "Ha, ha, you got Totten." True story. I may not have been the best athlete on the field but I was certainly the slowest. I was clumsy and uncoordinated and last at bat for good reason. But God chose me! He chooses all of us.

His purpose in choosing is that we have fellowship with Him in His Three Persons. He is our heavenly Father. He has made us holy in Christ, He directs and empowers us in holy living through His indwelling Spirit. Christ and the Holy Spirit both intercede for us constantly and with groanings that are beyond words (Hebrews 7:25, Romans 8:26, 34). He hears us when our agony is so great that we can't even verbalize it.

We are to be holy before Him. What is inside shows on the outside. Holiness will manifest itself in our speech and actions. When we are in His love, we can live in love with Him, ourselves, and others. Once we know that we are chosen by Him and are positioned in His love, we are empowered to have lives of holiness. We no longer have world worry.

Prayer – Dear Father, thank You for loving me, choosing me and empowering me to be holy.

December 10   Believe

John 14:1 *Let not your heart BE troubled; you believe in God, believe also in Me.*

> BE – to occur.

Q How do we avoid a troubled heart? We need to believe in Jesus.

> When we believe in God, we believe in Jesus. When we believe in Jesus, we believe in God. We need to believe and belive (intended).

> This verse tells us *"Let not your heart BE troubled …"* Being troubled is the opposite of being at peace. Being troubled is to have anxiety, to have world worry. When we are troubled, we are not trusting in God.

> We may be trusting in something else. If so, we have made that our god. If we think God is cruel, or if we think He is uncaring, we are guilty of blasphemous thinking.

> Don't let your heart be tied in a knot. We have studied Philippians 4:6-7 and we know how to handle anxiety. We can't read, study, and digest these verses often enough. The enemy constantly tries to unsettle us. Remember, not for everything but in *everything* … being thankful. If we are resentful we won't have the surpassing peace of God. And, we won't learn the lesson He has for us.

> When we believe in God, as He is, we believe that He is love, that He cares for us and that nothing enters our lives that doesn't first pass His throne. When we trust that God is in control, that nothing enters our lives before passing through His love, Philippians 4:6-7 makes sense. Whatever happens, we are to seek His will and His way and we will receive mind boggling peace.

> Rule # 1: Believe in God and you won't be troubled.

> Rule # 2: If anything troubles you, see Philippians 4:6-7.

> When we are anxious, we are disparaging God. INSTANT REPLAY - When we are anxious, we are disparaging God. Don't worry about anything. Trust Him.

Prayer - Dear Father, thank You that my belief in You calms my heart.

December 11   Found

Philippians 3:9 ... *and BE found in Him, not having my own righteousness ...*
but the righteousness that is from God by faith ...

> BE – to occur.

Q What is one advantage of being in Christ?

> We have the gift of God's righteousness.

> The righteousness that God gives to us comes through His gift of
> faith (Ephesians 2:8).

> Be sure to give careful thought to and acceptance of the fact that our
> faith is a gift from God. It is perfect and sufficient. In this faith there is
> no effort on our part to achieve acceptance. We are accepted
> through His grace. Satan had us hooked but we are off the hook of
> sin. We are released to SWIM. Happy fish!

> Not only faith, but also righteousness is a gift from God. That is
> fortunate because any effort on our part would be inadequate and
> insufficient and might generate spiritual pride. Having righteousness
> that is given by God means we don't have to be concerned about its
> quality or quantity.

> Because it is His grace that saves us, we are set free from efforts to
> be good enough for Him and we can devote our efforts to being
> righteous in Him. No amount of self-righteousness can equal the
> righteousness that God gives us. INSTANT REPLAY - No amount of
> self-righteousness can equal the righteousness that God gives us.

> Because of His activity in our lives we can be *found in Him.* This
> raises an interesting question. Where do people find us? Do they find
> us *in Him*? Or are we playing Hide and Go Seek with our faith? Let
> us be in plain sight with and *in Him.*

Prayer – Dear Father, may I always *be found in Him* in thought, word, and
deed.

December 12   Filled

Ephesians 5:18b-19 ... *BE filled with the Spirit ... singing and making melody in your heart to the Lord.*

Q How can I have this melody in my heart?

The melody becomes melodious

as we allow the Holy Spirit to fill us.

We see in Job 35:10 that *God gives songs IN the night.*

GOD gives songs. God GIVES songs. God gives SONGS.

A violin maker found one of his instruments, a beaten up violin, missing a string and a fret, in the back corner of an antique store. The sign read, "Slightly damaged, greatly reduced in value." He thought to himself, "I made this, I will fix it." With the Master's touch, the violin was restored. We can also be restored by the Master.

We are to let the wisdom of the word of God live in us with abundance so that we will sing a song of grace in our hearts *to the Lord* (Colossians 3:16). The wisdom of the word – the gospel – the good news – can live in us with abundant riches.

A troubled heart will not burst forth in song. We should be filled with the Spirit instead of resentment and doubt. When we are filled with the Spirit, a melody rings in our hearts.

Paul recognized the importance of emotions. Let your heart be a musical place.

Isaiah and Paul were in agreement. *For you shall go out with joy, and BE led out with peace; the mountains and the hills shall break forth into singing before you, and all the trees of the field shall clap their hands* Isaiah 55:12. *THANK YOU LORD!*

Let Christ dwell in your hearts. His filling drives out all else so we have the fullness of Christ

Prayer – Dear Father, I give my heart to You as an instrument in an orchestra so that Your melodies may ring out from me.

December 13   Accomplished

Ephesians 3:9-10 *... and to make all see what is the fellowship of the mystery, which from the beginning of the ages has been hidden in God ... the manifold wisdom of God BE made known ... according to the eternal purpose which He accomplished in Christ Jesus our Lord.*

        BE – to bring out into the open.

Q What is the manifold wisdom of God?

> God's manifold wisdom is what *He accomplished in Christ Jesus* – our salvation and eternal life.

> Paul writes, "We have a mystery". Those people who were called God's people have been joined with those who were not called His people. All those who wrongly thought they were part of God's kingdom, and those who knew they weren't part of His kingdom, are now brought together through the sacrifice of Christ.

> Paul unraveled the mystery when he wrote Romans 5:6-8: We were helpless, but in God's timing Christ died for those who were apart from God. Very few people would die even for a good person but God showed His love for us in that even while we were living lives apart from His ways and commandments, Christ gave His life for us. There is no greater love than this!

> Why should God want to gift us with forgiveness in Christ and shower us with all the workings of the Holy Spirit when we had rejected Him? Because He loves us! Can you believe it? I hope you believe it - because it is true for all of us. The mystery has been solved - made known, brought into the open – Christ died for our sins and brought us into relationship with God for now and eternity. The frozen have joined the chosen.

> God accomplished His purpose in Christ. Our relationship with Him is secure.

Prayer – Dear Father, thank You for accomplishing Your purpose in me.

December 14   Filled

<u>Ephesians 3:18-19</u> *You ... may BE able to comprehend ... what is the width and length and depth and height - to know the love of Christ which passes knowledge; that you may BE filled with all the fullness of God.*

BE – become able/filled.

Q How are we enabled to comprehend and be filled with God's love for us?

Through prayers that God would grant that we *comprehend, know,* and *BE filled.*

We understand because of our being in Christ and Him being in us. The thought that we are forgiven by God of the least to the most disgusting of sins, is hard to believe. After all, the guilt and shame have made us uncomfortable, unable to be free. To be forgiven and to have real joy, so easily, is amazing!

The Bible tells us many things that are beyond our human understanding. For instance, the trinity, how God is one but three at the same time. Paul's prayer is that we be able to comprehend the love of God. The wonderful thing is we don't have to understand these things in order for the Holy Spirit to manifest them in our lives. Beyond those things are L, J, P and the other six ingredients in the fruit salad given to us by the Holy Spirit (Galatians 5:22-23).

A plane has area, L x W. A container has volume, L x W x H. The love of God has L x W x H x D. This is like the love of Christ that passes knowledge and describes the fullness of God. There are no limits to the Length, Width, Height, and Depth of the love of God.

How do we obtain what *passes knowledge?* It is through <u>believing</u> and <u>receiving</u> Christ Jesus.

How can infinite love be packed into our finite bodies? It is through the power of the Holy Spirit. This also passes knowledge. Are you full? Running over? Spilling on to others?

Prayer – Dear Father, enable me to *comprehend* and *know,* understand and *be filled,* with the fullness of the love of Christ.

December 15   Grace

Philippians 4:23 *The grace of our Lord Jesus Christ BE with you all.*

Grace - undeserved merit.

BE – to exist in our lives.

Q How does grace BE with us?

One of the greatest things about God's grace is that it allows and fulfills our need for salvation (Ephesians 2:8). God created a God sized hole in us and only He can fill it.

Grace is with us in that assurance is given by the indwelling of the Holy Spirit.

When Paul was in prison, he was facing the end of his earthly life. At that time he wrote the Joy Letter. Philippians speaks of joy and being joyful more than any other of his letters. Joy is a deep down emotion based on righteousness. Whatever our circumstance we have the testimony of the Holy Spirit within us that we are in God's care and keeping.

Paul begins v23 and ends the sandwich of Philippians with the blessing of grace v1:2. It is his hope that all of his readers would live in an atmosphere filled with the constant knowledge of God's grace. This motivates us to respond with energetic joy. We are redeemed!

Remember the clear glass pitcher filled with water. When we are filled with, and surrounded by grace, we are blessfully (intended) grateful for whatever circumstance. We do not need to justify ourselves because God has justified us through Christ.

Sometimes Jesus is described as Lord and Savior. Here, Paul describes Jesus as Lord so that we would know that Jesus has the authority to extend His grace to us. For our southern siblings this grace is "with y'all".

Prayer – Dear Father, may Your Spirit empower me to extend Your grace to others so they may feel accepted and at ease in Your presence.

December 16   Seasoned

Colossians 4:6 *Let your speech always BE with grace, seasoned with salt ...*

As with many words, context is important. So called salty speech is not acceptable in polite society. As for Christians, we are *the salt of the earth* Matthew 5:13 and our speech is acceptable in any society.

BE – to exist.

Q How does *salt* help explain graceful speech?

Salt preserves, flavors, and is necessary for physical vitality. Low sodium negatively affects nerves and muscles. A lack of *salt* is a real detriment for the physical body, for the body of Christ, and for the world.

In this verse the focus is on speech - the words of our mouths are to be suitable to God (Psalm 19:14). It follows that our nonverbal communication should also be seasoned with the salt of grace. Grace is to life as salt is to speech. Some of the seasonings with salt are the looks on our faces, the tones of our speech, and the posture of our bodies. These traits, and more, should communicate the love of God.

I get a wry smile when I hear about an "adult movie" or "adult language." Really? There is nothing adult about sinful actions or trashy language.

Speech that is not seasoned is found in many putrid forms: gossip, bitterness, accusations, viciousness, biting words, undermining, demeaning, lewdness, and anger, to list a few descriptors. James, who is colorful, practical, and straight forward in his message describes the tongue as being an evil thing capable of defiling our entire being, the course of our lives, and is controlled by hell itself (James 3:6). Preserving and flavoring is better. You think?

We give grace to others because we act in the nature of Christ. We need to speak unto others as we would have them speak unto us.

Prayer – Dear Father, let the words of my mouth be acceptable in Your sight and manifest Your grace in the world.

December 17   All

1 Timothy 2:1 *Therefore I exhort first of all that supplication, prayers, intercessions, and giving of thanks BE made for all men ... for all who are in authority ...*

> BE – to enact.

Q What authorities should be the subjects of our prayers?

> All.

> Writing to his spiritual son, Paul urges consideration for those in authority. Regardless of political party, etc. We may not agree with someone's position but it doesn't say just to pray for those with whom we agree. Politicians, pastors, police, parents - the word *all* occurs again and again. Paul encourages:

>> that humble request be made for supplies for all men, even for those in authority,

>> that two way communication with God should occur,

>> that we should be concerned with the welfare of all other people, and

>> that we should be thankful for *all* who make society work. We may choke on this but we need to be faithful to God's instruction.

> Another word on exhortation is given in Hebrews 10:24-25. *And let us consider one another in order to stir up love and good works ... exhorting one another ...* We may wonder why we are exhorted to pray when God knows what He wants. What is necessary is for us to find out what He wants. Also, to bring forth an attitude of gratitude.

> When we encourage others, we bring our own faith and actions into consideration, and are more likely to function meaningfully in the body of Christ.

Prayer – Dear Father, may I be obedient to You in my prayers for all others.

December 18   Let

Ephesians 4:26 *BE angry and do not sin: do not let the sun go down on your wrath.*

BE – to occur.

Q Is anger permissible?   Yes, but with guidelines.

The heart is thought to be the center of our emotions because it responds so quickly to adrenalin and other hormones. Whenever the heart is mentioned in Scripture, we need to consider emotions. One theory of psychology says depression is the result of anger but anger, or any negative emotion, is caused by unmet expectations. Expectations that seemed reasonable at the time, can really shipwreck a person. All of our mistakes in life seemed reasonable at the time or we wouldn't have done them. A lot of my clients denied that, but think about it. The root of all anger, and any other unpleasant emotion, is unmet expectations. INSTANT REPLAY - The root of all anger, and any other unpleasant emotion, is unmet expectations.

We need to know that what Satan suggests seems to be a reasonable expectation but we need to get realistic. Negative emotions usually bring negative results. When there are evil thoughts, the first thought is Satan's doing. After that it is our response-ability. It isn't what happens, it is how we respond to what happens. Anger can often take control of the tongue so we are to listen carefully, think things over for a decent length of time, and then talk knowing that our anger doesn't necessarily agree with what God would do in a given situation (James 1:19-20). That is why God gave us two ears and one mouth.

God's anger is expressed hundreds of times in the Old Testament - mostly when His children disobey Him or someone is messing with His kids. We are created in God's image so there will be times we become angry. At those times we are to put a harness on our anger and use the adrenalin to produce a positive result.

And we are not to harbor anger. Let anger do its work in the day it occurs. Anger will be the enemy of sleep, so don't take it to bed with you. The word ANGER can give us a detailed plan on how to use it. Admit you are angry, avoid Negative results, think of a Good way to use it, Evaluate possible consequences, Resolve to act appropriately.

Prayer - Dear Father, thank You for anger. May I use it with response-ability.

December 19   Grace and Peace

Ephesians 1:2 *Grace to you and peace from God our Father and the Lord Jesus Christ.*

Ephesians 6:23-24 *Peace to the brethren and love with faith, from God the Father and the Lord Jesus Christ. Grace BE with all those who love our Lord Jesus Christ in sincerity. Amen.*

>   BE – to occur.

Q What is between these blessings? Paul began and ended Ephesians with wonderful blessings which we can accept for ourselves and share with others - a before and after blessings sandwich.

Grace and peace! Peace and grace, Grace is getting blessings we don't deserve! Peace is that which is beyond human understanding! We desire to have these gifts that are fulfilled in Christ. They are two of the elements of spiritual fruit (Galatians 5:22-23). Got 'em? If not, get 'em. Ask and you will receive.

Grace is necessary before peace can be realized. We need to KNOW that while these attributes are undeserved and beyond our own capabilities, they are real, available, and God desires that we have them. There is no need for stress or worry when we know that our loving Father only allows in our lives what is useful for His purposes. INSTANT REPLAY - our loving Father only allows in our lives what is useful for His purposes. He allows good things and good trials for our growth in Him (Matthew 6:34b). He only gives enough to grow on, not to frustrate us.

Peace with God, others, and ourselves, is necessary before love can be expressed. If we are bitter and unforgiving towards ourselves or others, it is difficult to love. We have to *love our Lord Jesus Christ in sincerity*. If we haven't accepted God's love and applied it to ourselves, we will project our self-loathing onto others. When we have accepted God's grace, peace, and love for ourselves, nothing can bother us. All this is possible because of God's gift of faith (Ephesians 2:8).

> *Peace to the brethren. Grace BE with* all who love God. Grace brings God's gifts to us in reality. Let us continually rejoice in God's good gifts!

Prayer - Dear Father, thank You for Your grace, peace, and love. I take hold of them for myself and extend them to those Whom you bring to me.

December 20   Diligent

<u>2 Timothy 2:15</u> *BE diligent to present yourself approved to God, a worker who does not need to BE ashamed ...* <u>Leviticus 11:44</u> *BE holy, for I am holy.*

BE – to occur.

Q How do we avoid shame and become approved before God?

Every action that we perform and every word that we say should be in the nature of Christ, and be a presentation of thankfulness to Him (Colossians 3:17).

We are to act in the nature of Jesus. Even if, sometimes, it goes beyond what seems reasonable in human nature. Not my will but God's will has become the bottom line for our prayers (Luke 22:42b). In all things we are to let our doings be a statement of thanksgiving to God.

We are to *BE diligent*, not slothful, making an earnest effort to make the results of our work an offering to God. We need to do this with humble pride, not *ashamed*, but willing to put Jesus' name on our work. It helps if we never do anything we will want to, or have to, lie about.

Satan has programmed his followers to try to shame people as being weak and stupid who are celebrating their strength and wisdom in Christ.

Think carefully about those who are passing judgment on you. Don't give them the authority of condemnation.

Our work is acceptable to God as we work out what God has worked into us (Philippians 2:12-13). In so doing we fulfill His desires. We would do well to adopt Colossians 3:17 as a motto for every aspect of our lives. Even if there is no other reason to do our job well, we do it as unto the Lord.

Prayer - Dear Father, may the words of my mouth and the actions of my body be delightful in Your sight.

December 21   Vigilant

1 Peter 5:8-9a   BE sober, BE vigilant; because your adversary the devil walks about like a roaring lion, seeking whom he may devour. Resist him ...

We celebrate the birth of Christ in a few days. The world will celebrate temporal commercialism but those of us who have accepted Christ's birth for its true meaning will have greater joy because the gift of Jesus is eternal.

> BE – to occur.

Q How do we avoid being devoured by the devil? We are to be clear-headed and thoughtful. The opposite is to be foggy-minded and careless. Accept the fact of spiritual warfare. We are to be alert and cautiously observant for questionable situations. The opposite is to be oblivious to Satan's evil intentions in our lives. We are told to watch out for Satan and to resist him.

Yesterday we were advised to be diligent. Today's word is *vigilant*. Both instructions have a sense of strong intent. We are to be at peace but not to live carelessly. We need to be open to the Spirit's warnings when evil acts and results are possible.

Have you ever wondered why the famous, well known bumper sticker was made? Because your adversary the devil wants to hurt you. There is an adversary (Ephesians 6:12, 1 Peter 5:8). That's where Murphy's Law came from. That's why things go wrong and sometimes the worst possible thing at the worst possible time seems to happen. But remember, God has control over Satan's intrusion in our lives and He can use them for good.

There is an Old Testament parallel to Peter's statement. There is a conversation between God and Satan. When God asked Satan what he was doing, Satan was rather evasive and simply said words to the effect that He was just wandering around (Job 1:7). We know from the rest of the story that Satan's intent was to mess with Job who was a man who found favor with God. The lesson to us is obvious.

Satan may come like a roaring lion or as a sneaky fox. He uses people and events to work his nasty purposes in our lives. He seeks to consume us and destroy our being. Watch the news on TV to see a continuum of destroyed people. As something rotten is not pleasing to our taste, God's goodness in our lives will be distasteful to Satan.

Prayer - Dear Father, thank You that being *in Christ* gives me protection from the enemy.

December 22   Revealed

Mark 4:22 *For there is nothing hidden which will not BE revealed, nor has anything been kept secret but that it should come to light.*

BE – to become.

Q Does that which happens in the dark stay in the dark?   No.

This is a common misconception that has become an advertising slogan almost bragging about sinful behavior. However, anything that happens anywhere is known to God. Everything that a person attempts to hide will be revealed.

Any hidden sin is like an infection, under a band aid, which can cause sepsis and death. The wages of sin is its fruit. Any evil that we do will cause irritation, self-loathing, and sleep problems. No wonder lack of sleep is such a problem in this country. Our lack of peace is a lie detector that tells us something needs to come to light. Not only might it come to light, it should come to light so it can be confessed and forgiven, so we can have peace. Take it to the Lord and don't leave with it.

We know that Jesus is light and life and that those whose minds are darkened do not understand Who Jesus is and what He is about (John 1:4-5). We understand that Jesus came to save us from darkness. Jesus is the Light of the world. Turning on the light is the same as turning off the darkness. If you want to turn off the darkness of your life, turn on the Light. God has given us an interior instrument panel such that when there is a problem, a light comes on. When you have a problem let the Light shine.

Being assured that He is quick to forgive us, we can come to Him and ask Him to inspect our lives and motives and ferret out any wickedness (Psalm 139:23). We can confidently let God perform open heart surgery knowing that His skillful, loving touch will heal us of all dis-eases.

Our lives will be so much better if we ask God to seek out and cleanse us of the impediments of sin.

Prayer - Dear Father, Make me aware of any *wicked way* in me and prevent it from destroying my joy and peace. May I never do anything I think I will want to lie about!

December 23   Helpful

<u>1 Corinthians 6:12</u> *All things are lawful for me, but all things are not helpful.*
All things are lawful for me but I will not BE brought under the power of any.

> BE – to become.

Q Is negative behavior acceptable to God?   No.

> This verse declares it to be our response-ability to avoid the power of sin.

> *All things are lawful for me* - Some translations put this phrase in quotation marks as if it were a phrase thought up by the Corinthians to excuse evil behavior because, after all, they were saved by grace so why should they worry about sin? Without quotation marks, it simply means what it says. I can do anything but I don't want to because not all things are helpful.

> How do *things* control us? Events take control if we give them permission. Nobody makes me sin. In order to sin, I need to give sin control. Nobady (intended) "Makes me mad" unless I give control of my emotions over to them. I choose not to do that. God allows us freedom to make decisions. We have the right to be wrong. But being wrong isn't right. INSTANT REPLAY - being wrong isn't right.

> Paul gave similar helpful instructions to the Romans. It doesn't make sense to willfully sin thinking that God's grace is bountifully available for forgiveness. Paul strongly opposes this erroneous thinking wondering how anyone could think that we could die to sin yet still live a life of sin (Romans 6:1b-2). Even <u>if</u> we can do anything, that doesn't mean we <u>should</u> do it. We are in Christ. It would be silly and counterproductive to do things that are harmful.

> Even if all things are lawful they should not control me. I won't give evil things power over me.

> One of today's mottos is, If it feels good, do it. Sound familiar? Our motto is, Only if it is in Christ, do it. Christians don't go about seeking how to sin carefully.

Prayer - Dear Father, help me to know what is helpful for my life and what is helpful for increasing Your kingdom.

December 24   Saved

<u>John 3:17</u> *For God did not send His Son into the world to condemn the world, but that the world through Him might BE saved.*

BE – to occur.

Q Why did God send His Son into the world?

To save the world; so by accepting Christ as Savior and Lord, the world would not be condemned.

Those who have a problem with condemnation should read the preceding verse (John 3:16). Condemnation should motivate us to seek salvation. Part of the work of the Holy Spirit is to convince us of our sinfulness so that we could have relationship with God, not so that He would condemn us (John 16:8b). They should take advantage of the conviction of their guilt, see conviction as a gift, repent, and confess.

Two eye opening examples from the crucifixion scenario were the experiences of Judas and Peter. Judas recognized his sin and went out and hanged himself. Peter recognized his sin and repented and accepted forgiveness. Judas looked into the mirror of the eyes of the Pharisees and saw condemnation; Peter looked into the mirror of the eyes of Jesus and saw salvation. What do you see?

God sent His Son that the world *through Him might be saved.* We have to recognize that salvation comes through Christ and be quick to accept this clear avenue to being a member of God's family.

Saved <u>from</u> what? - a life of desperation and an eternity separated from God when we are lost and directionless in this life.

Saved <u>to</u> what? - LIFE in this world and the next – cleansed by Jesus and filled with the power, gifts, and fruit of the Spirit.

Prayer - Dear Father, thank You for helping me know Your intent.

December 25   Joy   Have a merry and blessed Christmas!

<u>Luke 2:10</u> "Do not BE afraid, for behold, I bring you good tidings of great joy which will BE to <u>all</u> people. For there is born to you this day in the city of David a Savior Who is Christ the Lord."

> John wrote to non-Jewish readers using the concept of beginning. John 1 is the Christmas story for 'Gentiles.' And the Word became flesh and dwelt among us ... <u>John 1:14</u>. Merry Christmas! God has given us the greatest gift of all time, Jesus Christ, our Lord!!

> BE – to become.

Q What are the good tidings that dispel fear?

> A Savior, Who is Christ the Lord, is born! WE HAVE A SAVIOR! Savior = Great Joy!

> We might be frightened when the Holy Spirit flashes our sins upon us but let fright turn to joy and accept the Savior.

> The angels said, "Do not be afraid"; this is good news! - the good tidings tell of the ability to have a relationship with our God and Creator. Many people watch TV, listen to the radio, read the papers, and have apps on their phones to keep up with the news. The greatest news, that produces news which is favorable and overcomes that which is bad, is that we have a Savior and we need not fear anything negative. We don't need to be afraid of the message or the messenger because God loves us so much! Because He loves us with a love that is perfect, we don't have to be afraid because <u>His</u> love perfects our relationship (1 John 4:18). We have perfect love.

> Behold! - Look! - Understand! There is nothing for us to do except to accept - with great joy! For our part, Though now you do not see Him, yet believing, you rejoice with joy inexpressible and full of glory, receiving the end of your faith -- the salvation of your souls <u>1 Peter 1:8-9</u>. Believe today and be born again. As we celebrate Jesus' birth we can be born again All because the good tidings are for all people.

> Anyone who would disqualify him/herself from God's grace needs to turn their thinking to belief and absorb this promise.

Prayer - Dear Father, thank You that I am one of the all. I rejoice in my Savior and my salvation.

December 26   Indescribable

2 Corinthians 9:15 *Thanks BE to God for His indescribable Gift.*

Christmas has a tradition of gift giving. Let us not join the world in forgetting the real reason for the season. In algebra, X is the unknown. Christ-mas is not Xmas.

BE – to ascribe.

Q What are these gifts?

Here are some gifts that are truly worth opening:

Eternal life through Christ (John 3:16), even though

the gift of Christ is beyond description (2 Corinthians 9:15), and

The gift of Christ is beyond our ability to explain in human terms (Ephesians 3:8b).

Another gift

The indwelling power and help of the Holy Spirit (John 14:16).

Thanks be to God because these are gifts from Him,

and more gifts - L J P.

Christ's *Love* is beyond our ability to understand (Ephesians 3:19),

Even our *Joy* has no words that express it (1 Peter 1:8),

We have *Peace* that defies human explanation (Philippians 4:7).

WOW! Look at these verses again and again!

Beyond the language of the mind.

Filling the needs of the heart.

Indescribable, unsearchable, passing knowledge, inexpressible, surpassing understanding!

Prayer - Dear Father, words cannot express how grateful I am for all Your *indescribable* gifts.

December 27   Separate

2 Corinthians 6:17 *Come out from among them and BE separate, says the Lord. Do not touch what is unclean.*

BE – to become.

Q Are we to leave the world?

No, we are just not to be a part of *them.*

Paul is quoting Isaiah 52:11 and using the history of the Israelites to make a point with the Corinthians. Don't try to be birds of a feather with bad birds

We should not try to be like the world or to adopt the ways of the world in order to be attractive to the world. When you think about it, that way of thinking is silly if not stupid. Be like Christ so those around you can make a reasonable choice. Satan has talked many groups into watering down their message to the point that they are just like the world.

Sin is like Velcro; if part of us has a "Loopy" surface, sin has plenty of "Hooks" to snare us. Some lives are like oil and water, all shook up. Rest in Jesus so your thoughts and emotions can rise above the water. BE separate. There is a rat in separate. We need to separate ourselves from the rats of the world. We live in a fornication nation. Don't become part of it. We can be in it without being part of it.

Many passages of the Bible compare our relationship with God to a bride with her husband. Many of the statements in traditional marriage vows can be applied to our commitment to God. We, as the bride, are not to commit adultery with Satan. We are not to participate in any activity which is unclean. We are to keep ourselves only unto Him all the days of our life. We should not do what we think we are going to want to lie about.

Purity in marriage and purity in our relationship with God promotes love, joy and peace.

Prayer - Dear Father, help me to be still and to recognize Who is my God and to separate myself unto You.

December 28   Witnesses

<u>Acts 1:8</u> *But you shall receive power when the Holy Spirit has come upon you, and you shall BE witnesses to Me in Jerusalem and in all Judea and Samaria, and to the end of the earth.*

BE – to occur.

Q What empowers us to be witnesses?

The Holy Spirit will come upon us and give us power. We need to trust God and Jesus and know that the Holy Spirit is a wonderful gift. We must ask for, and receive, the Holy Spirit. In other devotions we have studied the fantastic power, gifts, and fruit of the Spirit. He is Jesus' presence in us in the world today.

Do not be anxious about how the Spirit will use you. Just immerse yourself in the word and the Body of Christ and God will provide opportunities to witness. We will be led to those outside the fold and to those inside the fold. Remember, other Christians need the heat and light that our log adds to the fire. We can be the ember in Re-member.

We *shall be witnesses to* and of Jesus in our homes, at work and play, in our neighborhoods, and anywhere in our sphere of influence. Like a pebble, or a boulder, cast in the water, our ripples will extend in all directions throughout the world. We may not know that what we do for one may be passed on to others. And that one may influence thousands, or another one, who may influence thousands, and so on. Do not hesitate to sow the seed on whatever soil. God will take care of the harvest. Paul (1 Corinthians 3:6) noted that many people may contribute to the work of redemption, but it is God Who brings it to completion. Trust that whatever you do, God will increase the part you play. Think of the feeding of the 5000 <u>Matthew 14:21</u>.

Prayer - Dear Father, wherever I am and whatever I do, I give it to You and trust You will use it for the increase of Your kingdom.

December 29   Treasure

Matthew 6:21 *For where your treasure is, there your heart will BE also.*

BE – location.

Q Where is your heart?

The heart is where your treasure is.

The mind and the heart are the two engines that pull the train. In this verse the heart is emphasized as the control center. How does finding emotional treasure identify the location of our hearts? We can help locate it by finding out what generates strong emotion.

What would you most hate to lose? What occupies your mind in the sleepless hours in the middle of the night? What would you give up everything for? Answering these questions can help you identify what is most precious to you and where your heart is.

The treasure doesn't have to be a material thing. The treasure may be lust, hate or resentment over real or perceived wrong. Some people sell their souls to the devil for an *idea. But:*

They should step back and ask what they bought (Matthew 16:26).

The kingdom of heaven is like a merchant seeking beautiful pearls, who, when he had found one pearl of great price, went and sold all that he had and bought it Matthew 13:46. In one sense, this parable describes God's desire to find us and purchase us for Himself. We came at a very high price, the blood of His Son (Acts 20:28).

The gifts of Christ and the Holy Spirit are the ultimate treasure.

Relationship with God is better than any world pearl regardless of the price. Relationship with God? - priceless! It is beyond our ability to purchase. It is a free gift from Him to all of us.

Prayer - Dear Father, thank You for Your priceless gift.

December 30   Judgment

Matthew 7:1 *Judge not, that you BE not judged. For with what judgment you judge, you will BE judged ...*

BE – to become.

Q What is the consequence of judging?

We'll be hit with our own hammer.

In a sense we make countless judgments each day - what to wear, what to eat, where to go. Many decisions are made for us by our life's circumstances. Therefore, this verse must be about something more profound. It must be about life and death matters.

We, and others, are always doing something that may intentionally or unintentionally cause a judgment to be made. The judgment may result in forgiveness that could build relationships or separation that could rip us apart.

On Christmas day was born a Savior, not a condemner.

One of the guiding principles in our consideration of judgment is our relationship with God. We can be in Christ and forgive or we can choose to shut the offending person out of our lives thus committing emotional murder.

We are to leave judgment to God because only He is capable of judging appropriately (Revelation 19:2). My judgments may be wrong. I don't know all the facts. God knows circumstances which are beyond our knowledge or wisdom to interpret. Judging dams up relationship. The "materials" of any interaction can be used to build a wall or a bridge. We are to be building bridges, not walls.

With what judgment we give, we will *be judged.* Give that a lot of thought. When we are offended, (an interesting word - off-ended) let us seek to involve Christ with us and the off-ender and see what can be done to bring the three of us together.

Prayer - Dear Father, thank You for placing my judgment on Christ.

December 31   Saved

Joel 2:32 (quoted in Acts 2:21) *And it shall come to pass, that whoever calls on the name of the Lord shall BE saved.*

>BE – to become.

Q Who shall BE saved?

>*Whoever calls upon the name of the Lord will be saved.*

>As we end the year, let us use the past year as a springboard for a new year in Christ. Each day, we see, not an ending, but another new beginning. If you have anything from last year hanging over you, realize that God makes everything *new* (Revelation 21:5).

>Have you called on the Lord? Do you know God's phone number? 555 537-3333 (Jeremiah 33:3). All you need to know is He wants you to give Him a call and He will answer and show you fantastic things which you haven't even thought of. Each day is a new beginning in Christ. Windshields are bigger than rear view windows for reason.

>Scripture tells us the two prepositional phrases, *on the name* and *of the Lord* explain how to qualify for salvation (justification). When we call on the nature of Christ, the promise of salvation is fulfilled. What Joel had prophesied has come to pass.

>John 3:16 trumpets the *whoever.* No one is left out. We need to pray for those in our own little world who aren't calling.

>*Whoever* calls out to Christ *shall be saved.* Shall means it will happen. Salvation language is Biblical and may sound strange to people outside the body of Christ. However, they might understand the concept of justification. Jesus justifies us, makes us just or righteous, in the eyes of God. Those who are ready to hear the message have been convicted by the Holy Spirit. Our job, as reconcilers, is to defend our faith and give reasons for our hope in Christ (1 Peter 3:15). The Holy Spirit will use our love, joy, and peace to influence them.

Prayer - Dear Father, help me be a winsome witness.

>Happy New Year!

>Ready for another round? Go to January 1. Happy New Year!

About the Author

Dr. Donald Totten's education, family background, and professional experience are the foundation for his rich, meaningful and inspirational thoughts for the Christian's daily walk with the Lord. He spent 30 years in the Michigan educational system teaching mathematics to gifted and talented students at the middle school level along with teaching experience at the high school, college, and post graduate levels. After retiring from teaching, he attended a Christian based university to earn the doctorate in Counseling Psychology. For the next 20 years he served the Lord in his private Christian counseling practice and finally retired for the second time at age 80. In more than 15 years of his teaching and counseling careers, he pastored different churches that experienced tremendous spiritual growth.

Donald has been married to his wonderful wife, Joan for over 60 years. Their two sons, Dr. Douglas Totten (optometrist), and Dr. Jeffrey Totten (principle engineer in a major corporation), are married to Catherine Totten (retired computer engineer and programmer), and Lori Totten, (dental hygienist). They have five grandchildren, Dr. Michael Totten, (general surgeon), Dr. Nicole Totten, (dentist), Zachary Totten (engineer in a major corporation), Kala Totten (BSN nurse), and Julia Totten (soon to be a doctor of optometry).

Preparation for Dr. Totten's careers was made possible by earning the BA degree in education, an MA in education, an MA in Psychology, a PhD in Psychology, and five quarters at a denominational seminary. Previously, Dr. Totten and his wife, Joan, co-authored The C.H.E.E.S.E Factor, published in 2006. This book was written from a Christian counseling perspective exploring reasons of why we are the way we are, and how to have a mentally and physically healthy life in Christ. They also published Math for Intelligent Students, Parents, Teachers a mathual (intended) to strengthen math skills and alleviate math anxiety.